T0154077

STROUD'S SLAVE LAWS

STROUD'S SLAVE LAWS

A SKETCH OF THE LAWS RELATING TO SLAVERY
IN THE SEVERAL STATES OF
THE UNITED STATES OF AMERICA

George M. Stroud

INPRINT EDITIONS
Baltimore

STROUD'S SLAVE LAWS

Second Edition, 1856

Published 2005 by
INPRINT EDITIONS

Introduction copyright 2005 by
Robert Johnson, Jr.

Library of Congress Card Catalog Number: 2004107006

ISBN-13 978-1-58073-007-5
ISBN-10 1-58073-007-8

Cover art by Michelle D. Wright

Printed by BCP Digital Printing
An affiliate company of Black Classic Press

ABOUT INPRINT EDITIONS

Our mission is to keep good books in print. We give life to books that might never be published or republished by making them available On Demand. Manuscripts and books are scanned, stored, and then printed as single or multiple copies from our digital library. When reprinting out-of-print books, we always use the best copy available.

INPRINT EDITIONS are especially useful to scholars, students, and general readers who have an interest in enjoying all that books have to offer. Our books are also a valuable resource for libraries in search of replacement copies.

You can purchase books or obtain a current list of our titles from:

INPRINT EDITIONS
c/o Black Classic Press
P.O. Box 13414
Baltimore, MD 21203
Also visit our website:
www.blackclassic.com

Introduction

Robert Johnson, Jr.

One year after the publication of *Stroud's Slave Laws*, the most significant legal treatise on American racism, Chief Justice Roger Brooke Taney of the Supreme Court of the United States, wrote that African people were property and had no rights that white people should respect. His decision in 1857, *Dred Scott v. Sandford*, made institutionalized racism national policy, and established for the nation the legal rationale for the enslavement and economic exploitation of people of African descent. [1]

Stroud's work comprehensively gathered into one volume prior southern slave laws that ultimately shaped the contours of Judge Taney's decision. Both men were lawyers, yet their views on slavery and the humanity of African people differed substantially. A slaveholder, Judge Taney served as law partner with Francis Scott Key, another slaveholder and the author of the *Star Spangled Banner,* before he was elected to the Maryland legislature. Judge Taney had served as a legislator from Maryland, Attorney General of Maryland, Attorney General of the United States, Secretary of the Treasury, and finally Chief Justice of the Supreme Court of the United States.

On the other hand, George McDowell Stroud, born on October 12, 1795 in Stroudsburg, Pennsylvania, had never acquired such laudatory positions in public service and was never a slaveholder. His father, Daniel was also born in Stroudsburg and was admitted to practice law at the age of 20. George enrolled at Princeton University as a junior in November, 1815 and graduated in 1817 as

1 See Don E. Fehrenbacher's *The Dred Scott Case: Its Significance in American Law and Politics* (New York: Oxford University Press, 1978), page 234.

Valedictorian. A year later he became a student in the law office of Judge John Hallowell and in 1819 was admitted to practice law in Philadelphia. In 1828 he married the Judge's daughter and subsequently served three terms as judge of the District Court of Philadelphia.[2] The first edition of his book was published when he was a practicing attorney and the second edition while he was a sitting judge.

Even before the Dred Scott decision, Stroud's book had extensive influence upon national legal thinking on the issue of slavery. For example, it is believed by some scholars that Harriet Beecher Stowe gained her knowledge of slave laws from Judge Stroud's work. Her *Uncle Tom's Cabin,* which was published in 1852, spurred in part, the development of the abolitionist movement in the nineteenth century. Her influence was so extensive that in 1862, President Abraham Lincoln invited her into the White House and told her that her book had started the Civil War.[3] For his part, Judge Stroud did not want any confusion on where he stood on abolitionism. He wrote in his first preface: "He is not now, nor ever has been, a member of any Abolition or Anti-Slavery Society. He has acted upon his own judgment. He has taken counsel of no one." Despite having written a book without the support of anti-slavery forces of the time, Judge Stroud clearly hoped that his work would be helpful to free states as they struggled with the issues of freedom and slavery in the new territories.

The book is written in a dispassionate and objective tone, although it is clear that Judge Stroud did not support slavery. Furthermore, there is no evidence that the work was written so that lawyers and slaveholders could have access to a comprehensive manual that contained all of the essential legal thinking on the question of slavery. The work could, however, be used for that

2 This biographical information was furnished to the author by Princeton's Seeley G. Mudd Manuscript Library, through the kind assistance of Rosemary Switzer, Special Collections Assistant.

3 Joan D. Hedrick, *Harriet Beecher Stowe: A Life* (New York: Oxford University Press, 1994), page vii.

purpose. In a blanket survey of slave codes of the period, he analyzed the statutes of Delaware, Maryland, Virginia, North Carolina, South Carolina, Georgia, Kentucky, Tennessee, Louisiana, Mississippi, Alabama and Missouri. He also drew upon works that had been written in many of the above states by judges. For example, he quoted extensively from *Brevard's Digest* by Judge Brevard of South Carolina. To illuminate the effects of slavery upon the masters, he also drew upon, to a lesser degree, non-legal writings such as Thomas Jefferson's *Notes on Virginia.*

However, it was in the legislative enactments of the southern states where Stroud found the most convincing evidence of a racist popular will. During this century, racism reached its apogee.[4] This base exploitation of African labor touched every facet of American life: religious, political, social, cultural, economic and legal. In fact, it was through the law that racism became institutionalized as the public policy of the United States.[5] Stroud's book on slave laws, therefore, exposed to the world, through its publications in 1827 and 1856, the diabolical nature of the legal enactments throughout the South that debased both African people and those who held them in bondage.

He wrote in his preface that many masters were, "little controlled by feelings of humanity, and less restrained by the precepts of religion,—many who, feeling power, forget right." It is for this reason that Stroud's book became such an important work of the nineteenth century, and continues to offer lessons of national importance today. The irony of the nineteenth century American life was the willingness of a substantial portion of the American population to ignore glaring precepts of morality, manifested primarily in the Christian message, and adopt a political,

---

4 George M. Fredrickson in *Racism: A Short History* , page 6, defined racism as the complete and permanent dehumanization of people of African descent. However, a more realistic definition can be found in Jemadari Kamara and Tony Menelik Van Der Meer's *State of the Race: "Creating Our 21st Century: Where Do We Go From Here?"*, page 376, where they and The People's Institute defined racism as "race prejudice plus power."

5 Robert Johnson, Jr., *Race, Law, and Public Policy, Second Edition* (Baltimore: Black Classic Press, 2002), pages 34-54.

socio-economic and legal system based upon human exploitation and moral degradation. The eminent African-American scholar W.E.B. Du Bois defined this fundamental contradiction in American life as a paradox of multiple dimensions:

> This way of thinking gave rise to many paradoxes, and it was characteristic of the era that men did not face paradoxes with any plan to solve them. There was the religious paradox: the contradiction between the Golden Rule and the use of force to keep human beings in their appointed places; the doctrine of the White Man's Burden and the conversion of the heathen, faced by the actuality of famine, pestilence, and caste. There was the assumption of the absolute necessity of poverty for the majority of men in order to save civilization for the minority, for that aristocracy of mankind which was at the same time the chief beneficiary of culture.[6]

In developing and sustaining this system, based upon racial subordination, southerners developed immoral legal concepts that gave legitimacy to their way of life. Stroud discussed in his work the legal rationales for the system of slave laws that purported to give legitimacy to the economic exploitation of African people. In developing his discussion, he relies upon several broad areas of legal discourse on several key areas: presumption of slave status; master-slave relationship; and gradual abolishment of slavery.

Presumption of Slave Status

One of the earliest means that southerners used to legitimize slave status was to create in law a presumption that "Negro" status equaled slave status. Stroud traces the earliest evidence of this legal concept to a Maryland statute in 1663. The presumption of slave status was perpetual, or in the language of the statute "durante vita." Children suffered the same fate as the parent. And if any "free-born English women" married a Negro, she would be obligated to serve the master of her husband and any children born to the union would

6   W.E.B. Du Bois, *The World and Africa* (New York: International Publishers, 1972), page17.

automatically become slaves. Central to this presumption of slave status was the common law concept that the condition of the child followed that of the father. In the year 1715 this legal approach was changed to reflect the mounting evidence of slave children being fathered by masters on the plantations. The resulting new statutory construction, that the status of the child followed that of the mother, insured that the master would benefit from his sexual exploitation of African women in two respects. One, he could have sex without the risk of emancipating any offspring that may result, and two, he could increase his slave population, and therefore his investment portfolio.

The presumption of slave status, according to Stroud, also found expression in northern states and extended to Indians. This debasement of native people ultimately led to the legal justification for genocide and the wholesale theft of native land by the European conquerors. For example, the Supreme Court of New Jersey in 1797 ruled that both Indians and Negroes could be slaves in the state, even though it was unclear in the law when and how they lost their freedom. The Court merely reasoned that any contrary interpretation of the laws of New Jersey would be "a great violation of the rights of property." In New Jersey, the law recognized that property rights superseded the human rights of African people. A review of nineteenth century laws, including Supreme Court decisions, found the racist capitalist class in America creating legal concepts that had no precedence in legal discourse. The concept of discovery was a classic example of this leap into legal fantasy or legal imperialism which allegedly gave European elites the right to claim the land of indigenous people because they "discovered" it first.[7]

Additionally, the laws throughout the country placed restrictions upon free Negroes as well. For example, in South Carolina if a free

---

7 Robert Johnson, Jr., *Race, Law and Public Policy, Second Edition* (Baltimore: Black Classic Press, 2002), pages 57-61. In the case of Cherokee Nation v. State of Georgia, the Supreme Court of the United States upheld a Georgia statute, passed in 1828, that allowed the confiscation of Cherokee land and their ultimate annihilation as a people. See State of Vermont v. Raleigh Elliott on pages 156-168 for a modern case on extinguishment of native rights and the law of discovery.

Negro concealed or harbored a runaway slave, he would have to pay a fine, which if not paid would result in the free Negro being placed up for public auction. In Virginia an emancipated slave must get out of the state within twelve months or he could be apprehended and sold and the proceeds given to the Literary Fund. Many of these laws, particularly in Virginia, arose as a result of slave revolts that forced the capitalist elites to develop and enforce laws that curtailed the rights of free Africans as well. These repressive laws became quite common after the slave revolts of Gabriel Prosser (1800, Virginia), Denmark Vesey (1822, South Carolina), Nat Turner (1831, Virginia) and other lesser known individuals.

Central to the classification of slave status was the recognition that slaves were not human beings, but property. Slaves could not purchase or inherit property. If they did receive property, it belonged to their master. They could make no wills. They could not marry. As property, slaves could be sold, pledged as collateral, tortured and put to death by the master. Mississippi was the leading state on the issue of slaves owning property. By statute, slaves were prohibited from cultivating cotton for their own use. Masters were subjected to fines if they allowed such practices to occur. The state of Louisiana explicitly established a rule that became universal throughout the South, that what a slave owned belonged to the master. In Tennessee, money acquired by a slave with the consent of the master, belonged to the master. In North Carolina, a master could claim the land that his slave received as compensation for public service in the Revolutionary War.

Master-Slave Relationship

In order to solidify the institution of slavery, the relationship of master and slavehad to be firmly and unequivocally established in civil law, which recognized the primary purpose of the master slave relationship as the quest for profit. In short, the relationship was established to promote and nurture the capitalist exploitation of African people for profit. The most penetrating discussion of this relationship between the rise of capitalism and the development of racism is Eric William's *Capitalism and Slavery*. In this monumental work, Williams postulates that slavery was primarily an economic institution and that "slavery was not born of racism: rather, racism was the consequence of slavery. Unfree labor in the New World was brown, white, black, yellow, Catholic, Protestant and pagan."[8] In 1829, the Supreme Court of North Carolina established this legal/economic principle, which quickly took precedence throughout the South, when it wrote: "The subject is one doomed in his own person and his posterity to ...toil that another may reap the fruits." The authority of the master, according to the Court, was "uncontrolled", and "absolute." On the other hand, submission of the slave had to be "perfect."[9]

At the heart of this relationship was the power of the master to conduct his business of slavery without legal interference. For example, he could determine what clothing and food the slave received and inflict whatever punishment he deemed appropriate. The master could freely delegate these powers to his agents. The status of the slave could be changed only by the master. It could be passed to the offspring and it lasted forever. The slave was therefore powerless to change his condition. He, in essence, would be a slave for life. From the first day that he recognized his status as a slave to the time when he relinquished his last breath, he was forever aware of his sense of nobodiness, of African inferiority and white supremacy.

"Negro acts," that governed the master-slave relationship, were passed in all of the southern states. These statutes were designed to protect slave property and to regulate, to some degree, the relationship of master-slave so as to prevent some unscrupulous masters from damaging the slave economy through excessive punishments or inactions. These statutes were never enacted to

8   Eric Williams, *Capitalism and Slavery* (New York: Capricorn Books, 1966), page 7.

9   The State v. Mann, 2 Devereux Rep. 263, 266. While these rules were relaxed in northern states, all of the original colonies of Britain sanctioned slavery, but abolished it long before the South. For example, Massachusetts ended slavery through legislation in 1641. For a comprehensive review of the master-slave relationship in the North, the leading text is A. Leon Higginbotham, Jr.'s *In the Matter of Color* (New York: Oxford University Press, 1978).

benefit the Africans or to promote humanitarian treatment. In 1740, South Carolina prohibited slave masters from working slaves more than fifteen hours per day. In 1806, Louisiana mandated that slaves be given half an hour for breakfast and two hours for dinner, during which time they could prepare their meals. These regulations also pertained to the quantity and quality of food provided to the slave. In Louisiana masters were required to give each slave, each month, one barrel of either Indian corn, rice, beans, or other grain. The same statutes required slaves to receive one pair of shirts and pants for both summer and winter months.

The right of the master to discipline his slave was so absolute in the South, that only two states, Louisiana and Kentucky, allowed slaves to petition the courts for a change of masters. However, even in these cases, such relief was rarely granted because a master must first be convicted of cruelty and second the remedy depended upon the sole discretion of the judge.

While these statutes imposed very few limits upon the power of the master to punish slaves, they strictly forbade the *willful*, *malicious* and *premeditated* killing of a slave. From as early as 1821 this type of killing was a capital offense throughout the slave holding states. If a slave died, however, as a result of *moderate correction* or an act of resistance or rebellion, the law did not treat these actions as punishable.

The authority to delegate power was central to maintaining the master-slave relationship. Louisiana was the sole state that passed comprehensive legislation on this important subject. All other states looked to it for guidance on how this power of control over the slave should be delegated to third parties.

Finally, slaves could not make or enter into contracts, including contracts for marriage. The relationship that slaves had among each other (*contubernium*) was not recognized in American southern slave law.

This caste status, based upon race, found expression in the courts of the South. For example, it was universally recognized that neither a slave nor a free person could testify against a white person in a court of law. This prohibition applied to all people of color and was not limited to Africans who were held in slavery. Consequently, a white person could inflict grievous harm upon African people with impunity unless another white person witnessed the offense and chose to testify in a court of law. African people, could, of course testify against each other.

The withholding of education from Africans, both slave and free, represented an integral part of the system to control both the body and mind of the slave. In *Narrative of the Life of Frederick Douglass*, we see the dire consequences that would result to both the slave and master, if the slave was allowed to learn to read and write. In *Narrative* Mrs. Auld has been caught by her husband teaching Douglass to read. Mr. Auld admonishes his wife:

> If you give a nigger an inch, he will take an ell. A nigger should know nothing but to obey his master- to do as he is told to do. Learning would *spoil* the best nigger in the world. Now…if you teach that nigger…how to read, there would be no keeping him. It would forever unfit him to be a slave. He would at once become unmanageable, and of no value to his master. As to himself, it could do him no good, but a great deal of harm. It would make him discontented and unhappy.[10]

According to Stroud, state legislatures across the South developed laws to prohibit not only instruction, but the assembling of Africans as early as 1740 (South Carolina). The laws gave magistrates the power to authorize the disruption of these "unlawful meetings" and to inflict no more than twenty lashes upon Africans and others engaged in "mental instruction." This prohibition of meeting for mental instruction applied during any time of the day or

---

10 Benjamin Quarles, Editor, *Narrative of the Life of Frederick Douglass: An American Slave, Written by Himself* (Cambridge: The Belknap Press of Harvard University, 1988), page 58.

night and even though a white person may have been present. The punishment for violating these statutes applied to everyone. It was a criminal offense for whites to teach a slave to read or write, to aid another in teaching or to support any slave in learning to read or write. Consequently, a white person could be prosecuted for giving even minimal support to teaching Africans, and for providing the place where the teaching occurred or funds that supported the teaching. This prohibition against instruction also applied to moral instruction as well. Some states prohibited moral education outright, while other states like Virginia decreed that an unlawful assemblage existed only when Africans gathered for worship under the leadership of a "negro."

Finally, submission to the will of the master was required in all of the states. This submission was precipitated by laws that provided severe punishment for each violation. In Georgia, for example, a slave could suffer the punishment of a whipping for striking a white person. For a second offense he was subjected to the death penalty. In South Carolina, in 1740, a white man could stop and question any slave who was off his plantation and not in the company of another white person. If the slave refused to submit to the examination he could be "apprehended and moderately" corrected. If the slave assaulted or struck the white person, he could be "lawfully killed."

This requirement of submission to the commands and wishes of the master had particularly harmful repercussions upon African women. Linda Brent, a slave woman, described these special problems faced by African women on the plantation:

> No pen can give an adequate description of the all-pervading corruption produced by slavery. The slave girl is reared in an atmosphere of licentiousness and fear. The lash and the foul talk of her master and his sons are her teachers. When she is fourteen or fifteen, her owner, or his sons, or the overseer, or perhaps all of them, begin to bribe her with presents. If these fail to accomplish their purpose, she is whipped or starved into submission to their will. She may have had religious principles inculcated by some pious mother or grandmother, or some good mistress; she may have a lover, whose good

opinion and peace of mind are dear to her heart; or the profligate men who have power over her may be exceedingly odious to her. But resistance is hopeless.[11]

The slave codes empowered any white person to accost slaves who were gathered together or traveling together on a "highroad", without a white person in their presence. In Maryland the white person could apprehend the slaves and inflict up to twenty lashings upon each. Slaves were also subjected to lashings if they were found outside their plantations and on land owned by another white man. Other offenses that would subject the slave to punishment would be traveling at night without a pass, or being found in another white man's "negro-quarters". The Africans found in the presence of the offending slave would be subject to lashings as well. Finally, whites could lawfully kill a slave who had run away and had been "outlawed". Most states authorized the killing of any slave who aided or abetted a runaway.

Abolishment of Slavery

Stroud ends his excellent book with a discussion of various efforts to abolish slavery. The Commonwealth of Pennsylvania was the first state to attempt abolition in 1780, stipulating that anyone born in the state after the passage of the statute would be free. The Massachusetts movement to end slavery stemmed from an interpretation of its Constitution's Bill of Rights. Other states quickly followed this trend. In 1784 Connecticut limited the years that a child born into slavery could be held in that status to age twenty-five. Stroud's discussion of the infamous Fugitive Slave Act of 1850 whereby the Federal Government attempted to make the issue of emancipation a federal issue and to require all states to respect the slave holder's rights in his slave property, also occupies a central part of the book's conclusion. Despite these efforts to limit slavery, by 1856, the date of his book's last publication, slavery as a

---

11 Linda Brent, *Incidents in the Life of a Slave Girl* (New York: Harcourt Brace Jovanovich, 1973), pages 51-52.

protected institution had become entrenched in American law with slave holding interests firmly in control of the legal discourse that guaranteed and protected their economic exploitation of African labor.

By the time of his death in 1875, Judge Stroud had seen the United States confront its racial divisions in a most violent manner, leading to the deaths of more than half a million men and women. He had witnessed the political transformation of America, whereby Africans were guaranteed through Constitutional amendments freedom and citizenship rights in the United States. One can only surmise what would have been the result if his compendium of the nation's slave laws had been written for the general public in addition to the legal community. Could this violence and delay in the granting of human and civil rights been avoided? Nevertheless, the work stands as a testimony to the pervasive and decadent scheme of racial subjugation and economic exploitation that became the social, economic and legal fabric of the United States.

In the twenty-first century, we can only hope that this young republic will reflect critically on this sordid past, and provide African descendants affirmative relief for this legally sanctioned, intentional and premeditated violation of human rights. Through George M. Stroud's exhaustive work in the nineteenth century, the legal evidence of this exploitation and denial of human rights has been ably documented. It is now time for policy makers to recognize this evidence as an essential part of the American historical experience and contextualize it within the national debate over affirmative action and reparations. If this happens, Stroud's work, 148 years after its last publication, could be utilized, along with the Dred Scott decision, as a legal/historical predicate for helping Americans to both understand their past and to move toward racial healing, which comes from confronting (not forgetting) the past; and from understanding the interrelationship between law and racism.

A

SKETCH OF THE LAWS

RELATING TO

SLAVERY

IN THE SEVERAL STATES OF THE UNITED
STATES OF AMERICA.

Second Edition,

WITH SOME ALTERATIONS AND CONSIDERABLE ADDITIONS.

BY

GEORGE M. STROUD.

PHILADELPHIA:
HENRY LONGSTRETH, 347 MARKET ST.
1856.

STEREOTYPED BY L. JOHNSON AND CO.
PHILADELPHIA.

PRINTED BY HENRY B ASHMEAD,
GEORGE ST ABOVE ELEVENTH.

PREFACE.

THE state of slavery in this country, so far as it can be ascertained from the *laws* of the several independent sovereignties which belong to our confederacy, is the subject of the following sheets. This comprises a particular examination of the laws of the states of Delaware, Maryland, Virginia, North Carolina, South Carolina, Georgia, Kentucky, Tennessee, Louisiana, Mississippi, Alabama, and Missouri. With respect to the remaining states, slavery in some having been abolished and in others never tolerated, a cursory notice of a few of their laws, chiefly important for the evidence which they furnish of the right of these states to the appellation of *non-slave-holding*, is all which the title or object of this work requires.

The District of Columbia, though in this connection not properly denominated *a state*, yet, from its important character in being exclusively within the jurisdiction of the Federal Government, deserves an equal share of attention. It happens, however, that this *District*, in regard to slavery as well as many other topics, is not regulated *integrally* by a code of laws enacted for the purpose by Congress, that body having, by an act dated February 27th, 1801, declared that the part of the District of Columbia which had been ceded to the United States by the state of Virginia should be governed by the laws which were then in force in Virginia, and that the other part, which had been ceded by the state of Maryland, should in like manner be governed by the laws then in force in Maryland. But few alterations have been made in the laws affecting the condition of slaves in either of the states just named since the date of the act of Congress; the quotations, therefore, given from their respective codes, being applied in conformity with the distinction established by the act of Congress, may, with but little hazard of error, be received as the laws of the District of Columbia.

Such provisions of the *Constitution of the United States* as might be fitly introduced into this sketch have been added in an *Appendix*. Several acts of Congress will be found inserted there also. These, however, are not numerous, since, from the peculiar relation which subsists between the Federal Government and the individual states, the former, except

3

within the District of Columbia and the *territories* not yet incorporated into the Union as *states*, is restrained from the exercise of legislative functions on all subjects of a character exclusively municipal.

The value of a work like the present must depend mainly upon the authenticity of its materials. On this point but little, if any, exception can be justly taken. The most approved code of each state was sought for, and, in most instances, obtained. The laws of Delaware, Maryland, Virginia, Georgia, Kentucky, Louisiana, Mississippi, Alabama, and Missouri, have been cited, from publications made under the express sanction of the several legislatures of these states. The laws of South Carolina have been drawn principally from a source entitled to equal consideration. I mean the Digest by *Judge Brevard.* This, however, having been issued from the press in 1814, it became necessary to procure a work which would indicate the changes effected by the legislature since that period. The *second* edition of *James' Digest* has been used for this purpose; and, though the *first* edition of this work is stated in Griffith's Law Register to have been imperfectly executed and not to deserve much reliance, yet, a *second* one having been called for, it seems fair to presume that in this the errors of the *first* have been corrected and its defects supplied.

Having been under the necessity of bringing together the laws of so large a number of independent states, it must be obvious that considerable difficulty existed in assigning to each part its proper place and giving to each its due effect, and, at the same time, preserving the appearance of symmetry in the whole. As the best method of meeting this difficulty, when the provisions of different codes on the same point were in the same language, or, as was most commonly the case, the same in substance but not in language, I have in general used a transcript from *one* code, and, having noted in immediate connection the work from which it was taken, have added successively references to the other codes. The words *"similar,"* and *"nearly similar,"* are sometimes interposed, the purpose of which needs no explanation. The titles of the different *Digests* being cited seemed to me to render a perpetual repetition of the *names* of the *states* unnecessary. In many occasions, therefore, these are omitted.

That the comments which I have offered on many of the laws might be the more readily understood, and their propriety judged of, I have, in almost every quotation which has been made, given the exact words of the law, omitting such only as were not essential to the perception of the legislative intent. Of the *actual* condition of slaves this sketch does not profess to treat. In representative republics, however, like the United States, where the popular voice so greatly influences all political concerns,—where the members of the legislative departments are dependent for their places upon *annual* elections,—the *laws* may be safely regarded as constituting a faithful exposition of the sentiments of the people, and as furnishing, therefore, strong evidence of the practical enjoyments and privations of those whom they are designed to govern. To the condition of the *passive* members of the community, such as slaves, this latter deduction is emphatically applicable. I speak of the case of slaves *generally*. Their condition will, no doubt, in a great degree, take its complexion from the peculiar disposition of their respective masters,—a consideration which operates as much *against* as in *favour* of the slave; for it cannot be denied that there are many persons but little controlled by feelings of humanity, and less restrained by the precepts of religion,—many who, "feeling power, forget right."

The very existence of slavery is calculated to produce the worst effects on the temper and morals of the masters. On this point, and, indeed, on the general treatment of slaves by their masters, the most decisive testimony is borne by MR. JEFFERSON, in his *Notes on Virginia.* "The whole commerce between master and slave," says he, "is a perpetual exercise of the most boisterous passions,—the most unremitting despotism on the one part and degrading submissions on the other. Our children see this, and learn to imitate it; for man is an imitative animal. If a parent had no other motive, either in his own philanthropy or his self-love, for restraining the intemperance of passion towards his slave, it should always be a sufficient one that his child is present. *But generally it is not sufficient. The parent storms, the child looks on, catches the lineaments of wrath, puts on the same airs in the circle of smaller slaves, gives a loose to his worst passions,* AND, THUS NURSED, EDUCATED, AND DAILY EXERCISED IN TYRANNY, CANNOT BUT BE STAMPED BY IT WITH ODIOUS PECULIARITIES."

PHILADELPHIA, *October 8th*, 1827.

PREFACE TO THE SECOND EDITION.

NEARLY twenty-nine years have elapsed since the original of *this sketch* was published. At that time the sentiment seemed to be universal throughout the United States, if not the whole civilized world, that in itself, as applied to reason able beings, involuntary servitude, except as a punishment for crime, was indefensibly wrong. In respect to its existence in these United States, it was everywhere spoken of as a moral and political evil.

But, as it had been introduced among us during the period of our colonial dependence on Great Britain, and the number of the bond had become very great,—as, by reason of native constitution or long-continued degradation, the coloured race was manifestly inferior to the white,—it was universally felt and acknowledged that the problem of their emancipation was exceedingly difficult to be *worked out*.

Of the *six* Presidents of the United States, *four* had been from a *slave-holding* state,—Virginia, the largest of the original thirteen, and *one* of the most, if not *the most*, influential of all. No one of these illustrious men was the advocate of slavery at any known period of his political history.

WASHINGTON has perpetuated his sentiments in the most unequivocal manner by liberating the great body of his slaves by his last will. JEFFERSON prepared and proposed a Constitution for Virginia, by which all born after the year 1800 were to be free. MADISON was unwilling that the word *slave* should have a place in the Federal Constitution, and, on his motion, it had been struck out from a *projected* article of that instrument. In respect to MONROE, no evidence, it is believed, exists to show that devotion to the cause of freedom, in its large and just sense, was less ardent in him than in the bosoms of his illustrious predecessors.

About the year 1830, for the first time, so far as my information extends, among men of the least political repute, it was announced by a governor of South Carolina that the institution of slavery was eminently useful and beneficent. And subsequently a Senator of the same state openly maintained the same doctrine. Later still, we have been presented with elaborate essays of the same general complexion from the pens of some of the most gifted and eminent scholars of the South.

The territorial dominion of the Federal Government has been greatly extended of late years. The augmentation of

6

the slave power—the political strength of the *slave-holding* states in comparison with the *free* states—was the great, if not the sole, incentive to these acquisitions of territory. The annexation of *Texas* was a Southern measure. The war with *Mexico* had a similar origin. *Cuba* has been and now is sought after by the same political interest, with an appetite which never palls. The *pecuniary* consideration which has been offered for it by peaceful negotiation throws in the shade the wildest extravagance of an insane imagination. Military expeditions have again and again been set on foot in Southern cities and by Southern men, for the forcible subjugation of this island, with the ultimate view of adding one more *slave-holding* state to the Union.

For no other purpose than the extension of slavery, a solemn compromise, which had existed for one-third of a century, between the slave-holding and the free states, has been recently abrogated. And already measures of unparalleled atrocity have been resorted to by the slave power, to deter and prevent the settlement of *Kansas* by freemen.

Without the co-operation in part of the North, the efforts of the South for the extension of slavery, which have succeeded, must have failed ; and further success will be checked if the North be but faithful to her own honour and interest.

The press, in one way or another, has contributed largely to a misapprehension of the real nature of this *peculiar institution,* so highly cherished of late years by the South. I do not allude here to the *editorials* of the *newspaper* press, nor to any special efforts by the conductors of these journals on this subject. The evil is done in an indirect way, without the purpose to mislead and without a suspicion that a wrong impression is likely to be produced. A weak or interested person visits the South, and brings back reports* of the happy

---

* After I had thus written, and was about to send it to the press, I chanced to look into *Mr. Olmsted's "Journey in the Seaboard Slave States,"* when my eye was caught by the statement, at page 108, that the LAWS of *Louisiana* "required the planter to give slaves 200 pounds of pork a year." This was derived from *report* while he was in *Virginia.* Thinking the error would be corrected when he should reach *Louisiana,* I turned to his account of what he saw and heard there. To my surprise, I found *repetitions,* at pages 650, 680, 690, and 700, of his previous statement. What I have said, *post,* page 47, is derived from the *Revised Statutes* of 1852, and shows that *meat* was not *then* (and, I presume, is not *now*) a part of the diet of slaves *required by law.*

If so intelligent a writer as *Mr. Olmsted* could be so misled, what confidence is to be placed in the gleanings of *anonymous* correspondents of the kind alluded to, on transient visits?

and contented condition of the slave population which he or
she has witnessed.   Much of this is true.   For there are, no
doubt, many humane masters and some contented slaves.   But
visitors are not apt, in polished life, to go where they are not
invited to go.   Their entertainment, as well as their proper
place, is in the parlour and not in the kitchen.   To follow a
gang of *field* negroes under the superintendence of an overseer
or a driver would be a poor pastime,—uncomfortable in a cool
day, and quite intolerable in a hot one.   What visitor would
think of *penetrating* the *negro quarters*, or be inquisitive as
to what clothes were worn in the *fields*, what food provided,
in what quantities, and how and when it was allowed to be
eaten,—when, how, and where were the indolent, the perverse
and the refractory punished?   Who would invite his guests to
so revolting a spectacle?

  " Nec pueros coram populo Medea trucidet
    Aut humana palam coquat exta nefarius Atreus."

  Again—we are told, in the *religious* periodicals, of the com-
mendable labours of the clergy to impart the truths of the
gospel to the slave.   I know nothing which can be more
worthy of their holy calling ; and I entertain no doubt of
the extent of their labours, and would fain cherish a belief
in their success.

  But who connects with the accounts of these praiseworthy
efforts the indisputable fact that the only mode of instruction
of *slaves* which the *law* of the South does not prohibit is *oral*
inculcation ?—that to precede or accompany this by *teaching*
the slave to *read* would be visited by severe penalties ?   Or
who bears in mind that no *public* provision is made for the
religious instruction of slaves by whites, whilst the feeble efforts,
for this purpose, of those of their own colour, are repressed
by law?

  These and the other manifold evils of slavery, which are
part and parcel of the institution, and, in the expressed opinions of its supporters, *inseparable* from it, seldom meet the
eye in the numerous and valuable publications which abound
in this age and country.

  This small volume is designed to supply the proper knowledge of the *peculiar institution.*   It is derived from the MOST
AUTHENTIC SOURCES,—*the statutes of the slave-holding states,
and the reported decisions of their courts of judicature.*

  The writer takes occasion here to state distinctly that he recognises in the fullest extent the great principle of our complex

government that each of the several states is sovereign and independent, except in so far as it has, by acceding to the national Constitution, surrendered any portion of such sovereignty; that *slavery* is a positive and peculiar institution of *each* of the states in which it subsists, over which the other states, neither separately nor collectively, nor the Federal Government itself, can rightfully exercise any power; and in respect, therefore, to the evils or the continuance of the institution, no citizen of a free state is in any degree or in any sense responsible.

But he does most firmly believe that *negro slavery*, as it exists in the slave-holding states of the Union, is a moral, social, and political evil of incalculable magnitude; and he as firmly believes that the free states have the constitutional right and power to prevent the extension of the institution into territories not yet erected into states. And, having this right and this power, the obligation is equally clear and imperative to make no truce, no compromise, no relaxation of effort, in the great struggle which is now waging for freedom on the uncontaminated soil over which the Federal Government has been invested with sovereign authority.

The labour of preparing this new edition has been undertaken from a strong conviction that such a work is a great need at the present time. Its publication rests upon the sole responsibility of the writer. He is not now, nor ever has been, a member of any *Abolition* or *Anti-slavery* Society. He has acted upon his own judgment. He has taken counsel of no one.

But, although the work has been prosecuted without the counsel of any one, the writer has been cheered in his labour with the hope that its publication will find a welcome and support throughout the whole of the free states of our Republic. He calls to mind the memorable contest in 1819–20, which resulted in the *Missouri Compromise*, when the people of these states stood together, as if moved by one mind, in stern opposition to the *extension* of slave territory. But for that compromise, the battle would have been fought with success then. Those who then profited by its deceptive promise of future peace have, by its repeal, forced the contest again. Will freedom or slavery now triumph? Will the free states suffer themselves to be deceived a *second* time?

PHILADELPHIA, Aug. 7, 1856.

ADVERTISEMENT TO THE FIRST EDITION.

THE laws of several of the states being contained in *Digests*, in citing them the names of the compilers have been generally given, and not the names of the states. Thus, the laws of *Georgia* are cited from *"Prince's Digest,"* 1 vol.; the laws of *South Carolina*, some from *"Brevard's Digest,"* 3 vols., and *some* from *"James' Digest,"* 1 vol.; the laws of *North Carolina*, from *"Haywood's Manual,"* 1 vol.; the laws of *Kentucky*, from *"Littell & Swigert's Digest,"* 2 vols.; the laws of *Louisiana*, to the year 1816, from *"Martin's Digest,"* 3 vols.; the laws of *Pennsylvania*, from *Purdon's Digest,"* 1 vol.; the laws of *Alabama*, from *"Toulmin's Digest,"* 1 vol. In *Virginia* and *Mississippi*, *Revised Codes* have been prepared, and are cited, *"Virg. Rev. Code,"* and *"Miss. Rev. Code,"* unless in some instances, where the name of the state is *prefixed* to the extract made, and *Rev. Code* only marks the citation. The *Civil Code of Louisiana* and *the Code of Practice* adopted in the same state are cited by their respective titles, and the *article* and *its number* given, but not the *page,* this being the *usual* and most convenient mode of reference as to these codes.

With respect to the laws of the other states, no explanation is necessary, as the name of the state is used.

ADDITIONAL WORKS CITED IN THE SECOND EDITION.

Code of Virginia of 1849.
Revised Statutes of Louisiana, 1852.
Morehead & Brown's Digest of Kentucky Statutes, to 1834, and *Loughborough's continuation of the same.*
Clay's Alabama Digest, 1843.
Caruthers & Nicholson's Statutes of Tennessee, 1836.
Revised Statutes of North Carolina, 1836–7.
Revised Statutes of Missouri, 1845.
English's Digest of the Laws of Arkansas, 1848.
Cobb's Digest of the Laws of Georgia, 1851.
Hartley's Laws of Texas, 1850.
Thompson's Digest of Florida, 1847.

CONTENTS.

CHAPTER I.

11

LAWS

RELATING TO SLAVERY.

CHAPTER I.

OF THE PERSONS WHO MAY BE HELD AS SLAVES, AND
UPON WHAT AUTHORITY THEY ARE SO HELD.

THE design of this sketch being merely to furnish
a connected view of the *laws* which relate to the
institution of slavery as it exists among us, it would
be supererogatory to enter upon a *particular* inquiry
into its *origin*. I shall introduce the subject to the
reader, by ascertaining what persons are included
under the denomination of slaves, and upon what
authority they are regarded as such. These propositions present but little difficulty; since positive
enactments of the several legislatures of the slave-
holding states constitute the authority; and the language by which they are enunciated is sufficiently
explicit to prevent any misapprehension of their
meaning.

The earliest law which I shall quote is taken from
the laws of Maryland. It is an act of the year 1663,
chap. 30, in these words: "All negroes or other
slaves within the province, and all negroes and other

slaves to be hereafter imported into the province, shall serve *durante vita;* and all children born of any negro or other slave, shall be slaves as their *fathers* were for the term of their lives." *Section* 2. "And forasmuch as divers free-born *English* women, forgetful of their free condition and to the disgrace of our nation, do intermarry with negro slaves, by which also, divers suits may arise, touching the issue of such women, and a great damage doth befall the master of such negroes, for preservation whereof, for deterring such free-born women from such shameful matches, *be it enacted, &c.* That whatsoever free-born woman shall intermarry with any slave, from and after the last day of the present assembly, shall serve the master of such slave during the life of her husband; and *that all the issue of such free-born women, so married, shall be slaves as their* FATHERS *were.*"

This law is remarkable for two particulars: First, the recognition of the common law doctrine, "partus sequitur *patrem,*" that the offspring follows the condition of *the father:* Second, the *pur auter vie* slavery to which it subjected the *white free-born English women* who might come within its provisions. The number of this *new* species of slaves must have been very small, and as the act had but a short duration, it is unnecessary to take further notice of this branch of it. With respect to the *offspring* of such marriages consummated while the act was in force, as these were made *slaves for life;* and as an act passed in 1681, for the purpose of repealing that of 1663, contained an *express saving of the rights acquired under the act of* 1663, *before the date of the repealing act, so* *far as concerned the enslavement of the woman* AND HER ISSUE, it is not improbable that some of their *descendants* are at the present day in that condition.*

---

* It is certain several such persons were held in absolute bondage until the year 1791, when (after the lapse of more than a century) it was finally decided by the highest court of judicature in the state, that for want of a *conviction* of the *white woman* who originally violated the law, her descendants were not slaves, and could not legally be retained as such. *See the case, Mary Butler vs. Adam Craig, 2 Harris and M'Henry's Reports,* 214 *to* 236. At a former period, (1770,) in a case in which the *parents* of the same Mary Butler were plaintiffs and petitioners for freedom, it was adjudged that they *were* slaves—their grandmother, a white woman, having been married to a negro slave in the year 1681, a short time prior to the repeal of the act of 1663. *Case of William and Mary Butler vs. Richard Boardman,* 1 *Maryland (Harris and M'Henry's) Reports,* 371 *to* 385.

A statement of one of the counsel for the petitioners in this latter case, as it serves to elucidate this anomalous portion of the history of slavery in Maryland, is here transcribed. "In the year 1676, the lord proprietary met the assembly in person; in 1677 he returned to England, and in 1681 he returned to this province, bringing Irish Nell" (Eleanor Butler, grandmother of the petitioners, who I presume were first cousins, as they were both petitioners for freedom as the descendants of the same parent, and were also husband and wife) "with him as a domestic servant. In 1681 she married," (a negro slave,) "and the repealing law was passed in the month of August immediately after the marriage, and his lordship interested himself in procuring the repeal, with a view to this particular case. The act of 1663 was repealed also, to prevent persons from purchasing white women" (as servants) "and marrying them to their slaves, for the purpose of making slaves of them" (and their offspring.) "The penalty is laid upon the masters, mistresses, &c., and the clergyman and the woman are intended to be favoured." This statement, though not very creditable to the early settlers of Maryland, is confirmed by the *preamble* to the repealing act, and also by the terms of the enacting clause; for it sets *free* any such white servant woman, and imposes a fine of ten thousand pounds of tobacco upon the master or mistress who should procure or connive at the marriage. *Act of* 1681, *chap.* 4.

The doctrine of "partus sequitur patrem" obtained in the province till the year 1699 or 1700,* when a general revision of the laws took place, and the acts, in which this doctrine was recognised, were, with many others, repealed. An interval of about fifteen years appears to have elapsed without any *written* law on this subject; but, in 1715, (*chap.* 44, *sect.* 22,) the following one was passed: "All negroes and other slaves already imported or hereafter to be imported into this province, and all *children now born or hereafter to be born of such negroes and slaves*, shall be slaves during their natural lives." Thus was the maxim of the civil law, "partus sequitur *ventrem*," introduced, and the condition of the *mother*, from that day up to the present time, has continued to determine the fate of the child.

This maxim of the civil law, the genuine and *degrading* principle of slavery, inasmuch as it places the slave upon a level with *brute* animals, prevails universally among the slave-holding states. The law of South Carolina may be quoted as follows: "All negroes, *Indians*, (free Indians in amity with this government, and negroes, mulattoes and mestizos, who are *now* free, excepted,) mulattoes or mestizos, who are or shall hereafter be in this province, and all their issue and offspring born or to be born, shall be and they are hereby declared to be and remain

---

* See the act of 1699, chap. 46, entitled "An act ascertaining the laws of this province," and the act of 1700, chap. 8, entitled "An act for repealing certain laws in this province, and confirming others."

forever hereafter absolute slaves, and shall *follow the condition of the mother.*" *Act of* 1740, *2 Brevard's Digest,* 229; similar in Georgia, *Prince's Dig.* 446, (*Act of* 1770;) and in Mississippi, *Revised Code of Mississippi, of* 1823, *page* 369; and see 1 *Rev. Code of Virg.* (*of* 1819,) *page* 421; *2 Litt. and Swi.* 1149–50, *Civ. Code of Louisiana, art.* 183. By this law, any person whose *maternal* ancestor, even in the *remotest* degree of distance from him or her, can be shown to have been a negro, or an Indian, or a mulatto, or a mestizo, *not* free at the date of the law, although the *paternal* ancestor at each successive generation may have been a *white free man,* is declared to be the subject of perpetual slavery. This is a measure of cruelty* and avarice which, to the reproach of our

---

* Under this law it may frequently happen that a person whose complexion is European may be *legally* retained as a slave. The well-informed mind will, upon a little reflection, perceive the justness of this conclusion. A competent judge of the subject, Don Antonio de Ulloa, whose opinion is confirmed by that of Mr. Edwards in his History of the West Indies, furnishes the following testimony: "Among the tribes which are derived from an intermixture of the whites with the negroes, the *first* are the *mulattoes;* next to these are the *tercerones,* produced from a white and a mulatto, with some approximation to the former, but not so near as to obliterate their origin. After these follow the *quarterones,* proceeding from a white and a terceron. The last are the *quinterones,* who owe their origin to a white and a quarteron. *This is the last gradation, there being no visible difference between them and the whites, either in colour or features;* NAY, THEY ARE OFTEN FAIRER THAN THE SPANIARDS." See *Edward's West Indies, book* 4, *chap.* 1. "A *quadroon* is the child of a *mestize* mother and a white father, as a *mestize* is the child of a *mulatto* mother and a white father. The quadroons are *almost entirely white:* from their skin no one would detect their origin; nay, many of them have as fair a complexion as

2*

republics, there is much reason to believe has no precedent in any other civilized country. "In

---

many of the haughty Creole females. Formerly they were known by their black hair and eyes; but at present *there are completely fair quadroon males and females.*"—*Travels through North America*, &c., by his Highness, Bernhard, *Duke of Saxe-Weimar Eisenach*, page 61, vol. ii. Thus the quinterones, who are only *four* removes from a negro ancestor, are found to be undistinguishable from the whites, either by colour or features. Yet even these, and the descendants of these to the remotest generation, are deemed slaves with us. In point of fact, *tercerones* are sometimes almost, if not entirely, white. An instance of this kind occurred in an individual, whose case underwent judicial investigation in the city of Philadelphia, in the year 1786; the report of which appears in 1 *Dallas' Rep.* 167, *Pirate alias Belt vs. Dalby.* The reporter's statement is given in these words: "The plaintiff, being the *supposed* issue of *white* and *mulatto* parents, attended the defendant to Philadelphia in the autumn of 1784, and presented *so pure a complexion,* that the attention of the Society (Abolition Society of Pennsylvania) was excited, &c. &c. Upon the trial it was given in evidence, that the plaintiff was born in Maryland of an unmarried *mulatto* woman" (who was a slave.)

I now quote another instance, of a most extraordinary character— of *white* children the immediate offspring of a *negro* mother; and though this may be looked upon as a *lusus naturæ,* to which no reasonable person would expect the general laws of society to be accommodated, yet, as it proves incontestably that *whites* are now in slavery in one of our states, under the *express* sanction of law, I will make no apology for introducing it. The instance to which I refer, is thus related by Laurence J. Trotti, in a letter to Professor James, of the University of Pennsylvania, dated November 15, 1825. "Some time in the year 1815, a *negro woman,* belonging to Mr. Allen, of Barnwell, *South Carolina,* was delivered by a natural unassisted labour of three children; *two* of them were *white* males, the other a perfectly *black* female. The two boys are now alive and full-grown for their age. Having, in company with other gentlemen, visited the *mother* and *children,* expressly to ascertain the truth of these facts, I have no hesitation in stating the above-mentioned circumstances as correct,"

Jamaica, the condition (of slavery) *ceases* by *express law* to attach upon the issue, at the *fourth* degree

&c. &c.   See *The North American Medical and Surgical Journal, No. 2, April*, 1826, *page* 466.   From the character of the Journal from which this account has been taken, and especially in reliance upon the judgment of the highly respectable gentleman to whom the letter is addressed, I have treated the whole relation as substantially true.   I confess, there is something (particularly the distance of time between the birth of the children and the date of the communication) which leaves room to doubt whether an imposition has not been practised on the *writer* of the letter—whether the *white children* were not born of *white parents;* yet, admitting this supposition to be correct, it would fortify the position, that our lawgivers should pay some respect to colour; for here are two *white* children who have been already in slavery more than ten years, and in all probability they will remain so during life.

An additional case may be here subjoined, illustrative of the general doctrine contained in this note.   An advertisement recently inserted in a newspaper published in the city of Philadelphia, offers a reward of one hundred dollars for the apprehension of a person alleged to be a runaway *slave,* who is thus described: —"Absconded from the subscriber on the 10th instant, a *very bright* mulatto man named Washington Thomas.   HE HAS SOMETIMES BEEN MISTAKEN FOR A WHITE MAN!!"   What the degree of distance of this person from an African ancestor is, does not appear; yet, though *more than once* taken for a white man, he is still claimed as a slave!!   See *Democratic Press of August* 13, 1827.

Take the following, among many similar cases, occurring in the slave states:—

"The *Salt River Journal,* at Bowling Green, Pike county, Mississippi, gives the following, which it correctly classifies as a peculiarly hard case:—' A case of a slave suing for his freedom, was tried a few days since in Lincoln county, of which the following is a brief statement of the particulars: A youth of about ten years of age sued for his freedom on the ground that he was a free white person.   The court granted his petition to sue as a pauper, upon inspection of his person. Upon his trial before the jury, he was examined by the jury and by

of distance from a negro ancestor. In other islands, (British West Indies,) the *written* law is silent on this head; but by established custom, the quadroons or mestizoes (so they call the second and third degrees) are rarely seen in a state of slavery." *Stephen's Slavery of the British West India Colonies delineated,* 27; *Edward's West Indies, book* 4, *chap.* 1. And, as in the Spanish and Portuguese colonies, slavery is in all respects milder than in those of the British, it is fairly inferrible that a regulation equally favourable to freedom, by custom, if not by express law, prevails there also. Of the French colonies and of the Dutch, I have not such information as will authorize an opinion which may deserve much reliance; yet in the *Code Noir* it is certain many provisions may be indicated, of a much more humane character than can be found in the codes of our slave-holding states, on kindred topics.

---

two learned physicians; all of whom concurred in the opinion that very little, if any, trace of negro blood could be discovered by any of the external appearances. All the physiological marks and distinctions which characterize the African descent have disappeared. His skin was fair; his hair soft, straight, fine, and white; his eyes blue, but rather disposed to the hazle-nut colour; nose prominent; the lips small and completely covering the teeth; his head round and well formed; forehead high and prominent; the ears large: the tibia of the leg straight; the feet hollow. Notwithstanding these evidences of his claims, he was proven to be the descendant of a mulatto woman, and that his progenitors on his mother's side had been, and still were, slaves; consequently he was found to be a slave. From the feeling manifested by the community where the trial was had, we presume his freedom will be purchased and his education provided for.' " See *Poulson's American Advertiser, Oct.* 16, 1834.

It has been already incidentally noticed, that by the common law,—the law of Villanage,—the offspring always followed the condition of the *father*: it has been also stated, and indeed the law which I have just extracted declares this principle in *unequivocal* terms, that, with respect to slavery among us, the condition of the *offspring* depends upon the condition of the *mother*. A consequence of this latter rule is, that whether born in or *out* of wedlock, the children are slaves whenever the mothers are so. But as to the child born *out* of wedlock, while from motives of public policy the *common law* prevents him from deriving any *benefit* from his parents, by way of *inheritance*, it declares, with a consistency strongly recommended by its humanity, that he shall not be obnoxious to the evils of slavery. Had these two maxims of the common law, *i. e.* that the offspring follows the condition of the father,—and that an illegitimate is always born free,—been permitted to retain their place in colonial jurisprudence, none but negroes of the whole blood (except from the rare instances of a matrimonial alliance between a free woman not black and an abject negro slave) would be numbered among the victims of slavery!! Every mulatto, except from the source just mentioned, would have been free—a destiny, at which, though it may have no claim to support it superior to what may be avouched for the *negro*, yet, inasmuch as it would have prevented the tremendous augmentation of our servile population, the evils of which are daily more and more felt, humanity and religion would have had cause to rejoice.

I am aware of a reply which may be given to
these remarks. It may be said, "True, on your
principles, no mulatto would be a slave—negroes
only would be such; still it would be necessary
only to encourage matrimony among slaves, and the
decrease of slaves, which you consider so important,
would not happen." Without stopping to show
that this view of the matter is not altogether correct,
it may be justly rejoined, that *this* very *encouragement
to matrimony* would, in itself, be of vast moment,
from *its moral effects;* and, furthermore, (what ought
by no means to be lost sight of,) since while the
parties to a marriage contract are in full life, neither
of them can lawfully enter into a similar contract
with a third person, the master's interest, or what he
conceives to be so, would in a great degree avert the
terrible calamity, which is now common—a separation of the parents of the same children—a separation of those who ought to be strictly and legally
husband and wife.

It may excite the surprise of some, to discover
Indians and their offspring comprised in the doom
of perpetual slavery; yet not only is *incidental* mention of them as slaves to be met with in the laws of
most of the states of our Confederacy, but in one,
at least, direct legislation may be cited to sanction
their enslavement. In Virginia, "By an act passed
in the year 1679, it was, for *the better encouragement
of soldiers*, declared, that what INDIAN PRISONERS
should be taken in a war in which the colony was
then engaged, should be *free purchase* to the *soldiers*
taking them. In 1682, it was declared, that all ser-

vants brought into this country, (Virginia,) by sea or land, not being *Christians*, whether negroes, Moors, mulattoes or INDIANS, (except Turks and Moors in amity with Great Britain,) and all INDIANS which should thereafter be SOLD by neighbouring Indians, or any other trafficking with us, *as slaves*, should be SLAVES *to all intents and purposes.*"* Per Judge Tucker, *in the case of Hudgins vs. Wright,* 1 *Henning and Munford's Reports,* 139.

And, in the state of New Jersey, it was decided by the supreme court, in the year 1797, "That *Indians* might be held as slaves." No law was adduced to show the origination of such a right, but it appeared by several acts of assembly, one of which was as early as 1713–14, that they were classed with

* "These acts," says Judge Tucker, speaking of the acts cited in the text, "continued in force till the year 1691, when, an act having been passed, authorizing a free and open trade for all persons, at all times and at all places, with *all Indians whatsoever*, it was decided by the courts, that this operated as *a repeal of the former acts.*" See 1 *Henning and Munford's Reports*, 139. The descendants of such Indians as were reduced to slavery under the sanction of the acts of 1679 and 1682, and during the time in which these were in force, may even at the present time be held as slaves in Virginia! ! But the decisions of the court protect all others. The highest court of judicature has decided, that "a *native* American Indian brought into Virginia *since* the year 1691, could not lawfully be held in slavery there, although such Indian was a slave in the country (Jamaica) from which she had been brought, previously to and at the time of her removal." *Butt vs. Rachel,* 4 *Munford's Reports,* 209. See also 2 *Henning and Munford's Reports,* 149, *Pallas and others vs. Hill and others,* in which cases the claim to freedom of at least *twelve* descendants of *native* American Indians, whose maternal ancestors had not been reduced to slavery till *after* 1691, was established.

negroes and mulattoes, *as slaves.* Chief-Justice Kinsey remarked, " They (Indians) have been so long recognised as slaves, in our law, that it would be as great a violation of the rights of property to establish a contrary doctrine at the present day, as it would in the case of Africans, *and as useless to investigate the manner in which they* ORIGINALLY lost their freedom." *The State vs. Waggoner,* 1 *Halstead's Reports,* 374 *to* 376.

In addition to the laws already cited, declaring who shall be deemed slaves, the codes of the slaveholding states exhibit a considerable number of enactments, by which FREE negroes, &c. are converted into absolute slaves. Thus, in *South Carolina,* if a *free* negro *harbour, conceal* or ENTERTAIN a runaway slave, or a slave charged "with *any* criminal matter," he shall forfeit the sum of ten pounds currency for the first day, and twenty shillings for every succeeding day, &c. And in case such forfeitures cannot be levied, or such free negro, &c. shall not pay the same, together with the charges attending the prosecution, such FREE *negro,* &c. shall be ordered by the justice *to be sold at public outcry,* and the money arising by such sale shall, in the first place, be paid for and applied towards the forfeiture, &c. to the owner, &c.; *and the overplus, if any, shall be paid by the said justice into the hands of the public treasurer,** &c. 2 *Brevard's Digest,* 237, *act of* 1740.

---

* I have, in the text, considered the whole of the 34th section of the act of 1740 as the law of South Carolina at the present time. A very recent proceeding in one of the judicial tribunals of that state,

So, "in case any slave shall be emancipated or set free, otherwise than according to the act (of 1800) regulating emancipations, it shall be lawful *for any person whatsoever to seize and convert to his or her own*

is my justification for so doing. The subjoined extract from the *Charleston Courier* of the 13th August, 1827, details the proceeding to which reference is here made: "A trial of much interest took place on Saturday last, at the City Hall, before a court composed of *John Michel, Esq., Justice of the Quorum, and two Freeholders.* The parties put upon their trial were *Hannah Elliott,* a free black woman, together with her daughter *Judy,* and her sons *Simon* and *Sam.* They were severally indicted *under the act of* 1740, for harbouring, concealing, entertaining two female children, aged about six and nine years, the property of a lady of this city, the extraordinary concealment and discovery of which was mentioned a short time since.

"After a patient investigation of all the circumstances of the case, the prisoners having the aid of able counsel, the court found them all guilty, and sentenced them, in accordance with the provisions of the aforesaid act, as follows: Hannah Elliott, with having harboured these slaves, for the term of two years; and her children with having harboured them respectively, for sixteen months each. The penalty under the act is a forfeiture of *ten pounds* currency for the *first* day, and *twenty shillings* currency for *every day after,* to the use of the owner of any slave so harboured, concealed or entertained. The act also provides, that, in case the forfeiture cannot be levied on such free negro, together with the charges attending the prosecution, the parties must be sold at public outcry, and the money arising from such sale be applied, in the first place, towards the forfeiture due to the owner, &c., and the overplus, if any, be paid into the public treasury."

Newspapers of later dates confirm this statement, and inform us, what might naturally have been anticipated, that the unhappy convicts, being unable to satisfy the enormous penalties which had been imposed upon them, were sold at public outcry, ten days after the trial, for slaves during life.

But, notwithstanding this decision of the Charleston court, I have no doubt that the act of 1740, *so far as concerns the offence of free negroes, mulattoes or mestizoes, in harbouring, concealing or entertaining a runaway slave,* NOT CHARGED WITH ANY CRIMINAL MATTER, *is re-*

3

26   FREE MADE SLAVES.

use, and *to keep as his or her property* the said slave so illegally emancipated or set free." 2 *Brevard's Digest*, 256.

---

pealed. On the 20th December, 1821, the legislature of South Carolina enacted a law in these words: "If any free negro, mulatto or mestizo, shall harbour, conceal or entertain any fugitive or runaway slave, and be convicted thereof before *two justices and five freeholders,* he shall suffer such corporeal punishment, not extending to life or limb, as the said justices and freeholders, who try such offender, shall in their discretion think fit." *See Acts of the Session of Dec.* 1821, *page* 20 ; *and James' Digest*, 390.

By comparing these two acts together, it will be perceived that they *agree* in the description of the offence to be provided against, while they *differ* in two important particulars : *first,* as to the tribunal before which offenders against the law are to be tried : *secondly,* in the punishment to be inflicted on conviction. Under the act of 1740, the tribunal consists of *one* justice and *two* freeholders, as is stated in another section of the same act : and the act of 1821 expressly directs a tribunal composed of *two* justices and *five* freeholders. By the former act, two (a majority) members of the court can convict or acquit : according to the latter, *four* are necessary for either purpose. On the supposition that both acts are in force, the offender may be tried and punished *twice* for one and the same offence—a conclusion which is forbidden by a principle of criminal jurisprudence, which has no exception in the laws of any civilized country, namely, that "no man can be placed in peril of legal penalties more than once upon the same accusation." 1 *Chitty's Criminal Law*, 452 ; 4 *Bla. Com.* 335. The provisions of the two acts are therefore manifestly inconsistent with each other, in which case, although words of express repeal are not used in the latter act, yet by implication it repeals the former, the *old* statute always giving place to the *new,* where both cannot stand together. 1 *Bl. Com.* 89. See *Rex vs. Cator*, 4 Burr, 2026 ; and *Rex vs. Davis*, Leach's Cases, 228 ; Dwarris on Statutes, 673–4.

The only argument by which the position that both acts are in force can be maintained, is, that the penalties are cumulative. This, however, can take place only where but *one* conviction is required ; whereas, it has been shown above that *two* are necessary according to these acts, inasmuch as *two distinct* tribunals for trial are appointed

And in Virginia, "If* any emancipated slave (infants excepted) shall remain within the state more than twelve months after his or her right to freedom shall have accrued, he or she shall *forfeit* all such right, and may *be apprehended and sold* by the overseers of the poor, &c. for the benefit of THE LITERARY FUND!!" 1 *Rev. Code*, 436, and see *Const. of* 1851.

In *North Carolina* he may be sold by order of court, and the proceeds be equally divided between the wardens for the poor and the *informer.* *Statutes of North Carolina*, 586.

And see Laws of *Florida*, by which a *free* negro or mulatto, if convicted of any crime or *misdemeanour*, the punishment of which shall not affect life or limb, if unable to pay the fine and costs of prosecution, the sheriff shall offer his services at public sale; "and any person who shall take such free negro or mulatto for the shortest period of time, paying the fine and costs of prosecution, shall be entitled to the services of such free negro or mulatto, who shall be held and taken *for the said period* of time *as a slave* to all intents and purposes whatever." Act of Feb. 10, 1832, *Thompson's Dig.* 542.

---

* The late President Jefferson, having by his last will emancipated five slaves, for whom he appears to have entertained much *personal* regard, in consequence of this section, made the following pathetic appeal to the legislature of his native State: "I *humbly* and *earnestly* request of the legislature of Virginia, a confirmation of the bequests to these servants, *with permission to remain in this State*, where their families and connections are, as an additional instance of the favour of which I have received so many other manifestations in the course of my life, and for which I now give them my solemn and dutiful thanks."

It is obvious that in this way, although convicted of a *misdemeanour* only, and this so slight in the eye of law as to incur a *mere fine*, a free negro may become a *slave* to the end of his life. And so, in the same state, for the *smallest debt* contracted by a *free* negro or mulatto, he may become a *slave* by sale under execution against him. *Ib.* 545, 546.

In Mississippi, every negro or mulatto found within the state, and *not having the ability** to show himself entitled to freedom, may be sold, by order of the court, as *a slave*. *Mississippi Rev. Code*, 389.

Maryland, in 1717, (chap. 13, sect. 5,) adopted these provisions : "If any *free* negro or mulatto *intermarry* with any white woman, or if any white man shall intermarry with any negro or mulatto woman, such negro or mulatto shall become *a slave during life*, except mulattoes born of white women, who, &c. shall become servants for seven years."

Another copious source of slavery—the condemnation under laws of several of the slave-holding states, made specifically for this purpose, of natives of Africa, brought into the United States in violation of the act of Congress of March 2, 1807, entitled "An act to prohibit the importation of slaves, &c. from and after the first day of January, 1808"—I shall defer the consideration of, to a subsequent chapter. *See the Appendix, chap.* 2.

Before quitting this chapter, it may not be amiss

---

* The extreme hardship of this law will be seen when I come to treat of the exclusion of negroes, mulattoes, &c. as witnesses, where the interest of white persons is in question.

to notice cursorily a species of SERVITUDE, (*growing out of slavery,*) which is peculiar, it is thought, to our country. It originated most probably in the *province* of Maryland, and will be readily apprehended from the subjoined extract from the act of that province in 1663, *chap.* 20, *sect.* 3: "All the ISSUE of *English* or other free-born women, that have already married negroes, shall serve the master of their parents till they be *thirty* years of age, and no longer." This act having been annulled in 1699 or 1700, was revived in *principle* by the *act of* 1715, *chap.* 44, *sect.* 26, with an extension of *one* year to the period of servitude fixed by the old law. The same provision shortly afterward recommended itself to the general assembly of *Pennsylvania*,* and may be found incorporated in an act passed March 5th, 1725–26, entitled "An act for the better regulating of negroes in this province." *North Carolina* in 1741, (ch. 24, §18,) imposed a servitude for the same space of time on the offspring of a *white* woman-*servant* and a *negro, mulatto,* or *Indian;* and this statute, although not in force *there* at the present time, continues to be the law of *Tennessee. Statutes of Tennessee,* 662. With respect to Maryland, it is necessary to add, that the progressive light of nearly a

---

* I have been careful to note with particularity the act of Assembly of Pennsylvania which gave rise to this species of servitude, chiefly because the late Judge Rush has inadvertently stated that *usage* was the authority upon which it was founded. See *Respublica vs. Negro Betsey et al.,* 1 *Dallas' Reports,* 475. And this mistake has been followed in a lecture before the Law Academy at the opening of the session of 1855–6, p. 22.

century and a half has at length enabled her to discover, as is declared in the act of 1796, *chap.* 67, *sect.* 14, that "it is contrary to the dictates of humanity and the principles of the Christian religion, to inflict personal penalties on children for the offence of their parents;" and this species of servitude has, in that state, been accordingly abolished.

CHAPTER II.

WITH the present chapter I propose to begin an examination of the nature and legal incidents of slavery. And in doing so, I will, in the first place, treat of the laws which regard the slave as *property.* This will comprehend such laws only as concern *the relation of master and slave.* Afterwards, those which treat of the slave as *a member of civil society* will be discussed.

The civil law—except where modified by statute or by usages which have acquired the force of law, —is generally referred to in the slave-holding states, as containing the true principles of the institution. It will be proper, therefore, to give an abstract of its leading doctrines; for which purpose, I use *Dr. Taylor's Elements of the Civil Law, page* 429:—"Slaves," says he, "were held *pro nullis: pro mortuis: pro quadrupedibus.* They had no head in the state, no name, title or register: they were not capable of being injured: nor could they take by purchase or descent: they had no heirs, and therefore could make no will: exclusive of

31

what was called their *peculium*, whatever they acquired was their master's: they could not plead nor be pleaded for, but were excluded from all civil concerns whatever: they could not claim the indulgence of absence *reipublicæ causa*: they were not entitled to the rights and considerations of matrimony, and, therefore, had no relief in case of adultery: nor were they proper objects of cognation or affinity, but of *quasi-cognation* only: they could be sold, transferred, or pawned as goods or personal estate; for goods they were, and as such they were esteemed: they might be tortured for evidence, punished at the discretion of their lord, or even put to death by his authority." This description is to be taken as applicable to the condition of slaves at an early period of the Roman history; for before the fall of the Roman empire, several important changes had been introduced favourable to the slave. By the *lex Cornelia de sicariis*, the killing of a slave became punishable. *Dig.* 488. *Cooper's Justinian*, 411. The *jus vitæ et necis* claimed by the master, was restrained by Claudius, the successor of Caligula. *Ibid.* The emperor Adrian prohibited generally cruel treatment towards slaves; and he banished Umbricia, a lady of quality, for five years, quôd ex levissimis causis *suas ancillas*,* atrocissime tractâsset. *Cooper's Justinian*, 412. Antoninus Pius applied the *lex Cornelia de sicariis*, specifi-

* Because for very slight causes she had treated her female slaves very cruelly.

cally to the masters of slaves; and the same law was strengthened by Severus and by Constantine. *Cooper's Justinian*, 412. Slaves might always induce an investigation by flying to the statues of the princes. *Ibid.*

I believe it will be found, upon a close comparison, that the condition of the slave, in our slaveholding states, *so far as the law may be invoked in his behalf*, is but little—if in any respect—better than was that of the Roman slave under the civil law. Take the following description of slavery, as given by the Supreme Court of *North Carolina* in 1829:—
" The end (of slavery) is the profit of the master, his security, and the public safety. The subject is one doomed in his own person and his posterity to live without knowledge and without the capacity to make any thing his own, and to toil that another may reap the fruits. Such services can only be expected from one who has no will of his own; who surrenders his will in implicit obedience to that of another. Such obedience is the consequence only of uncontrolled authority over the body. There is nothing else which can operate to produce the effect. The power of the master must be absolute to render the submission of the slave perfect. In the actual condition of things it must be so. There is no remedy. This discipline belongs to the state of slavery. They cannot be disunited without abrogating at once the rights of the master and absolving the slave from his subjection. It constitutes the curse of slavery to both the bond and free portions of our population ; but it is inherent in the relation

of master and slave." *The State vs. Mann, 2 Devereux Rep.* 263, 266.

The doctrine of *South Carolina* is equally strong. It is concentrated by *Wardlaw, J.*, in this single sentence :—"Every endeavour to extend to a slave positive rights is an attempt to reconcile inherent contradictions ; *for, in the very nature of things, he is subject to* DESPOTISM." *Ex parte* BOYLETON, 2 *Strobhart,* 41. He gives this as a quotation from *Kinloch vs. Harvey, Harper's Rep.* 514, with the commendation, " as is *well said."*

According to the law of Louisiana, "a slave is one who is in the power of a master to whom he belongs. The master may sell him, dispose of his person, his industry, and his labour: he can do nothing, possess nothing, nor acquire any thing, but what must belong to his master." *Civil Code, art.* 35. As to the master's power to punish his slave, a *limitation seems* to be contemplated by the following article :—" The slave is entirely subject to the will of his master, who may correct and chastise him, *though not with unusual rigour, or so as to maim or mutilate him, or to expose him to the danger of loss of life, or to cause his death." Art.* 173.—Yet, as will be fully demonstrated hereafter, no such limitation actually exists, or can by law be enforced.

With respect to the other slave-holding states, as none of these have adopted *èntire written codes,* enunciations of such a *general* nature as are exhibited in the quotations just made from the law of Louisiana are not to be expected. Nevertheless, the cardinal principle of slavery—that the slave is to be regarded

as a thing,*—is an article of property,—a chattel
personal,—obtains as undoubted law in all of these
states.   In South Carolina it is expressed in the
following language:—"Slaves shall be deemed, sold,
taken, reputed and adjudged in law to be *chattels
personal*† in the hands of their owners and posses-

---

* An apt illustration of this doctrine is presented in an act of Maryland, of 1798, Chap. CI. ch. 12, No. 12. The following is the language of this enlightened state: "In case the personal property of a
ward shall consist of specific articles, *such as* SLAVES, WORKING BEASTS,
ANIMALS OF ANY KIND, stock, furniture, plate, books, AND SO FORTH,
the court, if it shall deem it advantageous for the ward, may at any
time pass an order for the sale thereof," &c. &c. *See note A. post.* 296.

† In Louisiana, "Slaves, though movable by their nature," says the
civil code, "are considered as immovable by the operation of the
law." *Art.* 461.   And by act of Assembly of June 7, 1806, "Slaves
shall always be reputed and considered *real* estate ; shall be, as such,
subject to be mortgaged, according to the rules prescribed by law, and
they shall be seized and sold as *real* estate." 1 *Martin's Digest,* 612.
And in Kentucky, by the law of *descents,* they are considered *real* estate,
2 *Litt. and Sui. Digest,* 1155, and pass in consequence to *heirs* and not
to executors.   They are, however, liable *as chattels* to be sold by the
master at his pleasure, and may be taken in execution for the payment
of his debts. *Ibid. ; and see* 1247.   A law (act of 1705) similar to that
of Kentucky once obtained in Virginia, but it was repealed after a
short experiment. *See note to* 1 *Rev. Code,* 432.

In Massachusetts and Connecticut, and probably in the whole country
which used to bear the name of New England, the *harsh* features of
slavery were never known.   In Massachusetts colony, so early as in the
year of our Lord one thousand six hundred and forty-one, the following law was made: "It is ordered by this court and the authority
thereof, that there shall never be any bond slavery, villenage or captivity among us, unless it be lawful captives taken in just war, (such)
as willingly sell themselves or are sold to us ; *and such shall have the
liberties and* CHRISTIAN *usage which the law of* GOD ESTABLISHED IN
ISRAEL *concerning such persons doth morally require.*"   See *General*

sors, and their executors, administrators and assigns, *to all intents, constructions and purposes whatsoever.*" 2 *Brev. Dig.* 229; *Prince's Dig.* 446, *&c. &c.* Thompson, *Dig.* 183. The law is now the same in *Arkansas,* although for a time slaves there were regarded as *real* estate. *English's Dig.* 944. Absolute despotism needs not a more comprehensive grant of power than that which is here conferred. And though the particular design of the law-makers in framing this section was merely to declare of what nature— whether real or personal estate—slaves as *property*

Laws and Liberties of Massachusetts Bay, chap. 12, *sect.* 2. Though the phraseology of this law savour more of *Hibernia* than is supposed to be common to *New England,* yet its meaning is sufficiently palpable. That the law was not a dead letter, we have the authority which may be collected from an opinion delivered in the case of *Winchenden vs. Hatfield,* 4 *Mass. Rep.* 127–8, by Chief-Justice Parsons. "Slavery," says he, "was introduced into this country soon after its first settlement. The slave was the property of the master, subject to his orders, and to reasonable correction for misbehaviour. If the master was guilty of a cruel or unreasonable castigation of his slave, he was liable to be punished *for the breach of the peace,* and, I believe, the slave was allowed to demand sureties of the peace against a violent and barbarous master. Under these regulations, the treatment of slaves was in general mild and humane, and they suffered hardships not greater than hired servants."

And in Connecticut, Judge Reeve, speaking of slavery there, holds this language: "The law, as heretofore practised in this state, respecting slaves, must now be uninteresting. I will, however, lest the slavery which prevailed in this state should be forgotten, mention some things, that show that slavery here was very far from being of the absolute, rigid kind. The master had no control over the life of his slave. If he killed him, he was liable to the same punishment as if he killed a freeman. The master was as liable to be sued by the slave, in an action for beating or wounding, or for immoderate chas-

should be regarded, yet it is not on that account the less appropriate for the purpose to which I apply it. It is strictly consonant with an inflexible principle of their acknowledged law.

Viewing the language, "*that a slave shall be deemed a chattel personal in the hands of his owner, to all intents, constructions and purposes whatsoever,*" in this light, it is plain that the dominion of the master is as unlimited as is that which is tolerated by the laws of any civilized country in relation to brute animals,— to *quadrupeds,* to use the words of the civil law. How far the existing state of slavery, *as by law established and protected,* may conform to this deduction, will best appear by a more minute investigation of the subject. And in order to simplify the inquiry, and to enable the reader to arrive at a proper conclusion without difficulty, I shall subjoin, in distinct propositions, what will be found to be *corollaries* from the act of South Carolina; and, in connection with each of them, such laws as may be specifically applicable will be quoted, and their just bearing indicated.

Prop. I. The master may determine the kind, and

---

tisement, as he would be if he had thus treated an apprentice. A slave was capable of holding property, in character of devisee or legatee. If the master should take away such property, his slave would be entitled to an action against him, by his *prochein ami,* (next friend.) From the whole we see that slaves had the same right of life and property as apprentices; and that the difference betwixt them was this: an apprentice is a servant for time, and the slave is a servant for life." *Reeve's Law of Baron & Femme, &c.* 340–41.

4

degree, and time of labour, to which the slave shall be subjected.

Prop. II. The master may supply the slave with such food and clothing only, both as to quantity and quality, as he may think proper or find convenient.

III. The master may, at his discretion, inflict any punishment upon the person of his slave.

IV. All the power of the master over his slave may be exercised not by himself only in person, but by any one whom he may depute as his agent.

V. Slaves have no legal rights of property in things, real or personal; but whatever they may acquire belongs, in *point of law*, to their masters.

VI. The slave, being a *personal chattel*, is at all times liable to be sold absolutely, or mortgaged or leased, at the will of his master.

VII. He may also be sold by process of law for the satisfaction of the debts of a living or the debts and bequests of a deceased master, at the suit of creditors or legatees.

VIII. A slave cannot be a party before a judicial tribunal, in any species of action against his master, no matter how atrocious may have been the injury received from him.

IX. Slaves cannot redeem themselves, nor

obtain a change of masters, though
cruel treatment may have rendered
such change necessary for their personal safety.

Prop. X. Slaves being objects of *property*, if injured
by third persons, their owners may
bring suit, and recover damages, for
the injury.

XI. Slaves can make no contract.

XII. Slavery is hereditary and perpetual.

Preparatively to the separate discussion of the
above propositions, the remark may be made, as applicable to each, that the absence of a legislative
change as to the *law* of the proposition is always to
be taken as an implication that it exists as is therein
stated. For the *propositions*, it will be recollected,
are *corollaries* from the *express general* law.

Prop. I.—The master may determine the kind,
and degree, and time of labour, to which the
slave shall be subjected.

In *most* of the slave-holding states, the law is silent
on this topic. There can be no doubt,* therefore, as
I have just intimated, that it is given correctly in

---

* A strong illustration of this remark is supplied by the following
decision of the Supreme Court of *Alabama.* "The master or owner,
and not the slave, is the proper judge whether the slave is *too sick* to
be able to labour. The slave cannot therefore resist the order of the
master, or owner, to go to work." *State vs. Abram,* 10 *Alabama
Rep.* 928.

the terms of the proposition. As to the *silence* of the law, the codes of Georgia, South Carolina, Louisiana and Mississippi furnish exceptions; with what efficacy, will be shown in the succeeding observations. One of these exceptions is as follows:—

"If any person shall on the Lord's day, commonly called Sunday, employ any slave in any work or labour, (works of absolute necessity and the necessary occasions of the family only excepted,) every person so offending shall forfeit and pay the sum of ten shillings for every slave he, she or they shall so cause to work or labour." *Act of May* 10, 1770; *Prince's Dig.* 455; 2 *Cobb's Dig.* 981. So in *Mississippi*, under a penalty of two dollars. *Rev. Code*, 317; *Act of June* 13, 1822. And in *Arkansas* the penalty is *one dollar*. *English's Dig.* 369.

"Any owner or employer of a slave or slaves, who shall cruelly treat such slave or slaves, by unnecessary or excessive whipping, by withholding proper food and sustenance, by requiring greater labour from such slave or slaves than he or she or they are able to perform, or by not affording proper clothing, whereby the health of such slave or slaves may be injured and impaired, or cause or permit the same to be done, every such owner or employer shall be guilty of a misdemeanour, and on conviction shall be punished by fine or imprisonment in the common jail of the county, or both, at the discretion of the court." *Act of* 1833, 2 *Cobb's Dig.* 827.

The *ostensible* design of these laws is to afford protection to the slave. But, unfortunately for the oppressed, a single *fact* proves that the "*promised good*" is almost, if not altogether, illusory. *It is an inflexible and universal rule of slave law*, (to which more particular attention will be hereafter given,) founded in one or two states upon *usage*, in others sanctioned by *express legislation*, THAT THE TESTIMONY OF A COLOURED PERSON, WHETHER BOND OR FREE, CANNOT BE RECEIVED AGAINST A WHITE PERSON!!! It is scarcely necessary to add another word to substantiate the allegation, that these laws of Georgia ought to be considered entirely and unqualifiedly nugatory. By way of illustration, however, suppose a slave, *by the command of his master*, and through terror of his displeasure and punishment, is discovered on the Sabbath, employed in the ordinary labours of the field. It may be assumed that the master is apprised of the prohibition of the law. He knows *equally well*, too, that the testimony of a *white man* only can be produced against him. He will, of course, obey the dictate of common prudence,—a sufficient share of which, for this purpose, every man possesses,—*and issue his commands to the slave in the absence of a white man*. How, then, can he be convicted of this offence? or in what manner can the law be enforced? It must be a dead letter. It can serve no valuable end. For any benefit it yields the slave, it might as well not have been passed.

The same objections apply to the clause in the second section which has been cited, and which comes within the scope of the proposition under present consideration, *i. e.* "the requiring greater labour from such slave or slaves than he, she or they
4*

are able to perform." Indeed, the difficulty in effecting a conviction is increased, inasmuch as the charge is by the law of a *criminal* nature — every thing must therefore be *strictly* proved — the law itself must be *construed strictly*—and such a construction requires that the two other illegal circumstances enumerated in the section—*to wit, unnecessary and excessive whipping,—withholding proper food and sustenance* — should exist at the same time, and be proved against the master, to constitute the *single* crime of cruelty to the slave.

There is an obscurity and confusion in the penning of this law, which will strike every one with surprise, who is not in some degree acquainted with slave laws. There is an *omission*, too, which deserves notice. The cruelty of the *owner*, only, is made penal in the section; while the exaction of too much labour, &c. by the *overseer* or *agent*, is not provided against.

The negro act of *South Carolina*, passed in 1740, contains the following language as restrictive of the master's power in the exaction of labour from the slave. I copy, in addition to the *enacting part* of the section, the *preamble*, since it serves to evidence the *abuse* which obtained in this particular, at a very early period, when the labour of the slave was probably of much less value than it is at the present time. "Whereas many owners of slaves, and *others* who have the care, management and overseeing of slaves, *do confine them so closely to hard labour, that they have not sufficient time for natural rest:* Be it therefore enacted, That if any owner of slaves, or other person who shall have the care, management or overseeing of any slaves, shall work or put any such slave or slaves to labour more than *fifteen* hours in twenty-four hours, from the twenty-fifth day of March to the twenty-fifth day of September; or more than *fourteen* hours in twenty-four hours, from the twenty-fifth day of September to the twenty-fifth day of March, every such person shall forfeit any sum not exceeding twenty pounds, nor under five pounds, current money, for every time he, she or they shall offend herein, at the discretion of the justice before whom the complaint shall be made." , 2 *Brevard's Digest,* 243.

In Louisiana, the subjoined act was passed, July 7, 1806. "As for the hours of work and rest, which are to be assigned to slaves in summer and winter, the old usages of the territory shall be adhered to, to wit: The slaves shall be allowed half an hour for breakfast during the whole year; from the first day of May to the first day of November, they shall be allowed two hours for dinner; and from the first day of November to the first day of May, one hour and a half for dinner: Provided, however, That the owners who will themselves take the trouble of causing to be prepared the meals of their slaves, be, and they are hereby authorized to abridge, by half an hour per day, the time fixed for their rest." 1 *Martin's Digest,* 610–12.

The remarks which were made, in relation to the laws of Georgia, bear with equal force upon those of South Carolina and Louisiana, above cited. They are wholly inoperative, incapable of being

executed, and must, without doubt, give way to the
cupidity of the master, whenever circumstances excite the passion for gain. But to speak of, the law
of South Carolina: suppose it to be religiously observed; is not the measure as to the length of time
(for as regards the *kind* or *degree* of labour no regulation exists, and it would be futile to make any) excessive, and likely to destroy bodily energy? In a
matter of this nature, *exact* graduation is not easily
attainable; yet, judging from such data as I have
been able to collect, I think myself authorized in
the conclusion that *too much* is permitted. In the
island of Jamaica, besides many holidays which are
by law accorded to the slave, ten hours a day is the
extent of the time which the slave is compelled *ordinarily* to work. *See* 2 *Edward's West Indies, book* 4,
chap. 5. Also, *Consolidated Slave Act of Jamaica,
ibid. book* 4; *Appendix, section* 18. The regulations
of *penitentiaries*, in reference to the employment of
convicts at *hard* labour, furnish additional criteria de-
serving of our attention. And, happily, it is in my
power here to adduce the authority of at least three
slave-holding states, viz.: Maryland, Virginia and
Georgia, in conjunction with that of Pennsylvania
and New Jersey. In each of these states this law
has been adopted: "Such offenders (convicts) unless
prevented by ill health, shall be employed in work
every day in the year except Sundays and such days
when they shall be confined in the solitary cells; and
the hours of work, in each day, shall be as many as
the season of the year, with an interval of half an
hour for breakfast and an hour for dinner, will per-

mit; *but not exceeding eight hours* in the months of
November, December and January; *nine hours* in
the months of February and October, and *ten* hours
in the rest of the year. 1 *Virg. Rev. Code*, 624;
Prince's Digest, 382; *Laws of Maryland, Nov. Sess.*
1809, *ch.* 138, § 30; *Laws of New Jersey, revised and
published in* 1821, *page* 326; *Purdon's Digest of the
Laws of Pennsylvania, page* 324, (*act of April* 5, 1790.)
Hence it appears, that according to a statute which
was enacted upon the most solemn deliberation by
one legislature, and which has been adopted since
by four other distinct bodies of the same nature, *ten*
hours make up the *longest* space out of twenty-four
hours, which can be demanded for labour from *convicted felons*, whose PUNISHMENT was designed to consist chiefly of HARD LABOUR.   Yet the slave of South
Carolina, under a law professing *to extend humanity*
towards him, may be subjected to unremitting toil
for FIFTEEN HOURS within the same period!!
If we turn to Louisiana, the condition of the slave,
in this particular, will be found without melioration.
For, though the purpose of the act which I have
transcribed is declared to be to ascertain what hours
are to be assigned to the slave for *work* and REST, the
only *rest* which it provides is half an hour at breakfast and two hours at dinner.   At what time a third
meal is to be taken, whether at sunset or at mid-
night, is left to the master's pleasure.   And, judging
from our knowledge of the mode in which sugar is
made, and cotton raised and *pressed*, it is not too
much to say, that the going down of the sun is by
no means the signal of repose to the weary

slave.* And let it not be forgotten that the slave, within the short time allotted for *rest*, is under the necessity of preparing food for his meals!!

Prop. II.—THE MASTER MAY SUPPLY THE SLAVE WITH SUCH FOOD AND CLOTHING ONLY, BOTH AS TO QUANTITY AND QUALITY, AS HE MAY THINK PROPER OR FIND CONVENIENT.

Legislation having a direct reference to the subject of this proposition may be quoted from the codes of Louisiana and of North and South Carolina. Still, as the slave is entirely under the control of his master—is unprovided with a protector—and especially as he cannot be a witness, or make complaint in any known mode against his master, the *apparent* object of these laws may *always* be defeated. I might, therefore, spare myself any further attention to this proposition. But, for the information of those who have not resided in a slave state, I think fit to copy the authentic testimony of acts of assembly, as to the *quantity* and *quality* of food

---

* An extract from a Louisiana newspaper, dated New Orleans, March 23, 1826, will tend in some measure to confirm this remark. The words are these: "To judge from the activity reigning in the cotton-presses of the suburbs of St. Mary, and the *late hours* during which *their slaves work*, the *cotton* trade was never more brisk." Sugar-making is, I believe, generally more laborious than the cultivation of cotton. In an article on the agriculture of *Louisiana*, contained in "The Western Review," No. 2, (the editor of which is by no means unfavourable to slavery,) the following statement appears:—"*The work* (sugar-making) *is admitted to be severe for the hands*, (slaves,) *requiring, when the process of making sugar is commenced*, TO BE PRESSED NIGHT AND DAY."

which are directed to be provided for slaves. Thus in Louisiana, "Every owner shall be held to give to his slaves the quantity of provisions hereafter specified, to wit: *one barrel of Indian corn,* or the equivalent thereof in rice, beans or other grain, and a pint of salt, and to deliver the same to the said slaves in kind *every month,* and never in money, under a penalty of a fine of ten dollars for every offence." 1 *Martin's Digest,* 610, *act of July* 7, 1806; *Revised Statutes, p.* 522. In North Carolina a *much less* quantity of the same kind of food is deemed sufficient, as is *implied* from the following *curious* section of an act passed in 1753, and which is still in force: "In case any slave or slaves, who shall not appear to have been clothed and fed, [according to the intent and meaning of this act, that is to say, to have been sufficiently clothed, and to have constantly received for the preceding year an allowance not less than *a quart of corn per day,**] shall be convicted of stealing any corn, cattle, &c. &c. from any person not the owner of such slave or slaves, such injured person shall and may maintain an action of trespass against the master, owner or possessor of such slave, &c., and shall recover his or her damages, &c." *Haywood's Manual,* 524–5. In the *Revised Statutes* of

---

* In an action between an overseer and his employer, in South Carolina, the counsel of the overseer is reported to have used this language, speaking of the employer, who was the defendant. " He gauged his (the plaintiff's) and his family's stomachs very closely— *a peck of corn for each white person:—just a negro's allowance." Davis vs. Whitbridge,* 2 *Strobhart,* 236. The time here referred to was a *week.*

1836-37, p. 578, the part of this section which is contained within *brackets* is not found. In *lieu* thereof, the word *properly* is inserted before *clothed*.

The allowance of clothing in Louisiana seems to have been graduated by the same standard by which the quantity of food was determined in North Carolina. "The slave who shall not have on the property of their owners a lot of ground to cultivate on their own account, shall be entitled to receive from said owner *one* linen shirt and pantaloons (*une chemise et une culotte de toile*) for the summer, and a linen shirt and woollen great-coat and pantaloons for the winter." 1 *Martin's Digest*, 610; *Revised Statutes of* 1852, *p.* 522.

The other slave-holding states do not *pretend* to fix the kind and quantity of food and clothing to be furnished to the slave; but in South Carolina and in Georgia, the cruelty of denying to him a sufficiency of either is *attempted* to be guarded against. That full justice may be done to the humanity of the lawgivers of South Carolina, I extract a section of the law which professes to give redress to the injured slave: "In case any person, &c. who shall be owner, or who shall have the care, government or charge of any slave or slaves, shall deny, neglect or refuse to allow such slave or slaves under his or her charge sufficient clothing, covering or food, it shall and may be lawful for any person or persons, on behalf of such slave or slaves, to make complaint to the next neighbouring justice in the parish where such slave or slaves live, or are usually employed; and the said justice shall summon the party against

whom such complaint shall be made, and shall
inquire of, hear and determine the same; and, if the
said justice shall find said complaint to be true, or
that such person will not exculpate or clear himself
from the charge, by his or her own oath, which *such
person shall be at liberty to do in all cases* where
positive proof is not given of the offence, such
justice shall and may make such orders upon the
same, for the relief of such slave or slaves, as he in
his discretion shall think fit; and shall and may set
and impose a fine or penalty on any person who
shall offend in the premises, in any sum not exceeding twenty pounds, current money, for each
offence, to be levied by warrant of distress and sale
of the offender's goods," &c. &c. 2 *Brevard's Dig.*
241; similar in Louisiana, 1 *Martin's Dig.* 638-40;
Revised Statutes, 557.

Now, as the slave cannot be heard as a witness,
it is not very easy to see how *positive* proof as to the
insufficiency of food can be obtained; and, of course,
by the terms of the act, the master or overseer, by
his oath, may exculpate himself—may answer the
general charge by as general a denial —a matter
which an intrepid conscience, as all experience testi-
fies, will easily compass.

To what a degree of suffering slaves may be reduced, notwithstanding the provisions of this law,
the facts stated in a decision of the South Carolina
Reports as recently as 1848 give painful assurance.

A complaint under this section of the act of 1740
was made against the owner of twenty-one slaves
for not supplying them with sufficient food and

clothing. The magistrate decided against the owner, and imposed the statutory penalty. The owner appealed from the magistrate's order, and the case was thus brought before the Supreme Court. In the report of the case, this relation is made, which I give verbatim:—" The defendant did not give his negroes enough even of *meal,*—*the only provisions which he did give them.* *Five* bushels of meal *weekly,* the LARGEST quantity stated by any witness, even if not reduced in the ratio of three-eighths of a bushel in two bushels, to the standard of the defendant's measure, was plainly insufficient for a family of eight whites and twenty-one slaves. But it appears by the testimony of Jackson, the defendant's *overseer,* that this supply was not regular. The grown negroes had only a *quart* of meal a day. Many days he says they had no meal. Sometimes it gave out on *Thursday* and sometimes on *Friday.* They would then have a quart to last them till *Monday evening. The stinted allowance, when withheld, must have reduced the wretched slaves to famine.* For seventeen months, *Jackson* did not know that *shoes* had been given to them. Their feet were *frostbitten and sore.* During the same period *no clothes* were given to, them." STATE *vs.* BOWEN, 3 *Strobhart's Reports, pp.* 574, 575.

Here *positive* evidence was obtained by the oath of the *overseer,*—otherwise the defendant might have exculpated himself by his *own* oath, which, as he resisted the enforcement of the law until the court in the *last* resort had decided against him, there is too much reason to believe he would have done. But that the *overseer* was led to testify, it is not likely any relief could have been had by the *starving slaves.*

The act of Georgia remains to be considered. It will be seen, by recurring to the *latter* section of the law of this state, upon which I adventured a brief comment while speaking of the *first proposition* of this chapter, that among the *constituents* of the crime of cruelty by the master to his slave, are enumerated "*the withholding proper food and sustenance,*" and "*not affording proper clothing.*" For "withholding proper food and sustenance," it has been demonstrated, I trust, that the master is dispunishable. The *proof* cannot be had. Whether the slave be properly clothed may, however, be ascertained by *inspection.* But the enumerated circumstances of inhumanity—"*unnecessary or excessive whipping,*"—"*withholding proper food,*"—"*exacting more labour than the slave is able to perform,*"—"*not affording proper clothing*"—are neither severally nor aggregately a punishable offence; there must be superadded, both in fact and proof, the *effect* "*whereby*"—these are the words of the statute—"*the health of such slave or slaves may be injured and impaired*"!! It is, therefore, only in such extreme cases of suffering that the legislative penalty can be imposed.

Upon the topics of this proposition, another act of Georgia may be cited, the provisions of which are of a character so novel, that I shall be under the necessity of detaining the reader longer in its discussion than is altogether consistent with the plan of this sketch. The act is a brief one, and I transcribe it entire: "*Section* 1. From and after the passing of this act, (December 12, 1815,) it shall be the duty of the *inferior* courts of the several counties in this state, on receiving information, on *oath*, of any *infirm* slave or slaves being in a *suffering* situation, from *the neglect of the owner or owners* of such slave or slaves, to make particular inquiries into the situation of such slave or slaves, and render such relief as they in their discretion may think proper.

"*Section 2.* The said courts *may*, and they are hereby authorized, to sue for and recover from the owner or owners of such slave or slaves, the amount that may be appropriated for the relief of such slave or slaves, in any court having jurisdiction of the same; any law, usage or custom to the contrary notwithstanding." *Prince's Digest*, 460; 2 *Cobb's Digest*, 987.

By the terms of this act, the relief spoken of is confined to *infirm* slaves. The purpose of. this restriction I cannot perceive. It is unnecessary, however, to trouble ourselves with the inquiry, since to the *professed* objects of its bounty it is *scarcely possible* a benefit can result. As a preliminary to judicial investigation, the express directions of the first section require *information* to be given to the inferior judges *on oath*. I need not repeat that this must be the oath of a *white man.* A flagrant case it must be, it will occur to every reflecting mind, which will induce such a person to incur the enmity of a planter, by making a formal complaint, *on oath,* before the judges of the court, that "*an infirm slave is in a suffering condition from the neglect of his owner.*" But let it be granted that such complaint has been preferred by a competent person; it is, it will be observed, but an *incipient* proceeding, and, without the *inadmissible* evidence of the slave himself, how can the other requirements of the act be complied with? What kind of replies can be expected to the *"particular inquiries"* which the judges are directed to make? The charge is a grave one; it strikes at the *character* of the master: the evidence to support it should be proportionately cogent; it should be incontrovertible.

Improbable as I think I have shown the supposition to be, let it be further granted, that the complaint has been established by evidence satisfactory to the judges, and that, in conformity with the directions of the act, they have proceeded to "render such relief as they, in their discretion, have thought proper."

If the reader be in any degree conversant with judicial proceedings, he will be apt to conclude that this *latter* concession is an abandonment of the argument. And, truly, had the law under examination been founded on practical principles,—had it been framed, as all laws ought to be, to answer the behests of justice,—the concession would be open to this objection. Yet, unwilling as we may be to believe the reproach, it is impossible to shut out the conviction that the makers of the act did not design it to be efficient; otherwise, the *second* section would not have been appended. This section gives to the act, as has been before observed, a character altogether novel in jurisprudence. By the *first* section, it will be recollected, the *duty* is imposed on the judges of

5*

the inferior courts, after having made "particular inquiries into the situation of the suffering slave," *to render such relief as they should think fit.* One would naturally infer, that after a judicial tribunal had solemnly adjudged *"relief to be necessary for* AN INFIRM *slave in a* SUFFERING *condition from the* NEGLECT *of his owner,"* the hand of justice would not be tardy to enforce the decision. Very different, however, were the sentiments of the humane legislature of Georgia. No relief is administered. The *duty* of the judges is *at an end* by the determination *that relief is necessary!* They cannot order an *execution* upon their *judgment.* The harvest should have been ready for the sickle; but the seed has not been sown—the ground is not even prepared to receive it. The *judges* are authorized (not *commanded*) to assume the unheard-of character for *judges*—to become SUITORS in *another court*—"to sue for," says the second section, "and recover from the owner or owners of such slave or slaves, the amount that may be appropriated for the relief of such slave." No special provision is made for the payment of *costs,* in case these *plaintiff judges* should, from defect of evidence, or from any other cause, be unable to convince the ulterior court and jury that relief should be afforded. It results, of course, that they must defray them from their private resources, like all other unsuccessful parties to an action. The delay and uncertainty of the law, even in its ordinary mode of administration, where every reasonable facility for investigation is accorded, are *proverbial;* is it to be expected, then, with the obstacles to the

execution of this act which have been pointed out—
the exclusion of slave testimony when no other testimony would be likely to disclose the necessary
facts—the preferment of the complaint before one
set of judges whose decision, at *most*, leads to no
other result than that these judges *may* become *suitors*
in the cause before another distinct judicial tribunal,
with the certain inconvenience of loss of time, and
the *almost certain* loss of money, that a suit should
ever be terminated, or that it should be terminated
in favour of the slave? Legislation such as this is
worse than mockery.

Prop. III.—THE MASTER MAY, AT HIS DISCRETION,
INFLICT ANY SPECIES OF PUNISHMENT UPON THE PERSON
OF HIS SLAVE.

If the power of the master to the extent here implied were sanctioned by *express* law, we should
have no claim to the character of a civilized people.
The very being of the slave would be in the hands
of the master. Such is not the case; on the contrary, from the laws which I shall cite, it will be
fully evident, *that so' far as regards the pages of the
statute-book*, the *life* at least of the slave is safe from
the *authorized* violence of the master. The evil is
not that laws are wanting, but that they cannot be
enforced; not that they sanction crime, but that they
do not punish it. And this arises chiefly, if not
solely, from the cause which has been more than once
mentioned,—the exclusion of the testimony, on the
trial of a *white* person, of all those who are *not white*.
There was a time when, in all the old states in

which slavery is still maintained, the murder of a slave, whether by his master or a third person, was punished by a pecuniary fine only. South Carolina was the last of these states in which a change in this particular was made. Since then (Dec. 20, 1821) the *wilful*, *malicious* and *premeditated* killing of a slave, by whomsoever perpetrated, is a *capital* offence* in all the slave-holding states.

---

* Although it is strictly correct, as stated in the text, that the *wilful*, *malicious* and *premeditated* killing of a slave is a capital offence in all the slave-holding states, yet in several of these states the subject has occasioned much difficulty. Thus, in *Virginia*, even since the adoption of the distinction between the *degrees* of murder, on three occasions at least the legislature has defined murder in the *first* degree in such language as to show a variation of purpose to some extent at each particular time. Thus, by the revised code of 1819, "all murder which shall be perpetrated by means of poison, or by lying in wait or by duress of imprisonment or confinement, or by starving, or *by wilful, malicious and excessive whipping*, beating or other cruel treatment or torture, or by any *other* kind of wilful, deliberate and premeditated killing, or which shall be committed *in the perpetration* or attempt to perpetrate any arson, rape, robbery or burglary, shall henceforth be deemed murder in the *first* degree." 1 *Rev. Code*, (of 1819,) p. 616.

In 1847–48, the words are, "Murder committed by poison, lying in wait, duress of imprisonment, starving, *wilful and excessive whipping*, cruel treatment, or any kind of wilful, deliberate and premeditated killing, or in the *attempt* to commit any arson, rape, robbery or burglary, shall be murder in the *first* degree."

What is denominated *"The Code of Virginia"* is a very condensed body of statutable law, published under an act of Assembly of August 15, 1849, which did not, however, take effect until the 1st of July, 1850. The definition of murder of the *first* degree, according to this code, is "Murder by poison, lying in wait, imprisonment, starving, or any wilful, deliberate and premeditated killing, or in the commission or attempt to commit arson, rape, robbery or burglary." *Code of Virginia of* 1849, p. 723.

Such is the language of the statutes which have been made on this subject; and I have no doubt such is the real intent of the great mass of the

---

It will be observed that this last enactment leaves out "*wilful, malicious and excessive whipping, beating or other cruel treatment or torture,*" contained in the act of 1819, and "*wilful and. excessive whipping, cruel treatment*" of the act of 1847.

It is a remarkable fact that on *September* 1, 1849, whilst the act of 1847 was yet in force, one of the most, if not the most, *wilful, malicious and deliberate* murders was committed by the master of a slave, *by wilful and excessive whipping and cruel treatment,* which the criminal records of any country have transmitted. The case is reported in 7 *Grattan's Reports,* 679, under the name of *Souther's* case. The opinion of the court gives this narrative:—"The indictment contains fifteen counts, and sets forth a case of most cruel and excessive whipping and torture. The negro was tied to a tree and whipped with switches. When Souther became fatigued with the labour of whipping, he called upon a negro man of his and made him cob Sam with a shingle. He also made a negro woman of his help to cob him. And, after cobbing and whipping, he applied fire to the body of his slave, about his back, belly and private parts. He then caused him to be washed down with hot water in which pods of red pepper had been steeped. The negro was. also tied to a log, and to the bed-post, with ropes, which choked him, and he was kicked and stamped by Souther. This sort of punishment was continued and repeated until the negro died under its infliction."

The slave's offences, according to the master's allegation, were, "*getting drunk,*" and dealing with two persons,— *white men,*—who were present, and witnessed the whole of the horrible transaction, without, as far as appears in the report, having interfered in any way to save the life of the slave.

The jury found the master guilty of murder in the *second* degree. The court expressed a clear opinion that it was murder in the FIRST degree, under the act of 1847. What would have been held to be the proper verdict, had the existing law, in which "*wilful and excessive whipping,*" &c. are left out, been then in force, is very doubtful.

The language of the *Revised Statutes* of *North Carolina,* of 1836–37, ch. 34, § 9, p. 192, is this:—"The offence of *killing a slave* shall be

people in those states. But there is an inherent vice in the institution of slavery, which renders it exceedingly difficult, if not impossible, to give to the slave, by *general legislation*, equal protection with the *free*. In respect to *homicide*, the statute, *in terms*, may make no discrimination between the two classes, and yet the degree of protection which is

---

denominated and considered *homicide*, and shall partake of the same degree of guilt, *when accompanied with the like circumstances*, that homicide *does at common law*."

The common reader would naturally conclude from this provision, that if a master should *whip his slave to death*, the denomination of the crime would be *murder*, and the punishment *capital*. This would be a mistake. For, by the *common law*, "where a parent is moderately correcting his child, a *master his apprentice* or scholar, and happens to occasion his death, it is only *misadventure;* FOR THE ACT OF CORRECTION WAS LAWFUL." Now, it is a part of *slave* law that the master, or any one having the lawful control of a slave, may inflict corporal chastisement on him to any extent not affecting life or limb. *State vs. Mann*, 2 *Devereux*, 263. If death should ensue as a consequence of a corporal chastisement in such a case, the law would not infer that it was the *intention* of the master to cause it: the presumption would be the other way; for, being *his property*, why should he wish to destroy it? At all events, the question of *intention* would be for the determination of the jury; and what jury *anywhere*, but especially in a slave state, would infer, unless the instrument used would almost inevitably produce death, that the intention was to kill? "*Immoderate correction*" by a parent of his child, or a master of his apprentice, is not permitted by the common law, and would, therefore, be punishable in either of these cases, although the child or apprentice should not be killed by it. But there is no such law in respect to a slave. He may be beaten to any extent short of occasioning death or dismemberment, and his master is wholly dispunishable. The correction *to this extent* being *entirely lawful* as regards the slave makes such a broad distinction between *him* and the *apprentice*, that a conviction of a *master* for *murder* of his *slave* by *excessive whipping* is not to be expected.

thus afforded to the one and the other may be widely different.

The state of the law in *Missouri* supplies a perfect illustration of this remark. Thus, by Art. 3, § 28 of the *Constitution*, any person who shall *maliciously* deprive of life or dismember *a slave* shall suffer such punishment as would be inflicted for the like offence if it was committed on a *free white person*.

In exact accordance with this requirement, the statute on crimes, in treating of *homicide*, makes no mention of *colour* or *condition* of the person slain. *Sect.* 1. "Every murder which shall be committed by means of poison, or by lying in wait, or by any other kind of *wilful, deliberate* and *premeditated* kill ing, or which shall be committed in the perpetration or attempt to perpetrate any arson, &c. or other felony, shall be deemed murder of the *first* degree." *Sect.* 2. "All other kinds of murder at common law, not herein declared to be manslaughter or justifiable or excusable homicide, shall be deemed murder in the *second* degree." *Sect.* 3. "Persons convicted of murder in the *first* degree shall suffer *death;*—those convicted of murder in the *second* degree shall be punished by imprisonment in the penitentiary not less than *ten years.*" The 4th section defines *justifiable* homicide in the same undiscriminating language, but it is not necessary to extract it. The 5th section is in these words:—"Homicide shall be deemed *excusable*, when committed by *accident* or *misfortune*, in either of the following cases: *First*, in *lawfully* correcting *a child, apprentice, servant* or *slave.*" And it is afterwards provided, that where the "ho-

micide was committed under circumstances or in a
case where by any statute or the common law such
homicide was justifiable or *excusable*, the jury shall
return a general verdict of not guilty." *Revised
Statutes* of *Missouri*, 344–45; (and see *Arkansas Digest*,
p. 328, § 32, 33 and 34, *similar in effect*.)

The same language is used in regard to the correction of the *child, apprentice, servant* and SLAVE, and
the one word, *lawfully*, is prefixed as well to the
slave as to the *child* or *apprentice*. But what is *lawful*
correction of a *child* or *apprentice* is accurately defined and easily explained: the common law has
settled that, and the transgression of these limits is
an indictable offence. But there is no such limit in
regard to the power of the *master* over the *slave*. He
may use any instrument and may inflict any number
of blows which he may choose. This is a principle
of slave law, it is believed, of universal application.
In *North Carolina* it has been expressly affirmed by
the Supreme Court, and its *necessity* asserted and de-
fended in an elaborate opinion of the *Chief-Justice*,
on behalf of the whole court. *State vs. Mann*,
2 *Devereux Rep.* 263, 266.

In *Georgia* and *Tennessee*, the protection of the
master in the exercise of what the Supreme Court of
North Carolina designates his "*uncontrolled authority
over the body*" of his slave, is secured in a more *direct*,
but not a whit more effectual, way than in *Missouri*.
"If," says the statute of 1799, ch. 9, of *Tennessee*,
"any person shall wilfully or maliciously kill any
negro or mulatto slave, on due and legal conviction
thereof, &c. shall be deemed guilty of murder, as if

such person so killed had been a freeman, and shall suffer death without benefit of clergy." To which this proviso is added: "Provided, this act shall not be extended to any person killing any slave in the act of resistance to his lawful owner or master, or any slave *dying under moderate correction.*" *Statute Laws of Tennessee,* pp. 676, 677, published in 1836.

The Constitution of *Georgia* contains a provision substantially the same. "Any person who shall *maliciously* dismember or deprive a slave of life, shall suffer such punishment as would be inflicted in case the like offence had been committed on a free white person, and on the like proof, except in case of in-surrection of such slave, and UNLESS SUCH DEATH SHOULD HAPPEN BY ACCIDENT IN GIVING SUCH SLAVE MODERATE CORRECTION." Art. 4, § 12, and see, accordant with this proviso, act of Dec. 2, 1799, 2 *Cobb's Dig.* 982.

To style the *"correction"* of a slave which causes DEATH, *"moderate,"* is a solecism too monstrous for sober legislation. And yet such has been the law of two enlightened states for more than half a century. Had a statement of this nature appeared in the pages of a *foreign journal,* who is there among us that would not have indignantly repelled the charge as an *opprobrious falsehood?*

There is another point of view in which this *exception* as to death produced by the *moderate correction* of the slave claims an observation. I mean, in respect to the *protection* which it throws over the murderer when on his trial for killing a slave. Every one who has been the least attentive to trials

6

for *capital* offences, or who knows the human heart, is well aware that the *compassion* of a jury is ever ready to lay hold of a pretext to save themselves from the painful duty of *convicting* a fellow-being of a crime the punishment of which is death. Strong evidence will not, therefore, be required by them to induce the belief that the murderer's design was the *correction* of the slave; that possibly (and possibilities are usually urged as sufficient justification for acquittals, where life is in jeopardy) the measure bestowed was *moderate*, and, of course, the death must have been *accidental*.

In South Carolina, (act of 1740,) the legislature having by some means made the discovery, as they set forth in the law, that " cruelty is not only highly unbecoming those who profess themselves *Christians*, but is odious in the eyes of all men who have any sense of virtue or humanity,—to restrain and prevent barbarity being exercised towards slaves, enacted, " That if any person whosoever shall wilfully murder his own slave, or the slaves of any other person, every such person (*i. e.* the offender) shall, upon conviction thereof, forfeit and pay the sum of seven hundred pounds current money, and shall be rendered forever incapable of holding, exercising, &c. any office, &c. ; and in case any such person shall not be able to pay the penalty and forfeiture hereby inflicted and imposed, every such person shall be sent to any of the frontier-garrisons of the province, or committed to the workhouse in Charleston for the space of seven years, &c. &c. at hard labour." 2 *Brev. Dig.* 241. This pecuniary

mulct was the only restraint upon the wilful murder of a slave in this state, from the year 1740 to the year 1821,—a period of more than eighty years. But *wilful* murder, in the sense in which the epithet *wilful* is here used, it is not very likely would be often* perpetrated by the master. The species of murder, the cruelty of which can scarcely be exaggerated by any description, and which there is a strong probability would be not unfrequently chargeable upon the master or his overseer, is delineated in another section of the same act, and guarded against,— *how adequately*, the reader will judge for himself from the following quotation:—
" If any person shall, on a sudden heat or passion, or by *undue correction*,† kill his own slave, or the slave of any other person, he shall forfeit the sum

---

* Perhaps in this supposition I am mistaken. I find in the case of *The State vs. M'Gee*, 1 *Bay's Reports*, 164, it is said incidentally by Messrs. Pinckney and Ford, counsel for the state, " that the *frequency* of the offence (*wilful* murder of a slave) was owing to the *nature of the punishment*," &c. &c. *Relatively*, however, I have no doubt the latter species of this crime—i. e. *murder by undue correction*, &c.—must have been much more common. A reflection naturally suggests itself from the remark of Messrs. Pinckney and Ford which I have here transferred. This remark was made in 1791, when the above trial took place. It was made in a public place—a court-house—and by men of great personal respectability. There can be, therefore, no question as to its *verity*, and as little of its *notoriety;* nevertheless, thirty years elapsed before a change of the law was effected!

† The exact words of this section of the act of 1821 are, " If any person shall kill any slave *on sudden heat and passion*, such person, on conviction, shall be fined in a sum not exceeding $500, and imprisoned not exceeding six months."

of *three hundred and fifty pounds* current money."
2 *Brev. Dig.* 241.

The first-named of these sections, I have already
mentioned, has been repealed by an act of 1821,
which punishes the wilful, malicious and deliberate
murder of a slave, by death without benefit of
clergy. The latter section, so far as relates to the
killing of a slave on a sudden heat or passion,* has
been supplied by an enactment in the same year,
which DIMINISHES the *pecuniary* penalty to five hundred *dollars*, but authorizes an imprisonment not
exceeding six months. *James' Digest*, 392.

The law of *Alabama* is scarcely less objectionable.
For after enacting, "If any person shall, with malice
aforethought, cause the death of a slave by cruel,
barbarous or inhuman whipping or beating, or by
any cruel or inhuman treatment, or by the use of
any instrument in its nature calculated to produce
death, such killing shall be deemed murder in the
first degree," the following sections are found in
immediate connection:—"If any person, being the
overseer or *manager* of any slave or slaves, or having
the right to correct such slave or slaves, shall cause

---

* This differs from the section of the act of 1740, just quoted, in
leaving out the words "*by undue correction.*" The proper inference,
therefore, would seem to be, that killing a slave by *undue correction*
was not within the scope of the act of 1821, but was still subject as
to punishment to the act of 1740. But I find that it has been decided in South Carolina, by the highest tribunal there, "any killing
of a slave by *undue or excessive correction* is that kind of MANSLAUGH-
TER described in the act of 1821 by the words 'sudden heat and passion.'" *State vs. Fleming*, 2 *Strobhart Rep.* 464.

the death of the slave by such barbarous or inhuman whipping or beating, or by any other cruel or inhuman treatment, although without intention to kill, or shall cause the death of any such slave or slaves, by the use of any instrument in its nature calculated to produce death, though without intention to kill, unless in self-defence, such killing shall be deemed murder in the *second* degree.

" If any person, being the owner of any slave or slaves, shall cause the death of the slave by cruel, barbarous, or inhuman whipping or beating, or by any other cruel or inhuman treatment, although without intention to kill, or shall cause the death of any such slave by the use of any instrument in its nature calculated to produce death, though without intention to kill, unless in self-defence or in the use of so much force as is necessary to procure obedience on the part of the slave, such killing shall be deemed murder in the *second* degree." *Clay's Alabama Digest*, 413.

It is plain, upon the mere reading of these laws : 1. That it was the intention of the legislature to make a distinction in the *guilt* of killing a *slave* and a *freeman*. 2. That this is done by subverting the rule which obtains generally in criminal jurisprudence, that where there is the greatest probability of the commission of crime the strongest guard should be placed.

The life of the slave is in but little danger from *poisoning, lying in wait,* and such other means which imply coolness and deliberation; whilst his helpless condition exposes him to death by *cruel, bar-*

barous and *inhuman whipping,* begun without an intent to kill, and continued with a brutal indifference to consequences until death inevitably ensues. And yet this is not to be restrained by the fear of *capital punishment,*—nor yet the more aggravated atrocity of killing by "*the use of an instrument* IN ITS NATURE CALCULATED *to produce death,*" provided "the *master, overseer, manager,* or other person having the right to correct such slave," shall be the murderer.

Where the *life* of the slave is thus feebly protected, his *limbs,* as might be expected, share no better fate. I quote again from the act of 1740, of South Carolina. "In case any person shall wilfully cut out the tongue, put out the eye,* castrate, or *cruelly* scald, burn, or deprive any slave of any limb or member, or shall inflict *any other cruel punishment, other than by whipping or beating* with a *horsewhip,* cowskin, switch, or small stick, or *by putting irons on, or confining or imprisoning such slave,* every such person shall, for every such offence, forfeit the sum of one hundred pounds current money." 2 *Brevard's Dig.* 241. This section has, as far as I have been able to learn, been suffered to disgrace the statute-book from the year 1740 to the present hour. Amidst all the mutations which Christianity has effected within the last century, she has not been able to conquer the spirit which dictated this abominable

---

* How different was the Mosaic law!—"If a man smite *the eye* of his servant, or the eye of his maid, *that it perish,* he shall let *him go free for his eye's sake.* And if he smite out his man-servant's *tooth,* or his maid-servant's tooth, he shall let him go free for his tooth's sake." *Exodus, chap.* 21, *verses* 26, 27.

law. To say nothing of the trifling penalty for *mutilation*, what idea of humanity must a people entertain, who, by *direct legislation*, sanction the beating, *without ,limit*, of a fellow-creature with a *horsewhip* or *cowskin*, and the infliction of any torture which the ingenuity and malignity of man may invent, in the application of irons to the human body, and the perpetual incarceration, if the master so will, of the unfortunate slave, in a "dungeon-keep," however loathsome? Such, nevertheless, is the just interpretation of ,this law,—a law, too, which at the same time denominates these very acts, WHICH IT AUTHORIZES, *cruel* punishments.

Louisiana has borrowed the last section of the South Carolina law, with the exception of what respects mutilation, and making the penalty not more than five hundred dollars nor less than two hundred. *See* 1 *Martin's Digest*, 654. Whatever remarks, therefore, were made upon that law, will apply equally to this. Her new Civil Code effects no, reformation of the old law, but is content with the enunciation of a general principle, which is regarded, no doubt, as the quintessence of humanity. "The slave is entirely subject to the will of his master, who may correct and chastise him, though not with *unusual* rigour, nor so as to maim or mutilate him, or to expose him to the danger of loss of life, or to cause his death." *Civil Code of Louisiana, art.* 173. How far the power of the master is limited by the expression *unusual** rigour may be

---

* So lately as 1852 the legislature of Louisiana recognised the

easily inferred, when it is recollected that the law of South Carolina last noticed had been in full force in Louisiana for many years before, and was so at the time when the Civil Code was adopted. The Constitution of Mississippi bestows upon the general assembly power to make laws to oblige the owners of slaves to treat them with humanity—to abstain from all injuries to them extending to life or limb; and, in case of their neglect or refusal to comply with the directions of such laws, to have such slave or slaves sold for the benefit of the owner or owners. *Const. Mississippi, title Slaves, sect.* 1; *Rev. Code,* 554. In the exercise of the power thus granted, in the first and second clauses,—viz.: " to oblige the owners of slaves to treat them with humanity, and to abstain from all injuries to them extending to life or limb,'' the general assembly have passed this act:—" No cruel or unusual punishment shall be inflicted on any slave within this state. And any master or other person entitled to the service of any slave, who shall inflict such cruel or

---

practice of putting iron chains and collars upon slaves, to prevent them from running away. The act reads thus:—" If any person or persons, &c. shall cut or break any iron chain or collar, which any master of slaves should have used in order to prevent the running away or escape of any such slave or slaves, such person or persons so offending shall, on conviction, &c., be fined not less than two hundred dollars nor exceeding one thousand dollars, and suffer imprisonment for a term not exceeding two years nor less than six months.'' *Statutes of* 1852, pp. 210 and 552. It is worthy of special commemoration that the legislature of the same state, by the law given above in the text, from 1 *Martin's Digest,* 654, imposes a *much less* penalty for the infliction of "cruel punishments,'' of the most atrocious description, upon the slave.

unusual punishment, or shall authorize or permit
the same to be inflicted, shall, on conviction, &c.
be fined according to the magnitude of the offence, at
the discretion of the court, in any sum not exceeding five hundred dollars," &c. *Rev. Code*, 379,*
(*act of June* 18, 1822.)   Without the testimony of the
slave, I again remark, a law of this nature may be
regarded as nugatory. But, abstractedly considered,
what protection does it hold forth? "*Cruel*" and
"*unusual*," connected as they are by the disjunctive
"*or*," mean precisely the same thing,' and will be so
construed by the court. And what horrible bar-
barities may be excused under the name of *usual*
punishments, the reader will be enabled to judge by
recurring to the laws of South Carolina and Louisiana contained on the preceding pages.

But what reason can be alleged for not putting in
requisition at once the important power "to have
slaves sold from their owners who neglect or refuse
to comply with the directions of laws designed to
secure humane treatment to such slaves"? This
point will be the subject of separate examination
hereafter, and I forbear therefore enlarging upon
it now.

The Constitution of Missouri has gone beyond
that of Mississippi, in relation to the protection of
slaves from the inhumanity of their masters; for it
not only *empowers* the legislature "to oblige the
owners of slaves to treat them with humanity, and

---

* Alabama has a similar law, except as to the penalty, which is but
one hundred dollars. *Toulmin's Digest*, 631.

2*

to abstain from all injuries to them extending to life or limb," *art.* 3, § 26, *last clause,* (1 *Missouri Laws,* 48,) but it is made its DUTY *to pass such laws as may be necessary for this purpose.* If this injunction be regarded in its proper light, it will be incumbent on the legislature to remove the restriction which has been imposed on the reception of the testimony of all who are not whites. As yet, no law has been enacted on the authority of the article in the constitution; on the contrary, there is an act which confers upon the master a new mode of inflicting punishment on the slave, which *may be* perverted to subserve purposes most cruel. "If any slave resist his or her master, mistress, overseer or employer, or *refuse* to obey his or her lawful commands, it shall be lawful for such master, &c. to commit such slave to the common gaol of the county, there to remain *at the pleasure* of the master, &c.; and the sheriff shall receive such slave, and keep him, &c. in confinement, at the expense of the person committing him or her." 1 *Missouri Laws,* 309. While for the obvious reason that the master, if cruel and vindictive, can gratify his disposition in a manner *less expensive* and much less troublesome to him in its execution, and more severe towards his victim, I do not think it probable this power will be *abused,* yet, viewing man as he is, no law ought to justify and *assist* in the imposition of a punishment of this nature, to be prosecuted to any extent which a wicked heart may desire.

Upon a fair review of what has been written on the subject of this proposition, the result is found to be:—That the master's power to inflict corporal punishment to any extent, short of life and limb, is fully sanctioned by law, in *all* the slave-holding states—that the master, in at least two states, is *expressly* protected in using the *horsewhip* and *cowskin*, as instruments for *beating* his slave—that he may, with entire impunity, in the same states, load his slave with irons, or subject him to perpetual imprisonment whenever he may so choose—that for cruelly scalding, *wilfully* cutting out the tongue, putting out an eye, and for any other dismemberment, if *proved*, a fine of one hundred pounds currency only is incurred in South Carolina—that though in all the states the wilful, deliberate and malicious murder of the slave is now *directed* to be punished with death, yet, as in the case of a *white* offender none except whites can give evidence, a conviction can seldom, if ever, take place.

Prop. IV.—ALL THE POWER OF THE MASTER OVER THE SLAVE MAY BE EXERCISED, NOT BY HIMSELF ONLY IN PERSON, BUT BY ANY ONE WHOM HE MAY DEPUTE AS HIS AGENT.

Louisiana is the only state in which an act of Assembly has been passed on this topic. The language of the act may be cited as an appalling definition of slavery itself. "The condition of a slave being merely a passive one, his subordination to his master, and to all who *represent* him, is not susceptible of any modification or restriction, (except in what can excite the slave to the commission of crime,) in such manner, that he owes to his master

and to all his family a respect without bounds and
an absolute obedience, and he is consequently to
execute all the orders which he receives from him,
his said master, or from them." 1 *Martin's Dig.* 616.
In the other slave-holding states, the subjoined
extract from Mr. Stephen's delineation of slavery
in the West Indies, will, it is believed, accurately
express the law and the practice:*

---

* A case is reported among the decisions in the Supreme Court of
Appeals in Virginia, which, while it confirms the text, proves how
wantonly this power may be and is abused.   The statement prefixed
to the opinion of the court is in these words:—"*May* brought an
action of trespass vi et armis, in the Petersburg District Court, against
the appellants, (*Brown & Boisseau*,) for breaking and entering his
close, and *beating several of his slaves,* in the declaration named, *so that
he was deprived of their services for a long time,* and throwing down
his enclosures round his field, whereby his wheat, then and there
growing, was trodden down and injured by a great number of cattle
and horses, &c. &c.   A bill of exceptions states, that on the trial the
defendants offered, in mitigation of damages, the testimony of a witness, tending to prove that the *plaintiff had given a general permission
to Brown, one of the defendants, to* VISIT *his negro quarters, and to chastise any of his slaves who might be found acting improperly.*"   This
evidence was rejected, not that it was in itself improper, but on
technical objections, one of which was that it was offered, and according
to the state of the pleadings, if received, would go to the defence of
both Brown and *Boisseau*, whereas THE PERMISSION *was granted to*
BROWN *only; and the beating,* as had been previously shown, had been
inflicted *solely* by BOISSEAU,—"to whom," continues the report, "it
was admitted no such permission had been given."   *See* 1 *Munford's
Reports,* 288, *Brown & Boisseau vs. May.*   What more flagrant abuse of
the master's power of delegation could be practised than this,—to
grant a *general permission* to one *not* in the functions of an overseer,
or general deputy, to superintend the employment, &c. of the slaves,
(for this character is plainly denied to Brown, inasmuch as he is
charged with having *broken the close* of May, *i. e.* entered unlawfully,

"The slave is liable to be coerced or punished by
the whip, and to be tormented by every species of
personal ill-treatment, subject only to the exceptions
already mentioned, (*i. e.* the deprivation of life or
limb,) *by the attorney, manager, overseer, driver, and
every other person to whose government or control* the
owner may choose to subject him, as fully as by the
owner himself. Nor is any special mandate or
express general power necessary for this purpose;
it is enough that *the inflicter of the violence is set over
the slave for the moment, by the owner, or by any of his
delegates or sub-delegates, of whatever rank or character.*"
Stephen's Slavery, page 46.*

This power of deputation by the master is one of
the degrading and distinguishing features of *negro*
slavery. It was not permitted by the làw of *villanage*.
"The villein might have an action against any man
but his lord for beating him, except for just cause;
and it *was no legal defence in such action, to plead that
it was done by the command of the lord*" 9 *Coke's
Reports,* 76 *A;* and see *Stephen, supra*.

The most common delegate of the master is known
by the appellation of "*overseer.*" A description of
this class of beings is furnished by *Mr. Wirt*, in his
Life of Patrick Henry, page 34. Coming from this
source, there is no reason to suspect the character to

without his consent, upon his premises,) to visit his negro quarters,
and to chastise any of his slaves who might be found acting improperly!

* It has been decided by the Supreme Court of *North Carolina*, that
the *hirer* of a slave cannot be indicted for "a cruel and unreasonable
battery" on such slave. *The State vs. Mann,* 2 *Devereux Rep.* 263,

7

be surcharged *with cruelty*, and the following extract
is in the words of that author:—"Last and lowest,
(*i. e.* of the different classes of society in Virginia,)
a *feculum* of beings called '*overseers*,'—the *most abject,
degraded, unprincipled race,*—always cap in hand to
the dons who employ them, and furnishing materials for the exercise of their pride, insolence, and
spirit of domination."

Prop. V.—SLAVES HAVE NO LEGAL RIGHTS OF
PROPERTY IN THINGS REAL OR PERSONAL; AND WHAT-
EVER PROPERTY THEY MAY ACQUIRE BELONGS, IN
POINT OF LAW, TO THEIR MASTERS.

Of *negro* slavery only can this harsh doctrine be
affirmed. Among the Romans, the Grecians, and the
ancient Germans, slaves were permitted to acquire
and enjoy property of considerable value, as their
own. The Israelites, when in bondage to the
Egyptians, were allowed to acquire private property.
In the account of the plagues inflicted upon the
Egyptians in consequence of Pharaoh's refusal to
let the Israelites go to worship in the wilderness,
when the plague of *murrain* among the cattle is
threatened, it is said, "And the Lord shall sever
between the *cattle of Israel* and the cattle of Egypt,
and there shall nothing die of all that is the children's
of Israel." *Exodus* ix. 4. And in the sixth verse it
is added, "And all the cattle of Egypt died : but of
the cattle of the *children of Israel* died not one."
And see *Exodus* x. 9, 24, 25, 26 ; also *Ibid.* xii. 32, 38.
"The Polish slaves, even prior to any recent
alleviations of their lot, were not only allowed to

hold property, but were endowed with it by their lords." *Stephen's Slavery, &c.* 59, *citing Wraxall's Memoirs, vol.* 2, *letter* 21. In the Spanish and Portuguese colonies the money and effects which a slave acquires by his labour at times set apart for his own use, or by other honest means, are *legally* his own and cannot be seized by his master. *Ibid.* 60. And even in the *British* West India Islands, where the condition of slavery on the whole is not, perhaps, less severe than it is in the slave-holding sections of the United States, and where, in truth, the *unwritten* law is as above stated in this proposition, yet the feelings of the community there forbid its enforcement by the master. Since, however, to deprive the slave of any little articles of property which he might obtain by the exercise of his industry and skill, in the few moments of leisure occasionally indulged to him, has been thought of sufficient importance to call for *solemn acts* of the general assemblies in our slave-holding states, there seems but little reason to believe that humanity has opposed their execution and established a better practice there. I insert various acts of Assembly, which will evidence in what light this subject is viewed in the states so often alluded to. Thus, in *South Carolina,* "It shall not be lawful for any slave to buy, sell, trade, &c. for any goods, &c. without a license from the owner, &c.; nor shall any slave be permitted to keep any boat, periauger* or canoe, or

---

* *Periagua,* as this word should be spelled, is thus defined in the Encyclopædia, (first American edition, published by Mr. Dobson:)

raise and breed, for the benefit of such slave, any horses, mares, cattle, sheep or hogs, under pain of forfeiting all the goods, &c. and all the boats, peri-augers or canoes, horses, mares, cattle, sheep. or hogs. And it shall be lawful for any person what-soever to seize and take away from any slave all such goods, &c. boats, &c. &c. and to deliver the same into the hands of any justice of the peace, nearest to the place where the seizure shall be made; and such justice shall take the oath of the person making such seizure, concerning the manner thereof; and if the said justice shall be satisfied that such seizure has been made according to law, he shall pronounce and declare the goods so seized to be forfeited, and order the same to be sold at public outcry, one half of the moneys arising from such sale to go to the state, and the other half to him or them that sue for the same." *James' Dig.* 385–6; *Act of* 1740.

The act of the legislature of Georgia is in nearly the same words. *Prince's Dig.* 453; 2 *Cobb's Dig.* 979. And, lest perchance the benevolence of the master should sometimes permit the slave to hire

---

"A sort of large canoe made use of in the Leeward Islands, South America, and the Gulf of Mexico. It is composed of the trunks of *two* trees hollowed and united together, and thus differs from the canoe, which is formed of *one* tree." In this country, the distinction here mentioned between a canoe and periagua is not always observed. In "A series of letters from Timothy Flint, principal of the Semi-nary of Rapide, Louisiana, to the Rev. James Flint, of Salem, Mass.," I find the periagua described as "a vessel of from two to four tons, burden, hollowed *sometimes* from *one* prodigious tree, or from the trunks of two trees united, and a plank rim fitted to the upper part."

himself to another for his own benefit, Georgia has imposed a penalty of thirty dollars "for every weekly *offence* on the part of the master, unless the labour be done on his own premises," (*Prince's Dig.* 457,) and pay, besides, a *tax* of one hundred dollars. 2 *Cobb*, 1080. So in Kentucky, with a slight modification. 2 *Litt. & Swi. Dig.* 1159–60. See *Mississippi Rev. Code*, 375, and *Laws of Tennessee, Oct.* 23, 1813, *chap.* 135.

And in Virginia, if the master shall permit his slave to hire himself out, it is made *lawful for any person* and the *duty* of the sheriff, &c. to apprehend such slave, &c.; and the master shall be fined not less than ten dollars nor more than thirty, &c. 1 *Rev. Code*, 374–5; *Code of Virginia of* 1849. In *Missouri*, not less than twenty dollars, nor more than one hundred dollars. *Missouri Dig.* 1014; ,and see *Haywood's Manual*, 534; *Clay's Dig.* 541.

As early as the year 1779, North Carolina interposed as follows:—"*All horses, cattle, hogs or sheep, that, one month after the passing of this act, shall belong to any slave or be of any slave's mark, in this state, shall be seized and sold by the county wardens, and by them applied, the one half to the support of the poor of the county, and the other half to the informer.*" *Haywood's Manual*, 526. See *Mississippi Rev. Code*, 378, *and Kilty's Laws of Maryland, act of* 1723, *chap.* 15, § 6.

In Maryland, by act of *April sessions*, 1787, *chap.* 33, "any person who shall permit and authorize any slave belonging to him or herself, &c. to go at large or hire himself or herself, within this state, shall incur the penalty of five pounds (thirteen and one-third dollars) current money per month, except ten days at harvest." This penalty was increased to twenty dollars, excepting however an additional ten days in harvest. *Act of December sessions*, 1817, *chap*. 104, § 1. By both acts, a slave being a pilot is not included within the prohibition.

In Mississippi a slave is forbidden to cultivate cotton for his own use; and should the master permit him to do so he incurs a fine of fifty dollars. *Miss. Rev. Code*, 379.

And "if any master, &c. of a slave license such slave to go at large and trade as a freeman, he shall forfeit the sum of fifty dollars for each and every offence." *Mississippi Rev. Code*, 374; and see 2 *Missouri Laws*, 743; also, *Kilty's Laws of Maryland*, *act of April*, 1787, *chap*. 33. 'An equal fine is imposed upon a master *convicted* of permitting his slave to keep "*stock of any description.*" *Act of January* 29, 1825, *Pamph. Laws of Mississippi of* 1825.

The Civil Code of Louisiana coincides with the text in the following manner:—"*All that a slave possesses belongs to his master;* he possesses nothing of his own, except his peculium; that is to say, the sum of money or movable estate *which his master chooses he should possess.*" *Art.* 175; and see 1 *Martin's Dig.* 616. "Slaves are incapable of inheriting or transmitting property." *Civil Code, art.* 945. "Slaves cannot dispose of or receive by donation *inter vivos* or *mortis causa*, unless they have been previously and expressly enfranchised conformably to law, or unless they are expressly enfranchised by the act by which the donation is made to them." *Art.* 1462.

"The earnings of slaves and the price of their service belong to their owners, who have their action to recover the amount from those who have employed them." *Louisiana Code of Practice, art.* 103.

In *Arkansas* a statute has been passed in these words:—"Persons owning *slaves* in this state may permit such slaves to labour for *themselves* on *Sunday,* if such labour is done voluntarily by such slaves and without the coercion of the master, and *for the sole use* of the *slave.*" *Dig. of Statutes by English, p.* 370.

The decisions of the courts confirm the doctrine*

---

* There is an isolated case, of pretty early date, (determined in the Supreme Court of *South Carolina;* see 1 *Bay's Reports,* 260-3; *The Guardian of Sally, a negro, vs. Beatty,*) which is too interesting in *several* points of view to be passed by unnoticed. It is in opposition to the spirit of the laws, and to other *later* decisions of the courts, on which account, if no other reason could be assigned, it would be necessary to insert it. An outline of the facts of the case is thus given by the reporter. "This was a special action, in nature of ravishment of ward, to establish the freedom of a negro girl, according to the form proscribed by the act of the legislature for that purpose. The case was this:—A negro wench slave, the property of the defendant, by working out in town, *with permission of her master,* had by her industry acquired a considerable sum of money over and above what she had stipulated to pay for her monthly wages to her master; and, *having an affection* for a negro girl, Sally, she purchased her with this money which she had been for years accumulating, and gave her her freedom. For a considerable time after the purchase was made, the defendant never claimed any property in the negro girl,—never paid taxes for her, but, on the contrary, acknowledged he had no property in her. Some short time, however, before the commencement of the present action, when called upon to deliver up the girl as free, he refused; in consequence of which this action was brought. The court charged the jury in favour of the plaintiff; Chief-Justice Rutledge saying, in conclusion, 'If the wench chose to appropriate the savings of her extra labour to the purchase of this

of these acts of assembly; as in South Carolina, were it was held, "That slaves cannot take property by *descent or purchase.*" 4 *De Saussure's Chancery Report,* 266; *Bynum vs. Bostwick.* And in *North Carolina,*—"Slaves cannot take by sale, or devise, or descent. And *a devise of land, to be rented out for the maintenance of a slave, was adjudged to be void.*" 1 *Cameron's and Norwood's Reports,* 353; same decision, 1 *Taylor's Reports,* 209. Also in Maryland, a gift, bequest or devise made to a slave, by any *not* his owner, would be void. *See Dulany's opinion,* 1 *Maryland Reports,* 561. Though in this last state, such a devise of real or personal estate, made by the *owner* of the slave, has been held to entitle the slave to freedom, as the *implied* intention of the owner. *Hall vs. Mullin, 5 Harris and Johnson's Reports,* 190. In *Kentucky* it has been decided that although a

girl, in order afterwards to set her free, would a jury of the country say No? He trusted not. They were too humane and upright, he hoped, to do such manifest violence to so singular and extraordinary an act of benevolence.' The jury, without retiring from the box, returned a verdict for the plaintiff's ward, *and she was set at liberty.*" Which of these was neighbour to the oppressed negro girl?

I have called this an *isolated* case, and stated that it is in opposition to other *later* decisions. One of these, as recent as 1846, is reported in 2 *Richardson's Reports,* 424; *Elizabeth P. Gist vs. Maurice Tookey.* I quote merely the syllabus of the reporter. "The plaintiff's slave, William, made money *over and above* his wages, and placed it in the hands of the defendant to aid in purchasing his (William's) children. The children were purchased by the defendant. HELD, *that the plaintiff was entitled to recover the money from the defendant.* Notwithstanding any *promise* by the master that his slave shall have certain acquisitions, all the acquisitions of the slave in possession are the property of his master."

master gave permission to his slave to go at large and acquire property for himself, yet property so acquired belonged to the master. *Carter vs. Leeper*, 5 *Dana*, 261. And where a person, having obtained the *written* permission of a master to trade with his slave, purchased a horse from the slave, and the master sued him for the price of the horse, it was *held* that the horse belonged *not* to the slave, but to the master, and that he might recover the price of the horse if not paid to the slave. *Bryant vs. Sheely*, 5 *Dana*, 530.

A slave paid money, which he had earned *over and above his wages*, for the purchase of his children, into the hands of B., and B. purchased such children with the money. *Held*, that the master of such slave was, notwithstanding the money had been thus obtained and thus appropriated, *entitled to recover the* MONEY of B. *Gist vs. Toohey*, 2 *Richardson's*, (South Carolina) *Reports*, 424. And in *Tennessee*, money acquired by a slave with his master's consent belongs, nevertheless, to the master. *Jenkins vs. Brown*, 6 *Humphrey's Reports*, 299. What is earned by the slave, even though it be in the public service, as by services in the Revolutionary army, belongs to the master; as where a slave was allowed by his master to enlist in the *North Carolina* line, and for his services he received a grant of land, just as was bestowed on other enlisted soldiers, it was held that this land belonged to the master. *University vs. Cambreleng*, 6 *Yerger's Reports*, 79.

Prop. VI.—THE SLAVE, BEING "A PERSONAL CHAT-

TEL," IS AT ALL TIMES LIABLE TO BE SOLD ABSO-
LUTELY, OR MORTGAGED OR LEASED, AT THE WILL OF
HIS MASTER.

After what has been said with respect to the
master's power over his slave, it may seem to be of
but little consequence to the slave whether he remain for life subject to one and the same master,
or be transferred successively to many others. As far
as the master's treatment towards him is concerned,
this conclusion may be taken as generally correct.
But it must not be forgotten that the slave is a
human being, and, although his degraded condition
may have blunted or perhaps destroyed the nicer
sensibilities of our nature, yet is he susceptible of
many of the feelings which attach those of the same
species to each other, and even to insensate objects.
As man, he must be alive to the ties of consanguinity
and affinity. *As man*, he must know what friend-
ship is. *As man*, it is scarcely possible he should
not feel an attachment even *to place*. And *as man*,
the indulgence of these feelings cannot fail to con-
tribute largely to his happiness. To be torn from
such endearments, without the hope of a restoration,
and yet live, must inflict a pang agonizing beyond
description. The terror which his master's presence
inspires renders those of his own condition more
dear. Nevertheless, in the slave-holding states,
except in Louisiana, no law exists to prevent the
violent separation of parents from their children, or
even from each other.* In most other countries in

---

* One of the abolition acts of Pennsylvania (act of 29th of March,
1788) contains this provision :—"If any owner or possessor of any

which slavery is tolerated, the slave is employed in the cultivation of the soil, and cannot, by sale, be detached from it. Such is the case in the Spanish, in the Portuguese, and even in the French, colonies. The *Code Noir*, *art.* 47, (I quote from Stephen, not having the code before me,) prohibits the selling of the husband without the wife, the parents without the children, or *vice versâ.* In *voluntary* sales, made contrary to this regulation, the wife or husband, children or parents, though expressly retained by the seller, pass by the same conveyance to the purchaser, and may be claimed by him without any additional price.* *See Stephen's Slavery, &c.* 69.

---

negro or mulatto slave or slaves, or servant or servants, for a term of years, shall, from and after the first day of June next, separate or remove, or cause to be separated or removed, a husband from his wife, a wife from her husband, a child from his or her parent, or a parent from a child, of any or either of the descriptions aforesaid, to a greater distance than ten miles, with the design and intention of changing the habitation or place of abode of such husband or wife, parent or child, unless such child shall be above the age of four years, or unless the consent of such slave, &c. shall have been obtained and testified as hereinbefore described, (*i. e.* by acknowledgment before a magistrate, &c.) such person or persons shall severally forfeit and pay the sum of fifty pounds, with costs of suit, for every such offence, to be recovered by action of debt, &c. &c. *at the suit of any person* who will sue for the same, one moiety, &c. for the use of the plaintiff," &c. There is but little humanity, however, in this provision. Slaves separated from each other by a distance of ten miles might never see each other. Besides, the separation of children from their parents after four years of age is unwarrantable cruelty.

* "This law," says the compiler of the Annals of the Sovereign Council of Martinique, "has always been rigidly executed whenever a claim has been set up on the part of the purchaser. I have known slaves who have been sent to Guadaloupe or St. Domingo, to be

If the humanity of the French has adopted this law, why should not the citizens of our republics imitate so good an example? But it is foreign to my plan to dwell longer on this topic. I pass to a kindred proposition,—the source of perhaps greater evil.

Prop. VII.—THE SLAVE IS AT ALL TIMES LIABLE TO BE SOLD, BY PROCESS OF LAW, FOR THE SATISFACTION OF THE DEBTS OF A LIVING OR THE DEBTS AND BEQUESTS OF A DECEASED MASTER, AT THE SUIT OF CREDITORS OR LEGATEES.

In the British West Indies, where the law is similar to that which is expressed in this proposition, well-informed writers seem to regard the sales of slaves by *process of law* as productive of more cruel consequences than those which arise from *voluntary* alienation. Mr. Bryan Edwards, who, it will be recollected, *was the champion of slavery and of the slave trade*, in his *History of the West Indies, vol. 2, book 4, chap.* 5, after speaking of certain regulations which had been proposed for the melioration of slavery, uses this language:—"But these and all other regulations which can be devised for the protection and improvement of this unfortunate class of people, will be of little avail, unless, as a *preliminary measure*, they shall be exempted *from the cruel hardships* to which they are frequently liable, of *being sold by*

---

expatriated and sold, to reclaim their children remaining in our colony, with success, through the action of the purchasers in the colonies to which they were sent." *See Stephen's Slavery, 69 and 70, citing Annales de la Martinique, tome 1, p.* 285.

creditors, and made subject, in a course of administration by executors, to the payment of all debts, both of simple contract and specialty." This he stigmatizes as a "*grievance remorseless and tyrannical in its principles, and dreadful in its effects;*" the revival "in a country that pretends to Christianity of the odious severity of the Roman law, which declared sentient beings to be *inter res;* a practice injurious to the national character and disgraceful to humanity. A good negro," continues he, "with his wife and young family rising about him, is seized on by the sheriff's officer, forcibly separated from his wife and children, dragged to public auction, purchased by a stranger, and perhaps sent to terminate his miserable existence in the mines of Mexico; and all this without any crime or demerit on his part, real or pretended. He is punished because his master is unfortunate."

It would be in vain for me to attempt to augment the horror which every well-regulated mind must feel from this eloquent description of the cruelty of this law. For humanity's sake, I rejoice to say that the sphere of its operation is by no means co-extensive with the prevalence of slavery. With the exception of the British colonies in the West Indies, and I suppose at Demarara, and perhaps in the small islands belonging to the Dutch, it obtains only in the *republican states of North America !* * And

---

* From the generality of this remark the state of Louisiana must be excepted. It will be recollected that, at the beginning of this chapter, a law was extracted from the Civil Code of the state, by which slaves are declared to be *real* estate,—to be ranked among

8

here again I recur to Mr. Stephen, as ample authority. "Of the liability," says he, "of slaves to be
seized and sold separate from the land they cultivate,
by the master's creditors, for the payment of his
debts, it may safely, I believe, be pronounced that
a precedent to such cruel injustice is not to be found
in any part of the Old World." "Plantation slaves,
not only in the Spanish and Portuguese, but in the
French colonies also, are *real estate*, and attached to
the soil they cultivate, partaking therewith all the
restraints upon voluntary alienation to which the
possessor of the land is there liable; and they cannot
be seized or sold by creditors for satisfaction of the
debts of the owner." It has already been stated
that by the *Code Noir*, *art.* 47, the husband cannot
be sold without the wife, nor the parents without

---

immovable property. When, therefore, the owner of slaves is, as I
presume is most commonly the case, possessed of land, the slave cannot be separated from it by process of law. Besides this humane
regulation, there are several others which deserve to be signalized,
viz. :—"If, at a public sale of slaves, there happen to be some who
are disabled through old age or otherwise, and who have children,
such slaves shall not be sold but with such of his or her children
whom he or she may think proper to go with." 1 *Martin's Digest*,
612, *act of July* 7, 1806.

"Every person is expressly prohibited from selling separately from
their mothers the children who shall not have attained the full age
of ten years." *Ibid.* These provisions have probably been suggested
by a knowledge of the *much more* humane ones which are comprised
in the *Code Noir of Louis XIV.*, extracts from which are given in the
text of the former proposition. I call the *Code Noir much more humane;* for, though the slaves disabled by old age, &c., according to the
Louisiana law, are not *to be sold* apart from their children without
their consent, yet the master may *retain* them and *sell* their children,
and thus the like painful separation be effected.

the children. "Sales made contrary to this regulation, by process of law *under seizure for debts,*
are declared void." *See Stephen's Slavery, &c.,*
p. 68–9.

Since, then, from what has been said upon this
and upon the last preceding proposition, it appears
no restraint (except a partial one in the state of
Louisiana) is imposed upon the sale and transfer
of slaves,* but that these may take place, not only
at the will of the master, but against his will, *by
process of law, &c.*, sufficient authority is at once dis-
closed for the prosecution, to any extent, of the
inter-territorial slave trade which exists among us.
Many of the slave-holding states, however, while
they permit their citizens to sell their slaves to
whom they please, and to carry them where they
please, yet, for reasons of policy, have found it expedient to enact laws to prohibit, *in a great measure,*
the further introduction of them into their respective limits. Laws with this aspect have been
enacted in the states of Delaware, Maryland, North
and South Carolina, Tennessee, Kentucky, Georgia,
and Louisiana. The act of Assembly of North

---

* This—as most of the remarks in this work—applies exclusively
to those states in which laws for the abolition of slavery have not
been enacted. For in these latter states at least, whenever the
abolition of slavery has been, by a law, *gradual* in its operation,
it has been found necessary to prevent slaves from being carried
out of their respective limits. And in Delaware, though a slave-
holding state, slaves cannot be *exported* from the state without the
license of two justices of the Court of Quarter Sessions. *Act of June*
14, 1793, *ch.* 20.

Carolina, which, being one of the earliest,* has probably served as a precedent in the other states, deserves particular commemoration; and I therefore transcribe those sections which are important to the present inquiry:—

"*Section* 1. From and after the first day of May next, no slave or indented servant of colour* shall be imported or brought into this state by land or water; nor shall any slave or indented servant of colcar, who may be imported or brought contrary to the intent and meaning of this act, be bought, sold, or hired by any person whatever.

"*Section* 2.—Every person importing or bringing slaves or indented servants of colour into this state, after the said first day of May next, by land or water, contrary to the provisions of this act, shall forfeit and pay the sum of one hundred pounds for each and every slave or indented servant of colour so imported or brought. And every person who shall knowingly sell, buy, or hire such slave or indented servant of colour, shall, in like manner, forfeit and pay the sum of one hundred pounds for each and every slave, &c.; one moiety of which forfeiture shall be to the use of the state, and the other moiety to him or them who shall sue for the same, &c.

"*Section* 3.—It shall be the duty of all justices of the

---

* The law of Delaware bears date a few years anterior to that of North Carolina; but the provisions of the act of the latter state have been adopted, with but little variation, in the other states.

peace, sheriffs, coroners, constables or other judicial and ministerial officers of this state, to use all reasonable and lawful means to carry this act into effect, which if they or any of them neglect to do, it shall be deemed a misdemeanour in office. And any officer who shall fail, neglect or refuse upon application to perform the duties aforesaid, shall be held and deemed liable to the forfeitures inflicted on those who may import or bring a slave or indented servant of colour into this state in the first instance, and shall be proceeded against in the like manner and to the like effect."

To the generality of this prohibition the following exceptions are added:—

"*Section* 4.—Nothing in this act shall be construed to prevent any person or persons, being citizens of the United States, or subjects or citizens of foreign cuontries, who intend to reside and settle within the limits of this state, from bringing with him, her or them, such slaves or servants of colour as they may think proper; or to prevent such persons from travelling with their slaves, &c. through this state, in order to settle in another state; or to prohibit any citizen of this state, who may obtain slaves, &c. by marriage, gift, legacy, devise or descent, or who hath heretofore entered into *bona fide* contracts, from bringing the slaves or servants of colour so obtained or contracted for, into this state, by land or water."

And in order to guard against an abuse of the privileges conferred by these exceptions, it is made the duty of the persons coming within them to make oath, that the slaves introduced are not intended for traffic, nor in evasion of the act of Assembly above cited. *Haywood's Manual*, 533–4, *act of* 1794, *chap.* 2. And see 2 *Brevard's Digest*, 256 *to* 261 *inclusive*, (*acts of* 1800, 1802, & 1803;) *Laws of Maryland, act of* 1796, *chap.* 67 ; *Laws of Delaware, act of* 1787, *chap.* 145, § 7, *and act of* 1789, *ch.* 193; 2 *Litt & Swi.* 1162, *act of* 1815 ; *Prince's Digest*, 373–4,* *act of* 1817 ; *Louisiana, act of* 1826, (*see Pamphlet Laws.*)

The number of slaves admissible into the above states, in virtue of the proviso as to persons removing with slaves into the state, and in favour of those who may derive them by gift, descent, marriage or devise, it is probable would not greatly augment this species of population. It must, however, be evident, that while every coloured person is presumed to be a slave, and while a transfer of such is permitted without restraint among citizens of the same state, no matter how remote in distance may be the places of their respective residences, that it cannot be very difficult, especially with the pretext which is supplied by the proviso, to introduce within the extensive limits of most of the above states, as many slaves as any one, lured by a high price, may choose. At the present time, I presume there is but little temptation to prosecute this traffic in the states where the prohibitory law has been adopted; for a mart is open in the states of Alabama, Mississippi, Florida, Arkansas and Missouri, which is not likely

---

* The *African* slave trade was prohibited in Georgia in 1798, by an article of her Constitution, *art.* 4, § 11. But it was not until 1817 that the act of the legislature was procured for the prohibition of the *inter-territorial* traffic.

to be glutted for many years to come. And even *Virginia,** after having, in the year 1778, enacted an inhibition of the importation of slaves, with a few exceptions, within her borders, has recently resumed her ancient policy, and now proclaims her willingness to *receive* all those, not convicted of crimes, who have been " born within the United States, or any

---

* Between the years 1699 and 1772, the legislature of Virginia passed numerous acts to *discourage* the importation of slaves. The means resorted to for this purpose was the imposition of a considerable *duty* on imported slaves. *See* 2 *Tucker's Blackstone, Appendix,* 49, 50. The *royal negative* was exercised in relation to several of these acts, and it is abundantly demonstrated by Judge Tucker, that a *direct* effort by the *colony* would have been entirely unavailing. The fate of an act of this description which was attempted by the assembly of *Pennsylvania* in the year 1712 might be cited as additional proof of this disposition on the part of the crown. At the period of our Revolution, a strong conviction of the impolicy and inhumanity of the traffic in slaves seems to have existed in Virginia. And in the year 1778, as is stated in the text, an entire inhibition of the importation of slaves within her borders, except such as might be brought by *emigrants* to the state, or might be derived by her citizens from descent, marriage or devise, took place. This humane act, after having undergone by subsequent legislatures several revisions and slight mutations, without materially affecting its principles, was, in the year 1819, *almost* wholly annulled;—*wholly* it could not be, from the paramount force of the Constitution and laws of the United States. How humiliating the contrast which is exhibited by the provisions of this act of 1819, and the following quotation from the preamble to the Constitution of this state, promulgated on the 29th June, 1776:—"Whereas George the Third, king, &c., heretofore intrusted with the exercise of the kingly office in this government, hath endeavoured to pervert the same into a detestable and insupportable tyranny, by prompting our negroes to rise in arms among us,—*those very negroes whom,* BY AN INHUMAN USE OF HIS NEGATIVE, HE HATH REFUSED US PERMISSION TO EXCLUDE BY LAW."

territory thereof, or within the District of Columbia."
1 *Rev. Code,* 421–2, *act of* 1819; *Code of Virg. of* 1849,
p. 457.

I will conclude my observations on the subject
of this and the next preceding section, by holding
up for the imitation of those whom it may concern,
the conduct of the aborigines of our country, whom,
in courtesy to those for whom this is written, I shall
style *savages.* Speaking of the Seminole Indians,
the author of a small work published at Charleston,
South Carolina, in the year 1822, entitled *"Notices
of East Florida, with an account of the Seminole nation of
Indians, by a recent traveller in the Province,"* says,
"Another trait in their character is their great
indulgence to their slaves. Though hunger and
want be stronger than even the *sacra fames auri,* the
greatest pressure of these evils never occasions them
to impose onerous labours on the negroes, or to
dispose of them, though tempted by high offers,
if the latter are unwilling to be sold."

Prop. VIII.—A SLAVE CANNOT BE A PARTY BEFORE
A JUDICIAL TRIBUNAL IN ANY SPECIES OF ACTION
AGAINST HIS MASTER, NO MATTER HOW ATROCIOUS MAY
HAVE BEEN THE INJURY WHICH HE HAS RECEIVED
FROM HIM.

In a former part of this chapter, the several laws
which *profess* to give redress to the slave for cruelty
inflicted upon him by his master were brought
together, their principles discussed, and their inefficacy exposed. By none of these, it will be perceived, however, could the slave appear in any

CANNOT CHANGE MASTERS.   93

capacity against his master; and therefore, though they may seem to have some connection with this proposition, I do not deem it fit or necessary to make any comment upon them in this place. The law is unquestionably, as stated above, without any exception or limitation.

Prop. IX.—SLAVES CANNOT REDEEM THEMSELVES, NOR OBTAIN A CHANGE OF MASTERS, THOUGH CRUEL TREATMENT MAY HAVE RENDERED SUCH CHANGE NECESSARY FOR THEIR PERSONAL SAFETY.

This proposition holds good as to the right of *redemption* in all the slave-holding states; and equally true is it as respects the right to compel a *change of masters, except in Louisiana and Kentucky.* The Civil Code of Louisiana contains a regulation by which the latter privilege may sometimes, perhaps, be obtained by the slave. Yet the conditions upon which its extension to the slave depends are such, that it needs strong proof to induce the belief that the law has ever been called into action. For it requires as preliminaries—First, that the master be *convicted* of cruelty,—a task so formidable, that it can hardly be ranked among possibilities; and, secondly, it is afterwards *optional* with the judge whether or not to make the decree in favour of the slave. I extract the article of the code, which is in these words:—"No master shall be compelled to sell his slave, but in one of two cases, to wit: the first, when, being only co-proprietor of the slave, his co-proprietor demands the sale, in order to make partition of the property; *second, when the master shall be* CONVICTED *of cruel treatment of his slave,* AND THE JUDGE SHALL DEEM IT PROPER *to pronounce, besides the penalty established for such cases, that the slave shall be sold at public auction, in order to place him out of the reach of the power which his master has abused."* *Art.* 192. And in *Kentucky*, by act of 1830, a mode is pointed out by which, in case a jury should be of opinion that the owner of a slave has treated him *cruelly* and *inhumanly*, and so as to endanger *his life* or *limb*, such slave may be sold to another master. 2 *Morehead & Brown's Digest*, 1481–2.

In Turkey the law is still more favourable to the slave. "For he may allege *contrariety of tempers*, whereby they cannot live together, and the judge will decree that the patron shall carry his slave to market and sell him." *Life of Hon. Sir Dudley North*, p. 63 of vol. iii. of Lives of his three brothers, by Roger North, London edition of 1826.

The Constitution of Mississippi, as we have before seen, empowers the legislature to enact a law for the benefit of the slave in this particular;* yet, though the subject of cruelty by the master to his slave has claimed a portion of their attention, the humane design of the Constitution has been disregarded. This neglect, not only in Mississippi, but in the slave-holding states generally, is the more remarkable, inasmuch as in the codes of several of these same states a provision of this nature exists for the cases of *indented servants and apprentices*. *See particularly Prince's Digest*, 458. Such a regulation,

---

* See supra, page 68.

every one who will take the trouble to reflect on the subject must consider indispensable for the slave's protection.   What a mockery must it be to pass laws *professedly* to punish the master's cruelty to his slave, if the slave is still to be left in the power of the same master, exasperated by the punishment and disgrace which must ensue from conviction. " Would you," said Mr. Randolph, in his speech, delivered* in the House of Representatives, on the imprisonment of the Spanish officers ·in Florida, " would you send a slave who had been abused by his overseer to that very overseer for protection ?"

Prop. X.—SLAVES BEING OBJECTS OF PROPERTY, IF INJURED BY THIRD PERSONS THEIR OWNERS MAY BRING SUIT AND RECOVER DAMAGES FOR THE INJURY.

This is a maxim of the common law with respect to property in general, and it may, therefore, be assumed to be the law of all the slave-holding states in regard to slaves also.   Taken strictly, it does not operate as a shield to the slave against corporal aggression, unless the violence used is so great as to *deteriorate* the property of the master.† And so a decision of the Supreme Court of Maryland has established the law to be in that state:—

---

* February 27, 1822.

† *Kentucky* is an exception to the generality of this statement. The owner of a slave there, by act of Assembly of 1816, may bring an action of trespass against any one who shall whip, strike or otherwise abuse such slave without the owner's consent, " *notwithstanding the slave may* NOT *be so injured that the master may lose his or her services thereby.*" 2 *Morehead & Brown's Digest*, 1481.

" There must be a loss of service, or at least a
diminution of the faculty of the slave for bodily
labour, to warrant an action by the master."
1 *Harris and Johnson's Reports*, 4; *Cornfute vs. Dale.*

A case, the report of which may be found in
2 *Bay's Reports*, 70, by the name of *Sims White vs.
James Chambers*, was decided by the constitutional
Court of Appeals in South Carolina, in the year
1796, by which the master was enabled to sustain
his suit against a third person, for a·corporal injury
to his slave, although *a loss of service* was not *alleged
in the declaration.* The following is the statement
prefixed to the case by the reporter: — " Special
action in the case for beating the plaintiff's negro
man. It came out in evidence on the trial, that
the negro in question had the care of his master's
fishing canoe on Sullivan's Island, when the defendant went down to the landing-place, where it
was, and said he would take it and go out fishing
in it. The negro told him he could not have it,
as his master had given him orders to let no one
take it away, as he was in the constant habit of
using it himself, and he expected him down every
minute to go out in it. The defendant, however,
persisted in taking it away, *and the negro in obeying
his master's orders* in refusing to let him have it:
upon which some high words passed between them
on both sides, whereupon the defendant struck him
a blow with his fist, *and then took up a paddle, which
was in the canoe, and knocked him down, and afterwards
beat him very severely, which laid him up for several
days, before he was able to go about his master's business*

again." Having given the reader this statement of the facts in the case, it is fit that I should gratify his curiosity by a faithful record of the *verdict.* He will then be enabled to form some estimate of the degree of protection which is derived by the slave from his owner's right of action against third persons for brutal violence to the slave. The jury "found a verdict for *five* pounds sterling, and costs of suit"!!

Let not the *jury only* be reproached with this verdict. A whole community are implicated with them. A section of the negro act of 1740, which was in force when this decision was given, and is, indeed, the law of South Carolina at the present hour, has fixed a measure of damages which fully sustains the conduct of the jury. "If any negro or other slave, who shall be employed in the lawful business or service of his master, owner, overseer, &c. shall be beaten, &c. by any person or persons, not having sufficient cause or lawful authority for so doing, and shall be *maimed* or *disabled by such beating* from performing his or her work, such person or persons *so offending* shall forfeit and pay, to the owner or owners of such slave, the sum of *fifteen shillings current* money, *per diem*, for every day of his lost time, and also the charge of the cure of such slave." 2 *Brevard's Digest*, 231-2.

I do not find any provision on this subject among the laws of the other slave-holding states, except in Louisiana and Kentucky, (see *ante*, pp. 93, 94,) in the former of which an act of Assembly, in most respects analogous to that which I have cited from the code

9

of South Carolina, has been passed with a special penalty imposed for the *benefit* of the master, where the injury to the slave is of a most aggravated character. For "if the slave," (*maimed, &c.*) *be forever rendered unable to work*, the offender shall be compelled to pay the value of said slave, according to the appraisement made by two freeholders, appointed by each of the parties; and the slave thus disabled shall be forever maintained at the expense of the person who shall have thus disabled him, which person shall be compelled to maintain and feed* him agreeably to the duties of masters toward their slaves, as ordered by this act." 1 *Martin's Digest*, 630–2.

From the abstract of the cases decided in Maryland and in South Carolina, and especially from the laws which I have here quoted, it will be perceived that the protection of slaves from the violent and wanton assaults of those not their masters, &c. is scarcely to be looked for, as a consequence of the master's right to be compensated for the deterioration of his property in the slave. The purpose of these laws is not, in truth, the protection of the slave, but the vindication of the master's rights of property.† And yet in slave-holding countries this *right of action* in the master is not unfrequently pro-

---

* See, as to food and clothing, supra, pages 47, 48.

† By an extreme refinement of this principle, it has been held in North Carolina, that "patrols are not liable to the master for inflicting punishment on his slave, *unless their conduct clearly demonstrates* MALICE AGAINST THE MASTER." 1 *Hawk's Reports*, 418; *Tate vs. O'Neal.*

claimed to be a sufficient protection to the slave. It would be more just to say *that it is the only one which is accorded to him.*

Prop. XI.—SLAVES CAN MAKE NO CONTRACT. Besides such of the laws referred to under Proposition V. of this chapter as relate to *this* proposition, it may be added that a slave cannot even contract matrimony, (*Civil Code of Louisiana, art.* 182,) the association which takes place among slaves, and is *called* marriage, being properly designated by the word *contubernium*—a relation which has no sanctity, and to which no civil rights are attached.* "A slave has never maintained an action against the violator of his bed. A slave is not admonished for incontinence, or punished for fornication or adultery; never prosecuted for bigamy, or petty treason for killing a husband being a slave, any more than admitted to an appeal for murder." *Opinion of Daniel Dulany, Esq., Attorney-General of Maryland,* 1 *Maryland Reports,* 561, 563.

Prop. XII.—SLAVERY IS HEREDITARY AND PERPETUAL.

This is not merely a corollary from the clause of the act of Assembly which was quoted near the beginning of this chapter, but is the effect of an express declaration found in the same act of As-

---

* In accordance with this, it has been held in North Carolina by the Supreme Court, that a slave, who was *the wife* of another slave, might give evidence against him, even in a capital case. *State vs. Smith,* a slave ; 2 *Dev. & Bat.* 177.

sembly, which, having been already transcribed,
need not be here inserted.

That a child should be deprived of any of its *natural*
rights in consequence of its parent's misfortunes, is
surely not the deduction of reason from any known
principle applicable to the social condition of man.
Yet the *hereditary* nature of slavery has probably
been an incident of the institution in every age
and among every people where the institution has
been tolerated.* It was so with the Hebrews, both
before and after the Mosaic dispensation; it was so
with them during their bondage to the Egyptians;
the Helots of Sparta and the Roman slave suffered
the like injustice.

But the *perpetuity* of slavery—the natural pro-
duct of its *inheritable* quality—received a check by
the *Mosaic* polity. The Israelites having been miraculously freed from the yoke of the Egyptians, it
was ordained, in unequivocal terms, that a Hebrew
should not retain his brother whom he might buy
as a servant more than *six years against his consent*,
but that in the *seventh* year he should go out free,

---

* In Massachusetts, "several negroes *born* in this country of *imported* slaves demanded their freedom of their masters by suits at
law, and *obtained* it by judgments of the courts." *See Winchenden vs.
Hatfield, &c.*, 4 *Massachusetts Reports*, 128. But these cases can hardly
be ranked as exceptions to the general allegation in the text. They
appear to have been the effect of collusion between the masters and
the slaves. For, according to Chief-Justice Parsons, " the defence
of the master was faintly made; for such was the temper of the times
that a restless discontented slave was *worth little, and when his freedom
was obtained in a course of legal proceedings, the master was not holden
for his future support, if he became poor.*"

for nothing. If he came by himself he should go out by himself; if he were married (when he came) his wife should go out with him. *Exodus, ch.* 21, *ver.* 2, 3; *Deut. ch.* 15, *ver.* 12; *Jeremiah, ch.* 34, *ver.* 13. Besides this important regulation, *Hebrew* slaves were, without exception, restored to freedom by the *jubilee.* I am aware that the authority of respectable names may be avouched for the opinion that the benefit of the jubilee, as to this particular, was enjoyed by *all classes* of bondmen, according to the literal import of the command:—"Ye shall hallow the fiftieth year, and *proclaim liberty throughout all the land,* and UNTO ALL THE INHABITANTS THEREOF." *Leviticus, ch.* 25, *ver.* 10. With an anxious desire to sustain this opinion, if tenable, it appears to me that not only was such a privilege not required by the general purpose for which the jubilee was appointed, but the positive language of the 44th, 45th and 46th verses of the same chapter forbid such an inference. "The condition of *foreign* slaves was less favourable. Whether captives taken in war, purchased, or born in the family, their servitude was *perpetual.*" 1 *Milman's History of the Jews, book* 3, *p.* 124; 1*st Lond. edit.*

It seems, however, highly probable, that the term *perpetual,* in its proper and absolute sense, was not applicable to the slavery by the Israelites even of *the heathen* nations. For the command was given to Abraham, and was not abrogated by Moses:—"He that is born in thy house, and he *that is bought with thy money,* must be circumcised." *Genesis, ch.* 17, *ver.* 13. Jewish commentators agree that this com-

mand was strictly construed and carried faithfully
into practice. Thus, it is said by *Maimonides*,
"Whether a servant be born in the power of an
Israelite, or whether he be purchased from the heathen, the master is to bring them both into the
covenant. But he that is born in the house is to
be entered upon the *eighth day*, and he that is bought
with money on the day on which the master receives him, unless the slave be unwilling. For, if
the master receives a grown slave, and he be unwilling, his master is to bear with him, to seek to win
him over by instruction, and by love and kindness,
for *one year;* after which, should he refuse so long,
it is forbidden to keep him longer than the twelve-
month, and the master must send him back to the
strangers from whence he came; for the *GOD* of
Jacob will not accept any other than the worship
of a willing heart." *Maimon. Hilcoth Miloth, chap.* 1,
sect. 8. *See Gill's Exposition of the Old and New
Testaments, &c.*

And, according to *Genesis, ch.* 17, *ver.* 10, compared with *Romans, ch.* 4, *ver.* 11, by the rite of
circumcision, the recipient was consecrated to the
service of the *true GOD. See* 3 *Horne's Introd. to
Crit. Study of the Holy Scriptures,* 413. And on such
a one were, in consequence, conferred nearly all the
rights of a son of Abraham. "Although," says
the respectable author last quoted, "the constitution of the Jewish polity, and the laws of Moses,
allowed no other nations to participate in their
sacred rites, yet they did not exclude from them
such persons as were willing to qualify themselves

for conforming to them. Hence, they admitted proselytes who renounced the worship of idols and joined in the religious services of the Jews, although they were not held in the same estimation as Jews by birth, descent, and language." *Ibid.* 255. "When a stranger will sojourn with thee, and keep the passover to the Lord, let all his males be circumcised, and then let him come near and keep it, and he shall be as one that is born in the land." *Exodus, ch.* 12, *ver.* 48. On this passage in Exodus Dr. Jennings observes these two things. "First, that when a man became a proselyte, all his males were to be circumcised as well as himself, whereby his children were admitted into the visible church of GOD, in his right as their father. Secondly, *that upon this he should be entitled to all the privileges and immunities of the Jewish church and nation,* as well as be subject to the whole law. *He should be as one born in the land." Ridgely's Body of Divinity, vol.* iv. 193, note by Dr. Williams.*

Notwithstanding the bearing of these authorities, I would not be thought to speak of the conclusion which they tend to establish, with a confidence approximating to positiveness. The dealings of the Almighty with the heathen nations, through the instrumentality of his chosen people the Israelites, is a subject not to be discoursed upon with the freedom of ordinary criticism. And on this point

---

* The edition of the work from which the above is extracted was published under the sanction (as the title-page affirms) of *James P. Wilson, D.D.*, and the note is of his selection, and consequently may be considered as speaking his sentiments.

especially,—what effect had proselytism on the condition of heathen slaves held by Hebrews, there is an obscurity which leaves the mind unsatisfied.

But whether or not the proselyte heathen slave became entitled to freedom at the jubilee is of no importance to us, so far as we are concerned in respect to our duties to the enslaved. *As to us*, there exists *no people* who can be called *heathen*, in the sense in which that appellation was used by the Israelites. The master and the slave are of the same class—are both Gentiles. The only legitimate inference, therefore, which, in a comparison with the Mosaic regulations, analogy furnishes, is, that our conduct to slaves should be the same as was the conduct of the Israelites to *Hebrew* slaves.

CHAPTER III.

OF THE CONDITION OF THE SLAVE CONSIDERED AS A MEMBER OF CIVIL SOCIETY.

To speak of a slave as a member of civil society may, by some, be regarded a solecism. Such a condition, however, is recognised by the laws of the slave-holding states. To what extent, and for what purpose, it is recognised, will be sufficiently manifested in the course of this chapter; which, for the sake of perspicuity, will be arranged and examined under the following titles:—

I. A slave cannot be a witness against a white person, either in a civil or criminal cause.

II. He cannot be a party to a civil suit.

III. The benefits of education are withheld from the slave.

IV. The means for moral and religious instruction are not granted to the slave; on the contrary, the efforts of the humane and charitable to supply these wants are discountenanced by law.

V. Submission is required of the slave, not to the will of his master only, but to that of all other white persons.

VI. The penal codes of the slave-holding states bear much more severely upon slaves than upon white persons.

VII. Slaves are prosecuted and tried upon criminal accusations in a manner inconsistent with the rights of humanity.

I. A SLAVE CANNOT BE A WITNESS AGAINST A WHITE PERSON, EITHER IN A CIVIL OR CRIMINAL CAUSE.

I have had occasion very frequently to advert to this subject, as the cause of the greatest evils of slavery. Acts of Assembly, apparently intended to give protection to the slave from his master's cruelty, have been adduced, and yet shown to be altogether nugatory, in consequence of the rule of law which forms the title of this section. In truth, in our slave-holding states this exclusion is not confined to the evidence of *slaves;* but natives of Africa, and their descendants, whatever may be the shade of their complexion, and whether bond or free, are under the like degrading disability.* In a few of the slave-holding states the rule derives its authority from *custom;* in others, the legislatures have sanctioned it by express enactment. In Virginia there is an act of Assembly in these words:—"Any negro or mulatto, bond or free, shall be a good witness in pleas of the commonwealth for or against negroes or mulattoes, bond or free, or in civil pleas where free negroes or mulattoes shall alone be parties, *and in no other cases whatever.*" 1 *R. V. C.* 422. Similar in Missouri; 2 *Missouri Laws,* 600. In Mississippi; *Mississippi Rev. Code,* 372. In Kentucky; 2 *Litt. & Swi.* 1150. In Alabama; *Toulmin's Dig.* 627. In

---

* In *Texas* this restriction is confined to such persons to the *third* generation only. *Texas Dig.* 219–220.

Maryland; *Maryland Laws, act of* 1717, *ch.* 13, § 2 & 3, *and act of* 1751, *ch.* 14, § 4. In North Carolina and Tennessee; *act of* 1777, *ch.* 2, § 42.

Such being the law, it requires no extraordinary perspicacity to pronounce that its effects must be most injurious to the unhappy victim of slavery. It places the slave, who is seldom within the view of more than one white person at a time, entirely at the mercy of this individual, without regard to his fitness for the exercise of power,—whether his temper be mild and merciful, or fierce and vindictive. A *white* man may, with impunity, if no other white be present, torture, maim, and even murder his slave, in the midst of any number of negroes and mulattoes. Having absolute dominion over his slave, the master or his delegate, if disposed to commit illegal violence upon him, may easily remove him to a spot safe from the observation of a *competent* witness. Indeed, it is probable few *white* persons ordinarily reside upon the same plantation, since I find in most of the slave-holding states, the owners of slaves are compelled by a considerable penalty "to keep *at least* one white man on each plantation to which a certain number of slaves is attached,"—a law which would not have been necessary unless a contrary practice was prevalent. *See Prince's Dig.* 455, &c.

Plain and conclusive as this reasoning must be to the mind of any candid person, I think it best, nevertheless, to corroborate it by the direct testimony of several distinguished persons, whose means of information entitle them to speak with authority. Sir William Young, then Governor of Tobago, and

an advocate of slavery, thus expressed himself in
1811:—"Instances of bad treatment and cruelty, and
of unjust and immoderate punishment of slaves, I
think occur exclusively within the narrow trading
or household circle of unattached slaves; and, I am
sorry to say, have *frequently* been reported to me,
with circumstances of atrocity to be *believed*, though
(for reasons which I shall give) not to be *proved*,
against lower white or coloured people domineering
over from two to ten or more wretched beings, their
slaves. In such cases, what protection by law have
the slaves against the abuse of power over them by
Europeans or other free people? *I think the slaves
have no protection.* In this, and I doubt not in every
other island, *there are laws* for the protection of slaves,
and *good ones;* but *circumstances in the administration
of whatever law render it a dead letter. When the intervention of the law,*" he continues, "*is most required, it
will have the least effect;* as, in cases where a vindictive
and cruel master *has care* to commit the most atrocious cruelties, *even to murder his slave*, NO FREE PER-
SON BEING PRESENT TO WITNESS THE ACT. There appears to me a *radical defect* in the administration of
justice throughout the West Indies, *in whatever case
the wrongs done to a slave are under consideration;* or
rather, *that justice cannot in truth be administered, controlled as it is by a law of evidence which covers the most
guilty European with impunity, provided that when having
a criminal intent he is cautious not to commit the crime in
the presence of a free witness.* I should consider it as
inconsistent with the respect and deference I bear
to the sagacity and wisdom of the august body for

whose use this report is framed, to idly enlarge it with the enumeration of *humane laws* for the protection of slaves, *all rendered nugatory* by the conditions of evidence required in their administration." See for this extract from Sir William Young, Report, &c., *a note to page* 167 *of Stephen's West Indian Slavery, &c.,* *pages* 168–9. Mr. Stephen has collected the statements of many others holding official stations in the British West India colonies, all concurring in relation to this one point:—the inefficacy of all laws made for the protection of slaves, in consequence of the rejection of the testimony of slaves. I avail myself of an additional citation from this source. *The Chief-Justice,** &c. of the island of St. Vincent gives the following answer to parliamentary inquiries proposed to him in the year 1791 :—" The only instances in which their (slaves') persons *appear* to be protected by the *letter* of the law, are in cases of murder, dismemberment and mutilation; and in these cases, *as the evidence of slaves is never admitted against a white man, the difficulty of establishing the facts is so great that white men are in a manner put beyond the reach of the law.*"

I subjoin a further proof,—not that I consider the present topic difficult of explanation, but because what I now adduce is borrowed from the authentic records of a slave-holding state of our own country. The negro act of South Carolina contains the following preamble to one of its sections:—"Whereas, by reason of the extent and distance of plantations in

* Drewry Ottley, Esq.
10

this province, the inhabitants are far removed from
each other, and *many cruelties* may be committed on
slaves, because *no white person** may be present *to
give evidence* of the same," &c. 2 *Brevard's Dig.* 242.

After such admissions of the evils of this law, we
are naturally induced to inquire what reasons have
led to its adoption, and especially what can justify
its continuance.

It is *alleged* by its advocates that it is coeval with
the institution of slavery; and they add moreover,
as if this circumstance were of great moment, that
slavery has existed since the time of Noah. 2 *Brevard's Dig.* 222, *note.* That servitude *under some form*
is of a very remote antiquity, there can be no doubt;
but it cannot be established, it is believed, by proofs
at all worthy of reliance, that the rejection of the
testimony of the slave has always been a concomitant
evil.† If indeed it could be shown that such had,

---

* A similar state of things appears to have existed in 1826, in this
state.   In *State vs. Raines*, 3 *McCord's Reports*, 546, the court says,
"The slave and his owner or possessor is perhaps as much secluded
from the view of other white persons *now* as formerly. He is still
even now *for days and weeks*, in many parts of the country, left *entirely*
with the *master* or *overseer.*"

† Josephus, in book 4, chap. 8, § 15, of his Antiquities of the Jews,
(*Whiston's translation,*) states the law on this subject differently from
what we find it recorded in the Sacred Scriptures of the Old Testament.
The passage in Josephus stands thus:—"Let not a single witness be
credited, but three or two at least, and those such whose testimony is
confirmed by their good lives. *But let not the testimony of women be
admitted, on account of the levity and boldness of their sex; nor let servants
be admitted, on account of the ignobility of their soul, since it is probable
that they may not speak the truth, either out of hope of gain or fear of
punishment.*"   The authority of Josephus cannot be set in competition

in all ages, been the misfortune of the oppressed, it would not surely, on that account, carry conviction of the justice of the rejection to the mind of any one who rightly weighs the claims of humanity, and who believes that " to do justly and love mercy" are duties of inflexible and perpetual obligation.

Villanage, as it existed in England, furnishes no authority for the universal application of this rule. A villain was a good witness, in civil cases, against any one except his lord; see *Bro. abridg. tit. Villeinage,* 66; and, as he might *prosecute* his lord in *the king's*

---

with that of the Sacred Scriptures as they have descended to us. And, though he professes to give the law as established by Moses and left by him in writing, without any ornament or addition, yet it requires but little attention to discover that instead of the Pentateuch itself he has furnished a commentary upon it by the Scribes and Pharisees, whose "traditions," as we are told by unerring wisdom, had made "void the law." *See note to Whiston's translation on the text of Josephus above cited; also, 3d volume of Horne's Introduction to a Critical Study of the Holy Scriptures,* 112, (American edition.) When, therefore, we find the law of Moses, according to our canon, prescribes numerous rules for the treatment of servants or slaves, regulates with considerable minuteness judicial proceedings in general, and makes particular mention of the *number* of witnesses required to establish the truth, and yet is entirely silent as to the *competency* of women and servants as witnesses, it is fair to presume that no such disqualifications were ever sanctioned by the Jewish lawgiver. *See Deut. ch.* 17, *v.* 6; *and ch.* 19, *v.* 15, *et seq.* The judges, indeed, were expressly empowered to decide upon the *credibility* of witnesses,—to proceed in a summary manner against those who testified falsely, and to inflict retaliatory punishment upon them; from which I infer that both the accuser and accused had a *right* to produce their witnesses and compel the hearing of them, leaving the *judges*, like *our juries*, to decide upon the weight of their testimony.

name for violence done to his person, it is right to presume in such a case he must have been admitted as a witness against him also: *Coke, Litt.* 124, *a; Dulany's Opinion,* 1 *Maryland Reports,* 561; and, without doubt, in *criminal* cases generally, it was *no exception* to a witness that he was a villain or bondman. *Hawkin's Pleas of the Crown, book* 2, *chap.* 46, § 28; *Coke, Litt.* 126, *a.*

We must have recourse to the *civil law* for its probable origin. "The general rule of that law certainly was that a slave could not be a witness, though there were exceptions to it, founded in reason and policy; for men of that condition might be examined when the welfare of the state, in cases of weight and difficulty, required such a departure from general principles, or *when other evidence was unattainable.*" *Stephen's West India Slavery,* 171, *citing Voetius' Commentary on the Pandects.* This latter exception, it is obvious, destroys the rule, if we are to understand by it that a slave might be examined, in the defect of other proof, for the inculpation of any offender against the laws. And such I suppose to be the true meaning, since "slaves might always (among the Romans) induce an investigation, by flying to the statues of the princes:" *Cooper's Justinian,* 412; a privilege which would be of but little value, unless the slave could be examined as a witness against his injurer; and if thus admissible in his own case, with much more propriety could he be heard on behalf of third persons, where feelings of interest would not operate to bias him.

It may be safely averred, I *believe,* that this rule of

evidence, *to the extent in which it obtains in our slave-holding states*, cannot challenge for its support the authority of any country, either ancient or modern. For it must not be forgotten that it is not the evidence of slaves only which is rejected by it; it applies equally to coloured persons, or rather to the descendants of Africans, as well to those who are *free* as to those who are slaves. This being the case, I shall briefly discuss the propriety of it in its whole compass.* And first let us see upon what reason it is founded, in its application to slaves. It has been said the admission of such testimony is dangerous to the lives and fortunes of the whites. This charge, if adopted in its most obvious sense, would seem to imply the total destitution of veracity in the slave. But this conclusion must be too comprehensive, since even slaves are competent witnesses, not only against each other, but against free

---

* In *Virginia*, a very early statute places the exclusion on the ground that none but Christians should be witnesses; and even among those a certain description of persons were excluded. The statute I allude to, runs thus:—"*Popish recusants convict*, negroes, mulattoes and Indian servants, and others not *being Christians*, shall be deemed and taken to be persons incapable in law to be witnesses in *any case* whatsoever." *See* 3 *Henning's Statutes (of Virginia) at large*, 298, *act of October*, 1705, (4*th Anne*,) *sect.* 31. In *Maryland*, papacy, of course, is not subjected to the ban, but the like intolerance is nevertheless evinced:—"No negro or mulatto slave, free negro, or mulatto born of a white woman, during his time of servitude by law, or any Indian slave or free Indian natives of this or the neighbouring provinces, (shall) be admitted and received as good and valid evidence in law, in any matter or thing whatsoever depending before any court of record, or before any magistrate within this province, wherein any *Christian white* person is concerned." *Acts of* 1717, *chap.* 13, § 2.

persons of colour, without any restriction. *Law of Virginia*, 1 *Rev. Code*, already cited; *Prince's Digest*, 446; *Haywood's Manual*, 523; *Maryland Laws, act of 1751, chap. 14, § 4, &c. &c.*

If the objection is restrained to the testimony of the slave against *his master*, it presumes the predominance of the utmost depravity of heart in the slave,—a depravity which, in the gratification of a spirit of revenge,* would disregard the strongest moral sanctions. To concede this is to impute a highly criminal negligence to the master; for, having the absolute dominion of the slave, the dictates of humanity, as well as the plain precepts of the gospel, demand the bestowal of such attention to the religious instruction of the slave as, in ordinary cases, would prevent or extirpate such excessive malignity.

But, it is said, "the hope of gain," or "the fear of punishment," would probably induce the slave to testify falsely. "The hope of gain" will be felt chiefly, if not exclusively, in investigations touching the master's interest, — an objection which, if it be a valid one, degrades the master far below the level of the *suborned* slave. "The fear of punishment" is a more embarrassing difficulty,—so much

---

* And yet revenge does not seem to be more prevalent with blacks than with whites. CLARKSON, whose labours on behalf of the negro are so well known, makes the following memorable declaration:— "That he had not, after a diligent and candid investigation of the conduct of *emancipated* slaves, under a great variety of circumstances, comprising a body of more than five hundred thousand, a considerable proportion of whom had been suddenly enfranchised, found a *single* instance of *revenge* or abuse of liberty."

so, indeed, that it would perhaps be proper, as a general rule, to exclude such testimony when offered *on behalf of the master.*

To every other objection except the last, *under the peculiar restriction there mentioned*, TRIAL BY JURY is an ample refutation. It is scarcely conceivable that a being so degraded as a slave in the eyes of those who usually compose juries in the slave-holding states should, as a witness, operate serious injustice to a *white man*. Labouring under the prejudice with which he is likely to be viewed by *slave-owners*, it is fair to infer that, unless fortified by other *unexceptionable* witnesses, or by strong circumstances, a slave's testimony would ordinarily go for nothing. But, as has been well remarked by Mr. Stephen, "how many instances are there in which the evidence of a witness, who is liable in a much higher degree to distrust, is essential to the interests of justice, and may furnish a satisfactory ground of decision, even for the purposes of conviction in capital cases! Often is a necessary link in the chain of circumstantial evidence wanting, which the vilest man on earth might credibly supply, because the other circumstances have previously raised the highest presumption of its truth, and of its being a truth, too, within the knowledge of that witness. Sometimes, also, testimony which is very low in credit may justly derive great weight from the consideration that, if untrue, the opposite party possessed the means of refuting it by satisfactory proof, which he has not produced; and sometimes it is satisfactory, because it is strongly corroborated by other evidence, though neither would have separately sufficed." The examination of *accomplices in crime* against each other, instances of which are of daily occurrence in criminal courts, is an illustration of these principles.

In the ruder ages of society, courts of law viewed the *competency* of witnesses with great jealousy. Persons were prevented from giving testimony then, on objections which are now treated as of insufficient validity. For this improvement in judicial administration we are principally indebted to the ascertained practical excellence of trial by jury. Besides, husband and wife, who, *in general*, from motives of public policy and humanity, are forbidden or *excused* from testifying for or against each other, may, under some circumstances, from *necessity*, in legal contemplation,—*i. e. to prevent an entire failure of justice*,—be heard even in his or her own behalf. Such is the case where *personal* violence has been offered by the one to the other. The grant of a like privilege to the slave against his master, in particular, may be supported by reasons *at least* equally forcible. And such a right it seems probable obtained in *Massachusetts*, as far as we are informed, without inconvenience; on the contrary, I have no doubt, with decisive public advantage. See *supra, note to page* 35.

If trial by jury is a sufficient answer to the several objections against the admission of a slave's testimony, with much greater force may it be urged in reference to the competency of the *free negro*. Indeed, it is to me inconceivable upon what plausible ground the unqualified and universal rejection of the latter as a witness can be supported. It is without the precedent of any other country, it is believed, whether civilized or savage. The freedman was a competent witness by the civil law. He might even give evidence of what came to his knowledge before his enfranchisement,—a privilege not allowed by the same law to the man of full age in respect to what he learned during his nonage. *Stephen*, 181–2, *citing Voetius ad Pand. lib. 22, tit. 5, sect. 2.* In the West Indies, free negroes are received as witnesses in *civil actions* against *white* persons, (*Stephen*, 182,) a distinction of immense advantage, especially in a trial for freedom, where it can hardly be expected a white person would be able to testify as to the pedigree of a black.

While *this unqualified and universal exclusion* of the evidence of coloured persons prevails, it can be of but little use to enact severe penalties against kidnapping. *Secrecy* in this crime, in particular, will, as far as it is in the power of the perpetrator, be preserved; and if the free negro — the injured party — cannot be heard against the offender, from what other source can satisfactory evidence be expected? But change the law: *admit him* as a witness, *and kidnapping of all crimes would be* THE EASIEST OF DETECTION.*

---

* Too much force cannot be given to this argument. Remote as is the city of Philadelphia from those slave-holding states in which the introduction of slaves from places within the territory of the United States is freely permitted, and *where also the market is tempting*, it has been ascertained that *more than thirty* free coloured persons, mostly children, have been kidnapped here and carried away within

Confessedly great as are the evils of this harsh regulation, it will naturally be asked if a remedy of some description has not been attempted. To this it may be answered, that a preposterous and wholly inefficacious one, as may be easily demonstrated, has been devised in South Carolina and imitated in Louisiana. Having thus characterized it, it is fit I should exhibit it to the reader, that he may judge for himself; and for this purpose I give the section of the act of Assembly in which it is found, without abridgement:—"Whereas, by reason of the extent and distance of plantations in this province, the inhabitants are far removed from each other, and many cruelties may be committed on slaves because no white person may be present to give evidence of the same, unless some method be provided for the better discovery of such offence, and as slaves are under the government, so they

---

the last two years. Five of these, through the kind interposition of several humane gentlemen, have been restored to their friends, though not without great expense and difficulty; the others are still retained in bondage, and if rescued at all it must be by sending *white* witnesses a journey of more than a thousand miles. The costs attendant upon law-suits under such circumstances will probably fall but little short of the estimated value, *as slaves*, of the individuals kidnapped. That very many free negroes have been kidnapped in non-slave-holding states admits of but little doubt. Within the last few years *two* notorious cases — those of *Rachel and Elizabeth Parker*, sisters, born and brought up to full womanhood in Chester county, Pennsylvania—may be mentioned. With what difficulty and expense were they at length rescued and restored to freedom!

The interesting book, "*Twelve Years a Slave*," &c., of *Solomon Northrup*, who was kidnapped at Washington City, furnishes another most memorable example.

ought to be under the protection of masters and managers of plantations, *Be it enacted,* That if any slave shall suffer in life, limb or member, or shall be maimed, beaten or abused contrary to the directions and true intent and meaning of this act when no *white person* shall be present, or being present shall neglect or refuse to give evidence, or be examined upon oath concerning the same; in every such case the owner or other person who shall have the care and government of such slave, and in whose possession or power such slave shall be, shall be deemed, taken, reputed and adjudged to be guilty of such offence, and shall be proceeded against accordingly without further proof, *unless* such owner or other person as aforesaid can make the contrary appear by good and sufficient evidence, *or shall by* HIS OWN OATH *clear and exculpate himself;* which oath every court where such offence shall be tried is hereby empowered to administer, and *to acquit the offender* if clear proof of the offence be not made by *two* witnesses at least." 2 *Brevard's Dig.* 242.

The reader has probably anticipated my objections to the extraordinary provisions of this law. That the slave population were subjected to many cruelties, as is set forth in the preamble, in consequence of the exclusion of their testimony against their oppressors, I have no doubt; and that the legislatures were fully convinced of this I consider to be equally clear. But it is by no means clear that a remedy of the mischief was *intended* by the enactment of this section. It would detract from the *intellectual* character of the legislature to suppose so. Could it be reasonably expected that the presumption of guilt, which the act authorizes to be made, would lead to a conviction, when the party could purge himself of the accusation brought against him by his *own* oath? Of a crime which could be satisfied by a small pecuniary fine, *perhaps* it *sometimes* might; such instances, however, *one white person only in general being on the plantation*, would seldom be brought to the knowledge of the magistrate. But would the man *wicked* enough to commit murder, hesitate to screen himself from its penalties by a crime not *more* heinous certainly than that which he would thus conceal?* But this

---

* No one, I believe, will question the truth of this as a general remark. It is not, therefore, for the purpose of fortifying it, that I refer to a case, reported in the South Carolina reports of judicial decisions, in which the *exculpatory* oath was offered to be made by a person whom the court decided not to be within the *benefit* of the act, and who was, *immediately afterwards, upon good evidence, found guilty of manslaughter.* See *The State vs. Welch,* 1 *Bay's Reports,* 172.

I subjoin a later case, A.D. 1826, from the judicial reports of the same state, in which, notwithstanding by the *confession* of the prisoner he had been guilty of a most cruel murder, yet he offered to *exculpate* himself by his own oath. The court below refused to permit him to do so, and the jury found him " guilty of *manslaughter,* and recommended him to the mercy of the court."

The statements of the facts is in the words of the judge before whom the case was tried :—" On the trial of the case, the declarations of the prisoner were given in evidence, from which it appeared that the prisoner was taking the negro from Chester jail to Columbia, *at the request of his owner,* William Gray. That the negro had broken open Wall's store, in Columbia, and stolen money, and had run away; that he was a bad negro, and had been a runaway, and had been shot and had the shot still in him. That the negro turned sullen and refused to go farther, and the prisoner whipped him to make him go

is a view of the law far more favourable than its
true construction authorizes. For it is in terms
declared that the offender *shall be acquitted* upon
his own oath of innocence, *if clear proof of his guilt
be not made by* TWO *witnesses at least;* thus, in fact,
introducing a modification of the former law, *not
for the protection of the slave,* BUT FOR THE ESPECIAL
BENEFIT OF A CRUEL MASTER OR OVERSEER !

II.—A SLAVE CANNOT BE A PARTY TO A CIVIL SUIT.

It has been shown in a preceding part of the

---

along, and for no other purpose, *and gave him,* as the prisoner said,
five hundred lashes.

"That when the prisoner found he could not make the negro go
along by whipping, he tied the negro's legs to prevent him from going
off until the prisoner could go and get assistance. That the prisoner
requested two women, at the first house down the road, to go back to
the negro to prevent any one from cutting him loose.

"The witnesses on the part of the state testified that the negro died
about eight minutes after the two women reached him, and some time
before the prisoner with two other men returned. That the prisoner
bled at *the nose, mouth, and ears,* though there was no bruise or mark
of a blow about the head or body. That the negro appeared to have
been severely whipped below the small of the back, and the blood
appeared in several places which seemed to have been touched by the
end of the switches. *That several small switches and two or three
larger ones lay near, which appeared to have been much worn ; also a stick
with a small end and a larger end seemed to have been used.*"

For the prisoner, witnesses testified, "That the prisoner was a
HUMANE, *peaceable man, and a man of good character.*"

"The court charged that the prisoner *was not guilty of murder,* but
was under the second count, for killing a slave *in sudden heat and
passion.*"

The *Court of Appeals* decided that the prisoner *was entitled to
exculpate himself by his own oath;* and that the judge who tried the
case erred in *not permitting him to do so.* See *The State vs. Gay Raines,*
8 *McCord's Reports,* 533.

11

sketch that a slave can neither acquire nor retain property, as his own, contrary to the will of his master. It results, therefore, that he cannot be a party to a civil suit; for there is no species of civil suit which does not, in some way, affect property. There is, however, an authority, which for the purpose of convenient investigation may be classed as an *exception* to the above rule, given by the laws of all the slave-holding states, to persons *held as slaves* BUT CLAIMING TO BE FREE, *to prosecute their claims to freedom before some judicial tribunal.* I design, therefore, in this place to bring into view whatever relates to this subject.

The oldest law of this description appears to have been adopted by South Carolina in the year 1740. It begins with what has been already extracted, but which, for the sake of perspicuity, it will be proper to repeat:—"Be it enacted, That all negroes, Indians, (free Indians in amity with this government, and negroes, mulattoes and mestizoes *now* free, excepted,) mulattoes and mestizoes who now are or shall hereafter be in this province, and all their issue and offspring born or to be born, shall be and they are hereby declared to be and remain forever hereafter absolute slaves, and shall follow the condition of the mother, &c. &c. Provided, that if any negro, Indian, mulatto or mestizo, claim his or her freedom, it shall and may be lawful for such negro, Indian, mulatto or mestizo, or any person or persons whatsoever, on his or her behalf to apply to the judges of his majesty's Court of Common Pleas, by petition or motion, either during the sitting of the said court, or before any of the justices of the same court, at any time in vacation. And the said court, or any of the justices thereof, shall and they are hereby fully empowered to admit any person so applying to be guardian for any negro, Indian, mulatto or mestizo claiming his or her or their freedom; and such guardian shall be enabled, entitled and capable in law to bring an action of trespass, in the nature of ravishment of ward, against any person who shall claim property in, or who shall be in possession of any such negro, Indian, mulatto or mestizo; and the defendant shall and may plead the general issue in such action brought, and the special matter may and shall be given in evidence, and, upon a general or special verdict found, judgment shall be given according to the very right of the cause, without having any regard to any defect in the proceedings, either in form or substance. And if judgment shall be given for the plaintiff, a special entry shall be made, declaring that the ward of the plaintiff is free, and the jury shall assess damages which the plaintiff's ward hath sustained, and the court shall give judgment and award execution against the defendant for such damages, with full costs of suit; *but in case judgment shall be given for the defendant, the said court is hereby fully empowered to inflict* SUCH CORPORAL PUNISHMENT, NOT EXTENDING TO LIFE OR LIMB, *on the ward of the plaintiff, as they in their discretion shall think fit.* Provided, that in any action or suit to be brought in pursuance of the direction of this act, THE BURDEN OF THE PROOF *shall lay upon the plaintiff, and it shall*

124 SUIT FOR FREEDOM.

be always presumed that every negro, Indian, mulatto and mestizos, is a slave, unless the contrary be made to appear, (the Indians in amity with this government excepted, in which case the burden of the proof shall be on the defendant.)" 2 *Brevard's Dig.* 229–30. In Georgia the act of Assembly of May 10, 1770, is almost literally a copy of this of South Carolina. See *Prince's Digest,* 446 ; 2 *Cobb's Digest,* 971.

It is impossible for any humane and reflecting person to examine the provisions of the above law, without the conviction of its injustice and cruelty. The negro, &c. claims to be free ; and yet he can bring no suit to investigate his master's title to restrain him of his liberty, unless some one can be found merciful enough to become his guardian, subject, in any event, to the expense and trouble of conducting his cause, and in case of failure to the costs of suit.*

---

* In South Carolina, by an act passed in 1802, "the guardian" (in a trial for freedom) " of a slave," (who may have been *illegally* imported into the state, and is *on that account,* by the same law, declared to be *free,*) "claiming his freedom, shall be liable to *double* costs of suit, if his action shall be adjudged groundless ; and shall be liable to pay to the bona fide owner of such slave all such damages as shall be assessed by a jury and adjudged by any Court of Common Pleas." 2 *Brevard's Digest,* 260. And in Maryland, the attorney, in a trial for freedom, must pay all costs, if unsuccessful, unless the court shall be of opinion that there was probable cause for supposing that the petitioner had a right to freedom. *Act of Nov.* 1796, *chap.* 67, § 25. And, on such a trial, *the master* (the defendant) is allowed *twelve* PEREMPTORY challenges as to the jurors. *Ibid.* § 24. The same spirit of hostility to the claimant for freedom is manifested in Virginia, where, if any person be found *aiding* or *maintaining* a slave in the prosecution of a suit upon a petition for freedom, who shall fail to establish

His judges and jurors will in all probability be slaveholders, and interested, therefore, in some measure, *in the question* which they are to try. The whole community in which he lives may, so few are the exceptions, be said to be hostile to his success. Being a negro, &c., by the words of the act, the *burden of proof* rests upon him, and he is *presumed* to be a slave till he make the contrary appear. This is to be effected through the instrumentality of *white* witnesses, as has been just shown, exclusive of the testimony of those who are *not* white, even though they may be free and of the fairest character. And, lastly, notwithstanding all these obstacles to the ascertaining of the truth of his allegations, the terror is superadded, should he not succeed in convincing the judge and jury of his right to freedom, *of an infliction of corporal punishment to any extent short of capital execution, or the deprivation of a limb!!!* And in *Georgia*, "should death happen by accident in giving this legal (moderate) correction," according to the terms of the Constitution already quoted,* it will be no crime! Such legislation forcibly reminds us of the feast of Damocles; though, in all soberness, it may be said the conduct of Dionysius was supreme beneficence, compared with the *terms of mercy* contained in this act.

The harsh and unreasonable doctrine which *pre-*

---

his claim to freedom, every such person shall be liable to the owner in an action on the case for damages. *Code of Virginia*, (1849,) *p.* 465.

* See, *supra*, page 61.

sumes every negro, &c. to be a slave obtains, I
believe, with the single exception which will be
hereafter noticed, in all the slave-holding states.
In Virginia there is no statute to this effect, yet
so is the law as established by judicial decisions.
Thus, where in suits for freedom, brought by several
persons, whose descent was traced to a free *Indian*
woman, and where, as the reporters say, " On the
hearing, the late chancellor,* perceiving from his
own view that the youngest of the appellees was
perfectly white, and that there were gradual shades
of difference in colour between the grandmother,
mother, and grand-daughter, (all of whom were
before the court,) and considering the evidence in
the cause, determined that the appellees were
entitled to their freedom, and moreover, on the
ground that freedom is the birthright of every
human being, which sentiment is strongly incul-
cated by the first article of our political catechism,
the Bill of Rights,—*he laid it down as a general position, that whenever one person claims to hold another in
slavery, the onus probandi (burden of proof) lies on the
claimant.*" The Supreme Court of Appeals, to
which the case was afterwards carried, thought fit,
in reviewing the decision of the chancellor, to go
beyond the accustomed line of its duty, in order to
cast a stigma upon the just position which had been
asserted by him. The following is a copy of the
final judgment:—" This court, not approving of the

---

* The Honourable George Wythe, one of the *signers of the Declaration
of our Independence.*

chancellor's *principles and reasoning* in his decree made in this cause, except so far as the same relates to *white persons and native American Indians*, BUT ENTIRELY DISAPPROVING *thereof, so far as the same relates to native Africans and their descendants*, who have been and now are held as slaves by the citizens of this state; and discovering no other error in the said decree, affirms the same." *See the case, Hudgins vs. Wright*, 1 *Henning & Munford's Reports*, 133 to 143. In Maryland, a similar decision has been made, 3 *Harris & McHenry's Reports*, 501–2, *case of negro Mary vs. the Vestry of William and Mary's Parish, &c.*; so, in Kentucky, 2 *Bibb's Reports*, 238, *Davis vs. Curry;* and in New Jersey, 2 *Halsted's Reports*, 253, *Gibbons vs. Morse*, (*decided November*, 1821.)

In *North Carolina* this doctrine is received with some limitation, the presumption being confined to negroes of the *whole blood;* while those of *mixed* blood, *mulattoes, mestizoes, &c.*, are presumed free until the contrary is proved. The report of the case in which this principle is recognised is given in 1 *Taylor's Reports*, 164, *Gobu vs. Gobu.* The case itself is *unique*, and on this account, as well as to display the sound reasoning (as far as respects the *mixed* blood) of *Chief-Justice Taylor*, is transcribed at large.

"Gobu) Trespass and false imprisonment.
   vs. } Plea, that the plaintiff is a slave, &c.
Gobu)

"It appeared in evidence, that the plaintiff, *when an infant apparently about eight days old*, was placed in a barn by some person unknown, and that the defendant, *then a girl of about twelve years of age*, found him there and conveyed him home, and had kept possession of him ever since, treating him with humanity, *but claiming him as her slave.* The plaintiff was of an *olive colour, between black and yellow, had long hair and prominent nose."* These facts were ascertained by the court, by proof and inspection; upon which the judge gave the following charge:— " I acquiesce in the rule laid down by the defendant's counsel, with respect to the presumption of every *black* person being a slave. It is so, because the negroes originally brought into this country were slaves, and their descendants must continue slaves until manumitted by proper authority. If, therefore, a person of that description claims his freedom, he must establish his right to it by such evidence as will destroy the force of the presumption arising from colour. But I am not aware that the doctrine of presumption against liberty has been urged in relation to persons of *mixed* blood, or to those of any colour between the two extremes of black and white, *and I do not think it reasonable that such a doctrine should receive the least countenance:* such persons may have descended from Indians in both lines, or at least in the maternal; they may have descended from a white person in the maternal line, or from mulatto parents originally free; in all which cases the offspring, following the condition of the mother, is entitled to freedom. Considering how many probabilities there are in favour of the liberty of these persons, they ought not to be deprived of it upon mere presumption;

more especially as the right to hold them in slavery, if it exists, is in most instances capable of being satisfactorily proved."*

While I freely subscribe to the soundness of the views of this distinguished jurist in relation to persons of *mixed blood*, I cannot but dissent from the specious reasoning by which it is inferred that every *black* person should be presumed to be a slave. Slavery is an institution which all *profess* to disapprove. It violates every man's sense of right: it is at variance with the genius of our government. Its existence, therefore, in no case ought to be *presumed*. But more than this, it is well known that a large number of *black* persons are entirely free, even in the slave-holding states; the laws of our country recognise their right to freedom, and the power of the government has been wielded for their protection, as citizens, whenever a fit case has been brought to public notice. With what propriety of reasoning, then, can it be urged that their colour should, in legal contemplation, raise a presumption against their liberty? Even those who think it desirable to perpetuate slavery—who think it no evil to degrade and brutify a being endowed by his Creator with reason—need apprehend no violation of their legal rights of property by a contrary doctrine. What greater difficulty can exist, to satisfy the requisitions of the law in regard to the ownership of a slave, than obtains in regard to the ownership of

---

* The doctrine of this case was afterwards confirmed, so that it may be considered as the settled law of North Carolina. See 2 *Haywood's Rep.* 170, and *Scott vs. Williams*, 1 *Devereux's Rep.* 376.

ordinary chattels? Will it be alleged that fraud may be perpetrated by transferring a freeman as a slave? But is not an intelligent creature, endowed with the faculty of speech, at all times capable of admonishing a *purchaser* against such a deception? And, when a communication of this nature is made, ought it not to be heeded?

I am the more strenuous in opposition to this doctrine of presumption against liberty, because it is obviously the fruitful source of the abominable crime of *man-stealing*,—a crime which, in all nations, seems to have been viewed with abhorrence and visited with severe penalties. The wretch who, by art or force, is enabled to exhibit a person of African extraction—"with a colour not his own"—in his custody, and within the limits of a slave-holding state, is exempted from the necessity of making any proof how he obtained him, or by what authority he claims him as a slave. Inspection notifies to every beholder that the unhappy person *said* to be a slave is *presumed* so to be by the law of the land! Supplemental evidence is unnecessary; a forged bill of sale *may* be a convenience to satisfy the timid and over-cautious, but the law—the supreme wisdom of man—deems any thing more than *colour* quite superfluous. Is this *just?* Does it become a free and enlightened people thus to decree?—*thus to injure?*

By the laws of several of the slave-holding states, *manumitted* and other free persons of colour, however respectable their characters, may be arrested when in the prosecution of lawful business, and if *documentary evidence* of their right to freedom cannot

be immediately produced by them, they are thrown
into prison and advertised as *runaway slaves.* Should
no owner—as must always be the case, unless injustice is done—appear within a time limited by
law for the purpose, the jailer is directed to dispose
of them at public auction, as *unclaimed fugitive slaves,*
in order to derive from the proceeds of the sale the
means of defraying the expenses of their detention
in prison. The unrighteous doctrine of *presumption*
from colour steps in and consummates the iniquity,
and the freeman and his posterity are doomed to
hopeless bondage. See 2 *Brevard's Digest,* 235-6-7 ;
Mississippi Rev. Code, 376-7 ; *Laws of Maryland,** act

---

* The laws of Maryland here referred to, having excited much attention, in consequence of the arrest and imprisonment, in the District of Columbia, of a free black man, a citizen of the state of New
York, named Gilbert Horton, I am induced to transcribe them in this
place. The *sixth* section of the act of 1715, chap. 44, reads thus :—
"And for the better discovery of runaways, it is hereby enacted, &c.
that any person or persons whatsoever within this province, travelling
out of the county where he, she or they shall reside or live, *without a
pass* under the seal of the said county, for which they are to pay ten
pounds of tobacco, or one shilling in money, such person or persons,
if apprehended, *not being sufficiently known or able to give a good account of themselves, it shall be left to the discretion and judgment of such
magistrate or magistrates before whom such person or persons as aforesaid shall be brought* to judge thereof, and if, before such magistrate,
such person or persons so taken up shall be deemed and taken as a
runaway, he, she or they shall suffer such fines and penalties as are
hereby provided against runaways." *Section* 7.—"And for the better
encouragement of all persons to seize and take up all runaways, &c.,
all and every such person or persons as aforesaid, seizing or taking up
such runaways, *travelling without passes as aforesaid,* not being able
to give a sufficient account of themselves as aforesaid, shall have and
receive *two hundred pounds of tobacco,*" (by act of 1806, chap. 81,

of 1715, (*April session,*) *chap.* 44, § 6, 7, & 9—*act of* 1719, (*May session,*) *chap.* 2, § 2—*act of* 1802, (*November session,*) *ch.* 96, § 2.

§ 5, commuted for SIX dollars,) "to be paid by the owner of such runaway servant, negro or slave so apprehended and taken up; *and if such suspected runaway or runaways be not servants, and* REFUSE TO PAY THE SAME, *he, she or they shall* MAKE SATISFACTION BY SERVITUDE OR OTHERWISE, as the justices of the provincial and county courts, where such person shall be so apprehended and taken up, shall think fit." *Section 9.*—"That at what time soever any of the *said persons*—runaways—shall be seized by any person or persons within this province, such person or persons so apprehending or seizing the same shall bring or cause him, her or them to be brought before the next magistrate or justice of the county where such runaway is apprehended, who is hereby empowered to take into custody or otherwise him, her or them, to secure and dispose of as he shall think fit, until such person or persons so seized and apprehended shall give good and sufficient security to answer the premises the next court that shall first ensue in the said county, which court shall secure such person or persons till he or they can make satisfaction to the party that shall so apprehend or seize such runaways or *other persons* as by this act is required, except such person shall make satisfaction as aforesaid before such court shall happen; and that notice may be conveniently given to the master, mistress, dame or overseer of runaways taken up as aforesaid, the commissioners of the counties shall forthwith cause a note of the runaway's name, so seized and apprehended as aforesaid, to be set up at the next adjacent county court, and at the provincial court and secretary's office, that all persons may view the same, and see where such their servants are, and in whose custody."

The foregoing sections apply *equally* to the cases of all persons, whether *white* or *black*, who may be found travelling *without* passes, out of the county where their residences are; and all such, at the *discretion* of a magistrate, may be subjected to *i*mprisonment and amercement. But the last section of the same act, while it bears with a severity altogether at variance with the spirit of a free government upon *whites* unhappily circumstanced so as to come within the terms

III. THE BENEFITS OF EDUCATION ARE WITHHELD
FROM THE SLAVE.

In no country is education more highly valued, or

of the previous enactments, introduces a provision by which they *may
be restored to freedom, if entitled to be free*; and yet *negroes and
mulattoes, with the same rights,* are left without relief. "When any
person or persons *(except negroes and mulattoes)* shall be found
travelling without passes, *as aforesaid,* and shall be taken up as suspected runaways, and by any justice of the peace committed to the
custody of any sheriff or jailer within this province, it shall not be
lawful for any such sheriff or jailer to hold such person in custody
longer than six months; and if such person can, at any time within
the said six months, procure a certificate or other justification that he
or she is no servant, he or she shall and may, by order of any two
justices of the county where such person is committed to prison, *be
discharged* from any further imprisonment, *he or she serving such
sheriff or jailer, or his assigns, so many days as he, she or they were
in custody of such sheriff or jailer, or otherwise paying ten pounds
of tobacco per day to such sheriff or jailer for* THEIR IMPRISONMENT
FEES, and no more ; and paying unto such person or persons who
took up such person *two hundred pounds of tobacco, or serving him,
her or them twenty days in lieu thereof ;* and if any such sheriff or
jailer shall detain such person in prison after such order of the justices aforesaid, or the expiration of six months and payment of ten
pounds of tobacco per day as aforesaid, such sheriff or jailer shall be
liable to an action of false imprisonment." Iniquitous as this law is,
it is obvious that the object of the legislature could not be reached by
it. It offered, indeed, a bounty to the sheriff or jailer who, by neg-
lecting to give notice of the imprisonment of a *suspected* runaway,
might protract such imprisonment till the value of his services, even
though an absolute slave for life, would not be equal to the jail fees.
And yet, without some further legislation, the jailer himself would,
in case the person detained was not a runaway, or if a runaway
should not be demanded by his master, be made to suffer the loss of
such expense as might be incurred for the sustenance of the suspected
runaway during his imprisonment. The lure held out by the act to
the jailer probably produced the abandonment of the slave in some

12

its benefits more generally diffused, than in the
United States.   The Constitutions of nearly all the

instances by the master; and it became necessary, therefore, for the
legislature to repeal the act or to supply its defects. The latter part
of the disjunctive was naturally preferred ; and, on the eighth day of
June, 1719, after reciting, that "Whereas, by the act of Assembly
relating to servants and slaves, there is not any provision made what
shall be done with such runaway servants or slaves that now are or
hereafter shall or may be taken up and committed to the custody of
any sheriff within this province, where the master or owner of such
servant or slave, having due notice of such servant or slave being in
the custody of such sheriff, refuses or delays to redeem such servant
or slave, by paying their imprisonment fees, and such other charge as
has or may accrue for taking up such servant or slave," enacted
"That, &c. every sheriff that now hath, or hereafter shall have, committed into his custody any runaway servants or slaves, after one
month's notice given to the master or owner thereof of their being in
his custody, if living in this province, or two months' notice if living
in any of the neighbouring provinces, if such master or owner of such
servants or slaves do not appear within the time limited as aforesaid,
and pay or secure to be paid all such imprisonment fees due to such
sheriff from the time of the commitment of such servants or slaves,
and also such other charges as have accrued or become due to any
person for taking up such runaway servants or slaves, such sheriff is
hereby authorized and required (such time limited as aforesaid being
expired) immediately to give public notice to all persons, by setting
up notes at the church and court-house doors of the county where
such servant or slave is in custody, of the time and place for sale of
such servants or slaves, by him to be appointed, not less than ten days
after such time limited as aforesaid being expired, and at such time
and place by him appointed as aforesaid, *to proceed to sell and dispose
of such servant or slave to the highest bidder*, and out of the money or
tobacco which such servant or slave is sold for *to pay himself* all such
IMPRISONMENT FEES as are his just due for the time he has kept such
servant or slave in his custody, and also to pay such other charges,
fees or reward as has become due to any person for taking up such
runaway servant or slave ; and after such payments made, if any
residue shall remain of the money or tobacco such servant or slave

states make it the duty of the respective legislatures
to establish and support seminaries for learning

---

was sold for, such sheriff shall only be accountable to the master or
owner of such servant or slave for such residue or remainder as aforesaid, and not otherwise." *Laws of Maryland, act of* 1719, (*May
session,*) *chap.* 2.

Upon the enactment of this law the most unprincipled sheriff should
have been content. It became, indeed, not only *his* interest, but the
interest of *all other persons*, to apprehend and to commit to prison
coloured persons especially; for these might be detained for a longer
period than six months, whether free or not. The right of the
taker-up to his legal reward and other charges was secured to him by
a LIEN ON THE BODY OF THE PRISONER, and the sheriff or jailer *was
indemnified in the same manner against the loss of his imprisonment fees.*
And by prolonging the imprisonment until the fees should be swelled
to nearly the value of the prisoner, if *a slave*, the master, in many
instances, might be unable or unwilling to redeem him, and the sheriff's sale, which in such case is authorized, could easily be turned to
the account of some *favourite* of that officer, and eventually, by collusion, to his own pecuniary advantage. And should the *suspected runaway not* be a slave, yet in a land where, from his colour, he is *presumed*
to be so, and where others *like him* are daily "made merchandise of,"
the facility with which his imprisonment, aided by the provisions of
this act, might be rendered profitable to the sheriff, would be greatly
increased. But, whatever may have been the true cause, the prevalence of a practice on the part of sheriffs, *of prolonging the imprisonment of persons apprehended as runaways,* is evidenced by an act of
Assembly, passed *the twenty-second day of December,* 1792, entitled
"*An Act to restrain the ill-practices of sheriffs, and to direct their
conduct respecting runaways.*" The act sets forth that "Whereas it is
represented to this General Assembly, that the sheriffs of the respective counties have *neglected to advertise runaways, to the great injury
of the owners;* therefore, &c. That it be the duty of the several
sheriffs, &c., upon any runaway being committed to their custody, to
cause the same to be advertised in some public newspaper within
twenty days after such commitment, and to make particular and
minute description of the person, clothes, *and bodily marks* of such
runaway." "And if no person shall apply for such runaway within

adequate to the wants of the citizens. *Common schools are also provided "for the education of the*

---

the space of thirty days from such commitment, then it shall be the duty of such sheriff, if residing on the Western Shore, to cause the runaway to be advertised, as heretofore directed, in the Maryland Journal and Georgetown Weekly Ledger; and, if residing on the Eastern Shore, to cause the same to be advertised in the Maryland Herald and Maryland Journal, within sixty days from such commitment, and to continue the same therein until the said runaway is released by due course of law." *Maryland Laws of* 1792, (*November session,*) *chap.* 72.

In that part of the District of Columbia which was ceded by the state of Maryland to the federal government, the whole of these laws are still in force. Shortly after the date of *the cession,* however, the legislature of Maryland repealed the *act of* 1719, *ch.* 2, and the *act of* 1792, *ch.* 72, supplying their place by the following regulations, which, as it will be perceived, are in *principle* the same as the repealed acts:—"That it shall be the duty of the sheriffs (respectively) of the several counties of this state, &c. upon any runaway servant or slave being committed to his custody, to cause the same to be advertised in some public newspaper or papers printed in the city of Baltimore, the city of Washington, and the town of Easton, and in such other public manner as he shall think proper, within fifteen days after such commitment, and to make particular and minute description of the clothing, person, and *bodily marks* of such runaway." "If the owner or owners, or some person in his, her or their behalf, shall not apply for such runaway within the space of sixty days from the time of advertising as aforesaid, and pay or secure to be paid all such legal costs and charges as have accrued by reason of apprehending, imprisoning, and advertising such servant or slave, it shall be the duty of such sheriff, and he is hereby required and directed, *to proceed to sell such servant* or slave, and immediately to give public notice by advertisements, to be set up at the court-house door and such other public places as he shall think proper, in the county where such servant or slave is in custody, of the time and place for sale of such servant or slave, by him to be appointed, not less than twenty days after the time limited as aforesaid has expired, and at such time and place shall proceed to sell and dispose of such servant or slave to the highest

poor gratis." In several, perhaps in all, of the
free states, no distinction is made, in the distri-

---

bidder." *Laws of Maryland of* 1802, (*November session*,) *chap.* 96,
§ 1 & 2, (passed 8th January, 1803.)

By recurring to the sections of the law of 1715, above transcribed,
it will be seen that magistrates were empowered to decide, *in their
discretion*, whether the person apprehended *as* a runaway should be
deemed such and be accordingly committed to prison. Whether such
power had been abused, or whether a *proper exercise* of it had been
found *inconvenient* to *takers-up* and *sheriffs*, I will not presume to conjecture; but, in 1810, (*chap.* 63, § 1,) legislative interposition was
called into action in the following extraordinary measure:—"Any
court or any judge or justice of this state, before whom any negro or
mulatto shall be brought as a runaway, shall be satisfied, by *competent
testimony*, that the said negro or mulatto is *not* a runaway, before
it shall be lawful for the said court, judge or justice to discharge
the said negro or mulatto from the custody of the person or persons detaining the said negro or mulatto as a runaway, otherwise
than by a commitment to the jail of the county of which he is a
judge or justice."

The barbarous severity to coloured persons which pervades the
whole of the laws of Maryland on this subject has at length been
somewhat softened by an act passed February 3, 1818. It is in these
words:—"Hereafter, when any servant or slave shall be committed to
the jail of any county in this state, as a runaway, agreeably to the laws
now in force, and the notice required to be given by law by the sheriff
shall have been given, and the time for their detention expired, and no
person or persons shall have applied for and claimed said suspected
runaway, and proved his, her or their title to such suspected runaway,
as is now required by law, it shall be the duty of the sheriff forthwith
to carry such *slave or slaves* before some judge of the County Court or
judge of the Orphans' Court, with his commitment; and such judge is
hereby required to examine and inquire, *by such means as he may
deem most advisable*, whether such suspected runaway be a slave or
not; and if he shall have reasonable grounds to believe that such
suspected runaway is a slave, he may remand such suspected runaway
to prison, to be confined for such further or additional time as he may
judge right and proper; and if he shall have reason to believe that

bution of the public bounty towards this object, between white and coloured children ; but schools are constantly maintained for the reception and instruction of poor children of every class and complexion.

A different policy began very early in the slave-holding states. In none of these do the laws interpose to afford any aid or facility for the acquisition of learning to persons of colour, whether slaves or freemen. On the contrary, the extracts which I shall make from the laws of these latter states will satisfactorily demonstrate the truth of the proposition at the head of this section,—namely, that the benefits of education are *withheld* from the slave, and, I might add, from the free negro also.

Legislation on this subject began in South Carolina at a comparatively early date. By act of 1740 it was enacted as follows:—" Whereas the having of slaves taught to write, or suffering them to be employed in writing, may be attended with great

---

such suspected runaway is the slave of any particular person, he shall cause such notice to be given by the sheriff to such supposed owner as he may think most advisable ; *but if said judge shall not have reasonable ground to believe such suspected runaway to be a slave, he shall forthwith order such suspected runaway to be released;* and if no person shall apply for such suspected runaway after he may be so remanded, within the time for which he may be remanded, and prove his, her or their title as the law now requires, *the said sheriff shall, at the expiration of such time, relieve and discharge such suspected runaway;* and in either case, *when such suspected runaway shall be discharged, the expense of keeping such runaway in confinement shall be levied on the county, as other county expenses are now levied." Laws of Maryland, (December session of 1817,) chap.* 112, § 6.

inconveniences, *Be it enacted,* That all and every person and persons whatsoever who shall hereafter teach or cause any slave or slaves to be taught to write, or shall use or employ any slave as a scribe in any manner of writing hereafter taught to write, every such person or persons shall for every such offence forfeit the sum of one hundred pounds current money." 2 *Brevard's Digest,* 243.

This was followed, in 1800, (leaving the act of 1740 also in force,) by this enactment:—"Assemblies of slaves, free negroes, mulattoes and mestizoes, whether composed of all or any of such description of persons, or of all or any of the same and of a proportion of white persons, met together for the purpose of *mental instruction* in a confined or secret place, &c. &c., are declared to be an *unlawful meeting;* and magistrates are hereby required, &c. to enter into such confined places, &c. &c., to break doors, &c. if resisted, and to disperse such slaves, free negroes, &c. &c.; and the officer dispersing such unlawful assemblage *may inflict such corporal punishment, not exceeding twenty lashes, upon such slaves, free negroes, &c.,* as they may judge necessary for DETERRING THEM FROM THE LIKE UNLAWFUL ASSEMBLAGE IN FUTURE." 7 *Statutes of South Carolina,* 440. And another section of the same act declares "That it shall not be lawful for any number of slaves, free negroes, mulattoes or mestizoes, even in company with white persons, to meet together for the purpose of *mental instruction,* either before the rising of the sun, or after the going down of the same." *Ib.*

She has since added a larger and more direct prohibition, by act of December 17, 1834:—"If any person shall hereafter teach any slave to *read or write*, or shall aid in assisting any slave *to read or write*, or cause or procure any slave to be taught *to read or write*, such person, if a free white person, upon conviction thereof, shall for every such offence against this act be fined not exceeding one hundred dollars, and imprisoned not more than six months; or if *a free person of colour*, shall be whipped not exceeding *fifty* lashes, and fined not exceeding fifty dollars; and if *a slave*, shall be whipped not exceeding *fifty* lashes: and if *any free person of colour* or *a slave* shall keep any school or other place of instruction for teaching any slave or free person of colour *to read or write*, such person shall be liable to the same fine, imprisonment and corporal punishment as are by this act imposed and inflicted on *free persons of colour* and *slaves* for teaching slaves to read or write." 7 *Statutes of South Carolina*, 468.

In *Virginia*, according to the *Code* of 1849, "Every assemblage of negroes for the purpose of instruction in *reading* or *writing* shall be an *unlawful assembly*. Any justice may issue his warrant to any officer or other person, requiring him to enter any place where such assemblage may be, and seize any negro therein; and he or any other justice may order such negro to be punished *with stripes*.

"If a *white* person assemble with negroes for the purpose of instructing them to *read or write*, he shall be confined to jail not exceeding six months, and fined not exceeding one hundred dollars." *Code of Virginia*, 747–48.

Three statutes have been made *in Georgia* on this subject, all of which appear to be still in force. The *first* was in 1770, and is very similar to the act of *South Carolina* of 1740, differing chiefly in including in its prohibition instruction in *reading* as well as *writing*, and fixing the penalty at *twenty pounds* sterling. 2 *Cobb's Digest*, 981.

In 1829 it was enacted, " If any *slave, negro* or *free person of colour*, or *any white person*, shall teach any other slave, negro or free person of colour to *read or write* either written or printed characters, the said free person of colour or slave shall be punished by *fine and whipping*, or *fine* or *whipping, at the discretion of the court;* and if a white person so offending, he, she or they shall be punished with *fine* not exceeding *five* hundred dollars, and imprisonment in the common jail at the discretion of the court." *Ib.* 1001.

In 1833 this further legislation occurred:—" If any person shall *teach* any *slave, negro* or *free person of colour* to *read* or *write* either written or printed characters, or shall procure, suffer or permit a slave, negro or person of colour *to transact business for him in writing,* such person so offending shall be guilty of a misdemeanour, and, on conviction, shall be punished by *fine,* or *imprisonment* in the common jail, or both, at the discretion of the court." *Ib.* 828.

In *North Carolina*, "Any free person who shall hereafter teach, or *attempt* to teach, any slave within this state to *read* or *write,* the use of figures excepted, or shall *give* or sell to such slave or slaves *any books* or *pamphlets,* shall be liable to indictment, &c.; and upon conviction shall, at the discretion of the court, if a *white* man or woman, be fined not less than *one hundred* dollars, nor more than *two* hundred dollars, or *imprisoned;* and if a free person of colour, shall be *fined, imprisoned* or *whipped,* at the discretion of the court, not exceeding *thirty-nine* lashes, nor less than *twenty* lashes." *Revised Statutes,* ch. 34, § 74, p. 209. And for a similar offence *as to instruction,* a slave shall receive *thirty-nine* lashes on his or her *bare* back. *Ib. ch.* 3, § 27.

By act of Assembly, *of Louisiana,* passed in March, 1830, "All persons who shall teach or cause to be taught any slave in this state to *read* or *write* shall, on conviction thereof, &c., be imprisoned not less than *one* nor more than *twelve* months."

And in *Alabama,* "Any person who shall *attempt* to teach any *free person of colour* or *slave* to SPELL, *read* or *write,* shall upon conviction, &c. be fined in a sum not less than $250 nor more than $500." *Clay's Digest,* 543, *act of* 1832, § 10.

So far as I have at present the means of ascertaining, the laws of *Kentucky, Tennessee, Mississippi, Missouri, Arkansas, Florida* and *Texas* are silent on this subject. And in regard to the states in which prohibition has been thought expedient, there are *differences* which are very remarkable. Thus, in *Virginia* the owners of slaves are left at liberty to instruct them as carefully and extensively as they please. The prohibition has respect to the efforts of *third* persons.

South Carolina began with repressing instruction *in writing* only. The next step was aimed against *mental instruction* of every kind, conferred, or attempted to be conferred, *at an assemblage of slaves, free coloured persons* and *whites.* The owners, notwithstanding either of these laws, might, at their respective *homes,* have taught their slaves to *read,* without fear of molestation or complaint. And it has been stated on high authority that, in this way, not a few had acquired the capacity to read so as to take part in religious worship in Episcopal churches at Charleston. The last act, whilst it is to be inferred from it that *slaves* had been so instructed, (for it supposes that such were then among them, *capable of keeping school,*) has placed under the ban all efforts to instruct the coloured race,—*bond* and *free,*—whether in *reading* or *writing.*

North Carolina will allow slaves to be made acquainted with *arithmetical calculations,* whilst she sternly interdicts *reading* and *writing* to a *slave.* She makes it highly penal, also, to *give* or *sell any book* or *pamphlet* to a *slave.*

Alabama wars with the rudiments of reading. She forbids any coloured persons, bond or free, to be taught to SPELL, as well as to *read* or *write.*

Georgia carries her prohibitions beyond imparting *instruction* to coloured persons; for she subjects any one to *fine and imprisonment* "who shall procure, suffer or permit a slave, negro or person of colour to *transact* business for him *in writing."*

Again, the *punishments* are various. Some impose *pecuniary* fines only; others add *imprisonment,* whilst in one state nothing but *imprisonment* will satisfy. *Whipping,* as well as *fine* and *imprisonment,* is meted out unsparingly to the *free coloured* offender; and the unhappy *slave* is not to be *whipped* only, but must receive *thirty-nine* lashes on *his* or HER BARE BACK.

Such differences, in statutable enactments on the same subject, suggest several observations. One of the most obvious is, that a being whose desire for mental improvement is so strong as to require such powerful means of repression must have been intended for a higher destiny than "to live without knowledge and without the capacity to make anything his own, and to toil that another may reap the fruits;" and also that there is great reason to believe his subjection to the *uncontrolled* authority of another, which is alleged to be inherent and inseparable from slavery, must be both a *mistake* and an *injustice.*

Before quitting this subject, it is proper to say that where there is no legislation on the part of a *state* to debar the slave from mental instruction, the power may exist, and I presume generally does exist, in *incorporated cities*, to effect the same end by local ordinances. In *Savannah*, in 1818, an ordinance of this description, going beyond the *then* law of the state, was adopted, and may be yet in force. The *Port-Folio* for April, 1818, thus notices it:—"The city has passed an ordinance by which any person that *teaches* any *person of colour, slave or free*, to *read or write*, is subjected to a fine of *thirty dollars* for *each* offence; and *every person of colour* who shall keep *a school* to teach *reading or writing* is subject to a fine of *thirty dollars*, or to be imprisoned ten days and whipped *thirty-nine* lashes"!! p. 325.

With such legislative obstacles to his mental improvement, it ought to excite no surprise if a slave having the ability to read or write could not be found within a slave-holding state. But, apart from these obstacles of *law*, the condition of slavery is such that a slave capable of reading must be, in most of the states, a prodigy indeed. His life is ordinarily passed in incessant toil. The laws, as I have already shown, secure to him no portion of time in which he may employ himself at his pleasure. He is awaked from his slumbers, at the call of his master, often before the dawn of day; he continues his heartless labour, with but slight intermissions for rest and food, till night has closed around him. Hard-worked, and scantily fed, his bodily energies are exhausted; without an instructor and without books, (for he has not the means to procure them,) he must of necessity remain forever ignorant of the benefits of education.

IV.—The means for moral and religious instruction are not granted to the slave; on the contrary, the efforts of the humane and charitable to supply these wants are discountenanced by law.

One of the plain dictates of the Christian religion is a regard for the well-being of our fellow-creatures. It is, indeed, largely insisted upon as a *duty*, both in the Old and New Testament. No believer in the Christian religion can doubt that the knowledge of its precepts and promises may promote the happiness both here and hereafter of every accountable creature; nor will such a one deny that a negro, though

13

a slave, is a member of the human family,—is en
dowed with reason,—has a soul which is immortal,
and must be deemed accountable unto GOD "for
the deeds done in the body." How can such a
belief be reconciled with a practice which forbids
to the slave access to the gospel ?—which, *as far as
the master's power so to do extends*, shuts out from
him the knowledge of the means of his salvation ?

It has been shown, in the last chapter, that one
of the means to which allusion is here made—
namely, *mental instruction*—is in general entirely withheld from the slave. He cannot be expected, therefore, to learn the Scriptures, except as an *auditor*.
And yet in none of the slave-holding states are any
facilities afforded by the laws for this purpose. No
time is secured to the slave, nor any place provided
where he can assemble with his fellows to hear
"the glad tidings of salvation" preached.

It is idle to talk of *accompanying his master* to
church. Such a spectacle, I apprehend, is rarely
exhibited, except *for the special convenience of the
master*. The paucity of places for worship, in the
slave-holding states, compared with the number of
white inhabitants, prevents the exercise of this privilege to an extent at all commensurate with the religious wants of the slaves.

Besides, if no other impediment existed, the rude
mind of the slave could not comprehend a discourse
designed for the refined taste and enlarged capacity
of the master. Christianity demands that these
unfortunate beings should be taught to read; that
buildings should be erected for their assembling

together to worship their Creator; that teachers* who are willing and qualified to administer to their spiritual necessities should be encouraged to dedicate their time and talents to the pious service; that rest should be allowed to the slave at the seasons usually allotted among Christians for religious worship, and especially that laws should be made and *enforced* to prevent the exaction of labour from the slave to such a degree that his senses are overpowered by sleep the moment his body ceases to be active.†

If the *practice* of the slave-holding states is in accordance with the *laws*, the reverse of this picture will, it is believed, be found true in most respects. In a law enacted by the state of Georgia, December 13th, 1792, with the title "To protect religious societies in the exercise of their religious duties," it

---

* In *North Carolina*, no slave or *free coloured* person is allowed to preach. *Revised Statutes*, p. 580, § 34.

† Mr. Jefferson, in his "Notes on Virginia," speaking of slaves, makes the following remarks :—" In general, their existence appears to participate more of sensation than reflection. To this must be ascribed their disposition to sleep when abstracted from their diversions and unemployed in labour. An animal whose body is at rest, and who does not reflect, must be disposed to sleep, of course." *See Answer to Query* 14. I do not dissent from this doctrine. It is philosophically true. But, with the accurate knowledge which Mr. Jefferson possessed as to the actual condition of the slave, it seems strange that he should have omitted to include, as a reason why the slave, when "abstracted from his diversions and unemployed in labour," should be disposed to sleep, the fatigue induced by the severity of his labour. The disposition to sleep which is thus indicated as characteristic of the *black* is equally observable, as far as I am able to ascertain, among *the labouring class* of whites.

is required of every justice of the peace, &c., and every civil officer of a county being present, &c. &c., to take into custody any person who shall interrupt or disturb a congregation of *white persons* assembled at any church, &c., and to impose a fine on the offender; and in default of payment he may be imprisoned, &c. &c.; yet the *same law* concludes in these words:—"No congregation or company *of negroes* shall, under *pretence of divine worship*, assemble themselves contrary to the act regulating patrols." *Prince's Dig.* 342. In 2 *Cobb's Dig.* 851, the concluding words, "*contrary to the act regulating patrols,*" are omitted; but at page 982 of the same volume they stand as part of the law still in force, and the seventh section of the act *regulating patrols* is also given as an existing law. *Ibid.* 973. I have not been able to discover the law here referred to as the *act regulating patrols;* but the *editor of the Digest*, whom I presume to be fully competent to resolve the difficulty, quotes the seventh section of an act passed May 10th, 1770, "for ordering and governing slaves, &c.," as that intended to be designated by the legislature. This section begins with a recital, "Whereas the frequent meeting, &c. of slaves under the *pretence of feasting* may be attended with dangerous consequences," and proceeds to enact "That it shall be lawful for every justice of the peace, &c., upon his own knowledge or information received, either to go in person, or by warrant, &c. directed to any constable, &c., to command to their assistance any number of persons as (*which*) they shall see convenient, to disperse ANY *assembly or meeting of slaves* which *may* disturb the peace or endanger the safety of his majesty's subjects; and every slave which shall be found and taken at such meeting as aforesaid shall and may, by order of such justice, immediately be corrected WITHOUT TRIAL, *by receiving on the bare back twenty-five stripes with a whip, switch or cowskin,*"* &c. *Prince's Dig.* 447; 2 *Cobb,* 973. The terms of this prohibition in relation to the meeting of slaves for divine worship are, it must be admitted, not a little enigmatical; yet, with the aid of the twenty-five lashes of the cowskin, the most stupid negro will be rendered apt enough to comprehend their meaning.

In South Carolina, by a section already in part extracted, a prohibition, though not absolute in its terms, yet in effect, I suspect, it must have been nearly so, was made in 1800. The section reads thus:—"It shall not be lawful for any number of slaves, free negroes, mulattoes or mestizoes, *even in company* with white persons, to meet together and assemble for the purpose of mental instruction or *religious worship,* either before the rising of the sun or after the going down of the same. And all

---

* And while in Georgia slaves are thus discouraged from assembling together for the purpose of divine worship, the same state, in a spirit which I by no means condemn, has adopted the following as a standing rule for the government of the *penitentiary:*—"It shall be the duty of the keeper, &c. to furnish them (*i. e.* the convicts) with such moral and religious books as shall be recommended by the inspectors; to procure the performance of *divine service* on Sundays, as often as may be." *See Rule* 13*th for the internal government of the penitentiary of Georgia; Prince's Digest,* 386–7.

magistrates, sheriffs, militia-officers, &c. &c. are hereby vested with power, &c. for dispersing such assemblies," &c. 2 *Brevard's Dig.* 254–5.   Three years afterwards, upon the petition, as the act recites, of certain religious societies, the rigour of the act of 1800 was *slightly* abated by a modification, which forbids any person, before nine o'clock in the evening, "to break into a place of meeting wherein shall be assembled the members of any religious society of this state, *provided a majority of them shall be white persons*, or otherwise to disturb their devotion, unless such person, &c. so entering the said place (of worship) shall have first obtained from some magistrate appointed to keep the peace, &c. a warrant, &c., in case a magistrate shall be then actually within the distance of three miles from such place of meeting; otherwise the provisions, &c. (of the act of 1800, above cited) to remain in full force." 2 *Brevard's Dig.* 261.   If this *latter* act yields to the slave a privilege in assembling for divine worship beyond what he possessed before, it must consist, it appears to me, chiefly in preventing interruptions by persons who, acting from a sense of *official* obligation, might deem themselves compelled, by the provisions of the *former* act, to hunt out and disperse the congregations of negro worshippers wherever they might be found.   For it must happen, I apprehend, *very frequently*, that the *quorum* of *white* persons cannot with much certainty be depended upon.   And, in such case, the poor slave, disappointed in his expectations of the *quorum*, will be at once subjected to the terrible penalty of the twenty-five lashes of the cowskin on his bare back, well laid on! In Virginia, until the late revision, the law was:— " All meetings, &c. of slaves, free negroes and mulattoes mixing, &c. with such slaves at any *meeting-house*, &c. or any other place, &c. in the night, under any pretext whatsoever, are declared to be *unlawful assemblies;* and the civil power may disperse the same, and inflict corporal punishment on the offenders." This forbids *meetings* of slaves in the *night*. The following change has been recently made:— "Every assemblage of negroes *for the purpose of religious worship*, when such worship is conducted by *a negro*, shall be an *unlawful assembly;* and a justice may issue his warrant to any officer or other person, requiring him to enter any place where such assemblage may be, and seize any negro therein, and he or any other justice may order such negro to be punished *with stripes*." Code of Virginia, (of 1849,) p. 747. The prohibition in this statute is directed against meetings of negroes for religious worship, *when conducted by a negro ;* and this is forbidden absolutely at any time, *day or night.* And if any provision were made by the government to secure to the coloured race the benefit of divine worship, properly conducted by *white* clergymen, the prohibition of the statute would be of little or no consequence; *but no such provision exists.*

Mississippi has adopted the former law of Virginia, with a proviso that the master or overseer of a slave *may*, in writing, grant him permission to attend a place of religious worship at which the minister may be white and regularly ordained or licensed, or, at least, two discreet and reputable white persons, appointed by some regular church or religious society, shall attend. *Mississippi Rev. Code*, 390.

An opinion seems, at one period, to have obtained in many of the states, that by consenting to the *baptism* of his slave the master virtually enfranchised him. To remove the pretext which was thus furnished for withholding the administration of a rite so commonly practised among Christians, the following brief section was enacted in Maryland:— "Forasmuch as many people have neglected to baptize their negroes *or suffer them to be baptized*, on a vain apprehension that negroes, by receiving the sacrament of baptism, are manumitted and set free, *Be it enacted, &c.* That no negro or negroes, by receiving the holy sacrament of baptism, is thereby manumitted or set free, nor hath any right or title to freedom or manumission, more than he or they had before, any law, usage or custom to the contrary notwithstanding." *Act of* 1715, *ch.* 44, § 23. So, in the year 1711, the legislature of South Carolina deemed a similar act necessary. "Since," according to the language of the preamble, "charity, and the Christian religion which we profess, oblige us to wish well to the souls of all men, and that religion may not be made a pretence to alter any man's property and right, and that no persons may neglect to baptize their negroes or slaves or suffer them to be baptized, for fear that thereby they should be manumitted and set free, *Be it, &c. enacted,* That it shall be and is hereby declared lawful for any negro, or

Indian slave, or any other slave or slaves whatsoever, to *receive and profess* the Christian religion, and
be thereunto baptized." 2 *Brevard's Dig.* 229.   The
section then provides that such profession of religion
and submission to baptism shall not be construed to
effect an emancipation of any slave, &c.*

---

* The doubts which gave rise to these laws of Maryland and South
Carolina probably originated in two judicial investigations which had
occurred in England a short time previously.   The first of these is
reported in 3 *Modern Reports*, 120–1, (A.D. 1686–7,) and is there thus
stated:—"Sir Thomas Grantham bought a monster in the Indies,
which was a man of that country who had the perfect shape of a
child growing out of his breast, as an excrescency, all but the head.
This man he brought hither, (*i. e.* to England,) and exposed to the
sight of the people for profit.   The *Indian* turns *Christian*, and was
baptized, and was detained from his master, who brought a *homine
replegiando*, (*i. e.* a writ by which his title to retain the man as property might be legally tested.)   The sheriff returned that he had
replevied the body, &c.   *And then the Court of Common Pleas* BAILED
HIM."   How the case was ultimately disposed of does not appear;
but the proceeding even thus far was calculated to excite a fear lest
the profession of Christianity and the administration of baptism might
be decided to entitle the slave to the privileges of a freeman.

In 1696, the question *whether the baptism* of a *negro slave*, WITHOUT
THE PRIVITY OR CONSENT OF HIS MASTER, emancipated the slave,
underwent an elaborate discussion before the judges of the King's
Bench.   Owing to a misconception of the *form* of the action, a final
decision was not given, and the plaintiff being, of course, unsuccessful on that occasion, the doubts which had resulted from the
former case were strengthened rather than impaired.

The arguments of the counsel for the defendant are sufficiently
curious to deserve transcription:—"Being baptized according to the
use of the church, he (the slave) is thereby made a Christian, and
Christianity is inconsistent with slavery.   And this was allowed even
in the time when the Popish religion was established, as appears by
Littleton; for in those days, if a villain had entered into religion, and
was professed, as they called it, the lord could not seize him; and

I know of no exception to the general bearing of the foregoing laws and observations, unless the following concise enactment of the legislature of Louisiana may be thought to form one:—"It shall be the duty of every owner to procure to his *sick* slaves all kinds of temporal and *spiritual* assistance which their situation may require." 1 *Martin's Dig.* 610. Giving to this provision the most favourable interpretation, it is but a kind of *death-bed* charity.

V.—SUBMISSION IS REQUIRED OF THE SLAVE NOT TO THE WILL OF HIS MASTER ONLY, BUT TO THE WILL OF ALL OTHER WHITE PERSONS.*

the reason there given is, because he was dead in law, and if the lord might take him out of his cloister, then he could not live according to his religion. The like reason may now be given for baptism being incorporated into the laws of the land; if the duties which arise thereby cannot be performed in a state of servitude, the baptism must be a manumission. That such duties cannot be performed is plain; for the persons baptized are to be confirmed by the diocesan, when they can give an account of their faith, and are enjoined, by several acts of Parliament, to come to church. But if the lord hath still an absolute property over him, then he might send him far enough from the performance of those duties, viz.: into Turkey, or any other country of infidels, where they neither can or will be suffered to exercise the Christian religion." In conclusion, the counsel remarks, "It is observed among the *Turks* that they do not make slaves of those of their own religion, though taken in war; and if *a Christian be so taken, yet if he renounce Christianity and turn Mahometan he doth thereby obtain his freedom.* And if this be a custom allowed among infidels, then baptism, in a Christian nation, as this is, should be an immediate enfranchisement to them, as they should thereby acquire the privileges and immunities enjoyed by those of the same religion, and be entitled to the laws of England." See 5 *Modern Reports*, 190–1; *Chamberline vs. Harvey.*

* On page 33 an extract from the opinion of the Supreme Court .

While the institution of slavery exists, every thing like resistance to the master's lawful authority should be decisively checked. Strict subordination must be exacted from the slave, or bloodshed and murders will unavoidably ensue. The laws of the slave-holding states demand, however, a much larger concession of power to the master than is here granted: they demand that the life of the slave shall be in the master's keeping; that the slave, having the physical ability to avoid the infliction of a barbarous and vindictive punishment by his master, shall not be permitted to do so. They go, indeed, *even beyond this :* they place the slave under the like restriction in relation to *every white* person, without discrimination as to character, and with but little consideration as to motives. Thus, it is enacted in Georgia:—"If any slave shall *presume* to strike *any white* person, such slave, upon trial and conviction before the justice or justices, according to the directions of this act, shall for the *first* offence suffer such punishment as the said justice or justices shall in his or their discretion think fit, not extending to life or limb ; and for the *second* offence suffer DEATH." *Prince's Dig.* 450 ; 2 *Cobb's Dig.* 976. The law of South Carolina (2 *Brevard's Dig.* 235) is in the same words, except that *death* is not made the punishment of the *second,* but

of *North Carolina* was given, in which the *implicit obedience* of a slave to his master or *any other having the control of him by his master's consent* was asserted in the most unqualified terms. This is a principle of slave law generally recognised in the slave-holding states. See *Commonwealth vs. Turner;* 5 *Randolph's Rep.* 678 ; and see also the cases given in *note* to this *sketch, post, p.* 296, *et seq.*

of the *third*, offence. In both of these states a proviso is annexed to this law, which shows plainly
that, however wanton or dangerous may be the at-
tack upon the *slave*, he is still compelled to submit:
—" Provided always that such striking, &c. be not
done by *the command and in the defence of the person
or property of the* OWNER, OR OTHER PERSON *having the
care and government of such slave*, in which case the
slave shall be wholly excused, and the owner or
other person, &c. shall be answerable as if the act
had been committed by himself."

In Maryland, *act of* 1723, *chap.* 15, § 4, a justice
of the peace, for this offence, may direct the offender's
ears to be cropped—and this, though he be a *free black*.
In Kentucky the same general principle is recognised, though enforced by penalties much less severe;
yet there, as in Maryland, free coloured persons are
included :—" If any negro, mulatto or Indian, bond
or *free*, shall, at any time, lift his or her hand in opposition to any person not being a negro, mulatto
or Indian, he or she so offending shall for every
such offence, proved by the oath of the party before
a justice of the peace of the county where such
offence shall be committed, receive thirty lashes on
his or her bare back, well laid on, by order of such
justice." 2 *Litt. and Swi. Dig.* 1153. Nearly similar
to this law of Kentucky was that of Virginia, from
the year 1680 to the year 1792, at which latter date
the following exception was added:—" except in those
cases where it shall appear to such justice that such
negro or mulatto was *wantonly* assaulted, and lifted
his or her hand in his or her defence;" (1 *Rev. Code*,

426–7;) and, by the last revision of her code, "a negro shall be punished with stripes" (not exceeding *thirty-nine*) "if he use *provoking language* or menacing gestures to a *white* person," (*Code of Virginia*, 754;) and laws conceived in the same spirit are to be found in all, or nearly all, the codes of the slave-holding states.

There is a section of a law in Louisiana, which, though in terms applying to *free* persons of colour only, may be properly cited to evidence the sentiments which are entertained there on this subject. The gravity with which the strange principle it asserts is declared will of itself excuse its introduction here, though not altogether congruous with the main object of this sketch:—"Free people of colour ought never to insult or strike white people, nor presume to conceive themselves equal to the whites; but, on the contrary, they ought to *yield to them on every occasion*, and never speak or answer them but with respect, under the penalty of imprisonment, according to the nature of the offence." 1 *Martin's Dig.* 640–2.

My chief objection to these laws is, that they furnish a *pretext*, and (may I not say?) an *inducement*, to an ignoble mind to oppress and to tyrannize over the defenceless slave. He must patiently endure every species of personal injury which a white person, however brutal and ferocious his disposition,— be he a drunkard, or even a maniac,—may choose to offer.

Several of the slave-holding states have adopted laws which are highly objectionable for the reason

14

just given. The subjoined may be taken as a specimen:—"If any slave shall *happen* to be slain for refusing to surrender him or herself, contrary to law, or in unlawful resisting any officer or *other person* who shall apprehend or endeavour to apprehend such slave or slaves, &c., such officer or *other person so killing such slave as aforesaid*, making resistance,* shall be and he is by this act *indemnified* from any prosecution for such killing aforesaid, &c." *Maryland Laws, act of* 1751, *chap.* 14, § 9.

And by the negro act of 1740, of South Carolina, it is declared:—"If any slave who shall be out of the house or plantation where such slave shall live or shall be usually employed, or without some white person in company with such slave, shall *refuse to submit* to undergo the examination of *any white* person, it shall be lawful for any such white person to pursue, apprehend, and moderately correct such slave; and if such slave shall assault and strike such white person, such slave may be *lawfully killed*"!! 2 *Brevard's Dig.* 231.

VI.—THE PENAL CODES OF THE SLAVE-HOLDING STATES BEAR MUCH MORE SEVERELY UPON SLAVES, THAN UPON WHITE PERSONS.

A being ignorant of letters, unenlightened by religion, and deriving but little instruction from good example, cannot be supposed to have right concep-

---

* It has been decided in *North Carolina* that it is *justifiable* to KILL a *slave* resisting or OFFERING to resist his master by force. 2 *Haywood's Rep.* 54.

tions as to the nature and extent of moral or political
obligations. This remark, with but a slight qualification, is applicable to the condition of the slave.
It has been just shown that the benefits of education
are not conferred upon him, while his *chance* of acquiring a knowledge of the precepts of the gospel is
so remote as scarcely to be appreciated. He may
be regarded, therefore, as almost without the capacity
to comprehend the force of laws; and, on this account,
such as are designed for his government should be
recommended by their simplicity and mildness.

His condition suggests another motive for tender-
ness on his behalf in these particulars. *He is unable
to read*, and, holding little or no communication with
those who are better informed than himself, how is
he to become acquainted with the *fact* that a law
for his observance has been made? To exact obedience to a law which has not been promulgated—
which is unknown to the subject of it—has ever
been deemed most unjust and tyrannical. The reign
of Caligula, were it obnoxious to no other reproach
than this, would never cease to be remembered with
abhorrence.

The lawgivers of the slave-holding states seem, in
the formation of their penal codes, to have been un-
influenced by these claims of the slave upon their
compassionate consideration. The *hardened convict*
moves their sympathy, and is to be *taught* the laws
before he is expected to obey them;* yet the *guiltless*

---

* "It shall be the duty of the keeper (*i. e.* of the penitentiary) on
the receipt of each prisoner, *to read to him or her* such parts of the

slave IS SUBJECTED TO AN EXTENSIVE SYSTEM OF CRUEL ENACTMENTS, OF NO PART OF WHICH, PROBABLY, HAS HE EVER HEARD.

Parts of this system apply to the slave exclusively, and for every infraction a large retribution is demanded; while, with respect to offences for which whites as well as slaves are amenable, *punishments of much greater severity are inflicted upon the latter* than upon the former.

With very few exceptions, the penal laws, to which slaves *only* are subject, relate not to violations of the moral or divine laws; positive institution is their only sanction. Thus,* if a slave is found beyond the limits of the town in which he lives, or off the plantation where he is usually employed, without the company of a white person, or without the written permission of his master, employer, &c., *any person* may apprehend him and punish him with

---

penal laws of this state as impose penalties for escape, and *to make all the prisoners* in the penitentiary *acquainted with the same.* It shall also be his duty, on the discharge of such prisoner, *to read to him or her such parts of the said laws as impose additional punishments for the repetition of offences.*" *Rule* 12*th for the internal government of the Penitentiary of Georgia* — *sec.* 24 *of the Penitentiary act of* 1816; *Prince's Dig.* 386.

* It is proper to say that while the statement which follows in the text was, it is believed, entirely accurate in 1827, when it was prepared and published, changes have since been made in the laws of these states, by which many of the smaller offences here mentioned have been withdrawn from the power of the *police.* This is especially true in respect to *Virginia*, to a considerable extent in *North Carolina*, and in a slight degree in some of the other states. The gain to the *slave*, however, in this way, is of but little value, inasmuch as the power of the *master and his agents* remains *almost without restraint.*

whipping on the bare back, not exceeding twenty
lashes. 2 *Brevard's Dig.* 231; *Prince's Dig.* 447.
In Mississippi, a similar punishment, by direction of
a justice of the peace. *Mississippi Rev. Code,* 371.
So also in Virginia and Kentucky, at the discretion
of the justice, both as to the imposition of the punishment and the number of stripes. 1 *Virg. Rev. Code,*
422; 2 *Litt. and Swi. Dig.* 1150; and see 2 *Missouri
Laws,* 741, § 2, and *ibid.* 614.

And if a slave shall be out of the house, &c., or
off the plantation, &c. of his master, &c., without
some white person in company, &c., and shall refuse
to submit to an examination of *any white person, &c.,*
such white person may apprehend and *moderately
correct* him; and if he shall assault and strike such
white person, he may be lawfully killed. 2 *Brev.
Dig.* 231; *Prince's Dig.* 447, § 5, *act of* 1770, *and*
p. 348, *No.* 43, *title Penal Laws;* 2 *Cobb's Dig.* 785,
972.

If a slave shall presume to come upon the plantation of any person, without leave in writing from his
master, employer, &c., not being sent on lawful business, *the owner* of the *plantation* may inflict ten lashes
for every such offence. 1 *Virg. Rev. Code,* 422–23;
Mississippi Rev. Code, 371; 2 *Litt. and Swi. Dig.*
1150; 2 *Missouri Laws,* 741, § 3; and see *Maryland
Laws, act of* 1723, *chap.* 15, §§ 1 *and* 5.

It shall be lawful *for any person* who shall see more
than seven men-slaves, without some white person
with them, travelling or assembled together in any
highroad, to apprehend such slaves, and to inflict
a whipping on each of them not exceeding twenty

lashes apiece.* 2 *Brev. Dig.* 243; *Prince's Dig.* 454.
In Delaware, more than *six* men-slaves meeting together, not belonging to one master, unless on lawful business of their owners, may be whipped to the extent of twenty-one lashes each. *Delaware Laws*, 104.
If a slave or Indian shall *take away* or *let loose* any boat or canoe† from a landing or other place where

---

* It is with extreme regret I have been apprised by the newspapers that this law has been recently introduced into the Floridas by our territorial government there. The humanity which the Spaniards manifest towards their slaves rendered such a measure unnecessary during the many years in which these provinces were under their dominion. Scarcely is the power of our republic recognised there by the *free*, when a more galling oppression proclaims its existence to the *slave*. Well, indeed, might even the inhabitant of our slave-holding states blush with shame, when a sense of justice wrung from him the humbling confession which he thus recorded:—" The indulgent treatment of their slaves by which the Spaniards are so honourably distinguished, and the ample and humane code of laws which they have enacted, and also *enforce*, for the protection of the blacks, both bond and free, occasioned many of the Indian slaves (*i. e.* of East Florida) who were apprehensive of falling into the power of the Americans, (*i. e.* citizens of the United States,) and also most of the free people of colour who resided in St. Augustine, to transport themselves to *Havana as soon as they heard of the approach of the American authorities.*" See "*Notices of East Florida, with an account of the Seminole nation of Indians, by a recent traveller in the Province,*" p. 42. From the tenor of many of his remarks, the writer is evidently an inhabitant of one of our slave-holding states.

The foregoing note was inserted in the *first* edition of this sketch. The Florida statute referred to may be found incorporated in the revision in 1847, *Thompson's Digest*, 540.

† To take away a canoe, &c. for the temporary accommodation of the taker, with the intention of returning it again in a few minutes, is a very common practice in countries (such as South Carolina was at the date of this law, *i. e.* 1695–6) where, from the paucity or poverty of the inhabitants, few bridges have been erected. The offence, how-

WHIPPING FOR NO OFFENCE.163

the owner may have made the same fast, for the *first* offence he shall receive thirty-nine lashes on the bare back, and for the *second* offence *shall forfeit and have cut off from his head* ONE EAR.* 2 *Brev. Dig.* 228.

For keeping or carrying a gun, or powder, or shot, or a *club*, or *other weapon whatsoever*, offensive or defensive, a slave incurs for each offence thirty-nine lashes, by order of a justice of the peace, (2 *Litt. & Swi.* 1150; 1 *Virg. Rev. Code*, 423; 2 *Missouri Laws*, 741, § 4;) and in North Carolina and Tennessee, twenty lashes, by the nearest, constable, *without* a conviction by the justice. *Haywood's Manual*, 521.

For having *any article* of property for sale, without a ticket of permission from his master, *particularly specifying* the same and authorizing it to be sold by the slave, ten lashes, by order of the captain of the patrol*lers*, (2 *Litt. & Swi.* 981;) and if the slave be taken before a magistrate, thirty-nine lashes may be ordered. *Ibid.* So in North Carolina and Tennessee, (*Haywood's Manual*, 529; and see *Mississippi Rev. Code*, 390;) and in Florida, "if any slave shall *barter*, buy, sell or *deliver* any thing of value, (except brooms, baskets or fabrics of straw or rush,) without the consent *in writing* of his master, &c., *thirty-nine stripes* may be inflicted upon him." *Thompson's Dig.* 540–41.

A slave being at an *unlawful assembly*,† the captain

---

ever, of the poor slave or Indian would be consummated even though the owner should not make the discovery, and of course suffer no inconvenience, till after the canoe, &c. had been returned.

* *Cutting off the ears* is no longer a punishment in *South Carolina. Act of Dec.* 19, 1833.

† The augmentation of crimes under the name of *unlawful assemblies*

of patrol*lers* may inflict ten lashes upon him. 2
Litt. & Swi. 981; 2 *Missouri Laws*, 741, § 2, and *ibid.*
614. If taken before a magistrate, he may direct
thirty-nine lashes. 2 *Litt. & Swi.* 981.

For travelling by himself from his master's land
to any other place, unless by the most usual and
accustomed road, the owner of the land on which
such slave may be found is authorized to inflict forty
lashes upon him. *Haywood's Manual*, 518, (*act of*
1729.) For travelling in the night, without a pass,
forty lashes, (*ibid. ;*) or being found in another person's
negro-quarters or kitchen, forty lashes, (*ibid. ;*) *and
every negro in whose company such vagrant slave shall be
found incurs also twenty lashes.* (*Ibid.*)

Any person may lawfully kill a slave who has
been *outlawed** for running away and lurking in

---

is a favourite measure of despotic governments for the suppression
of liberal principles. In this country, the experiment has never been
tried by statutory provisions, except in reference to the black population. The reader will recollect that in the chapter treating of education and religious privileges, several acts of the slave-holding states
were given, in which these *unlawful assemblies* were spoken of. A
complete enumeration of the *crimes* thus created (for all of which
slaves are severely punished) would swell this branch of the subject
beyond its appropriate limits.

* Such was once the law of Virginia also. "In 1705, two justices
of the peace were authorized by proclamation to *outlaw* runaways,
who might thereafter be *killed* and destroyed by any person whatsoever, by *such ways and means* as he might think fit, without accusation
or impeachment of any crime for so doing." Speaking of this law
and some others of a kindred nature, Judge Tucker, professor of law
in the University of William and Mary, Virginia, observes—"Such
are the cruelties to which a state of slavery gives birth; such the
horrors to which the human mind is capable of being reconciled by

swamps, &c. &c. *Haywood's Manual*, 521–2; *Revised Statutes*, 577–8.

For hunting with dogs, in the woods even of his master, the slave is subjected to a whipping of thirty lashes. *Haywood's Manual*, 524, (*act of* 1753.)

A slave *endeavouring** to entice another slave to

---

its adoption." And, again, says the same respectable writer, "In 1772, some restraints were laid upon the practice of *outlawing* slaves,—requiring that it should appear to the *satisfaction* of the justice that the slaves were outlying and *doing mischief. These loose expressions of the act left too much in the discretion of men not much addicted to weighing their import.* In 1792, every thing relative to the outlawry of slaves was *expunged* from our code, and *I trust will never again find a place in it.*" See *Appendix to Blackstone's Commentaries, second part, p.* 56–7. How long will it be before such sentiments prevail in North Carolina?

* The original section creating this *crime* was in these words:—"Every slave who shall endeavour to delude or entice any slave to run away and leave this province, every such slave and slaves, and his and their accomplices, aiders and abettors, shall, upon conviction as aforesaid, suffer death." 2 *Brevard's Digest*, 233, *act of* 1740. After an experiment of eleven years' duration, the legislature relented so far as to declare, "That whereas by, &c. of the act entitled, &c. it is (among other things contained) enacted 'That every slave who shall endeavour to delude or entice any slave to run away and leave this province shall upon conviction suffer death,' which is a punishment too great for the nature of the offence, as *such offender might afterwards* alter his intentions, Be it therefore enacted, That such part of the said paragraph as relates only to slaves endeavouring to delude or entice other slaves to run away and leave this province shall not operate or take effect, unless it shall appear that such slave (so endeavouring to delude or entice other slaves to run away and leave this province) shall have actually prepared provisions, arms, ammunition, horse or horses, or any boat, canoe or other vessel *whereby their intention shall be manifested.*" 2 *Brev. Dig.* 244, *act of* 1751. It is hardly necessary to remind the intelligent reader that the *principle* upon which the act of 1740 was founded is retained in the amendment of

run away, if provisions, &c. be prepared for the purpose of aiding in such running away, shall be punished with DEATH. 2 *Brevard's Dig.* 233 and 244. And a slave who shall aid and abet the slave so endeavouring to entice another slave to run away shall also suffer DEATH. *Ibid.*

If a slave harbour, conceal or *entertain* another slave being a runaway, in South Carolina and Georgia, he is subjected to corporal punishment to any extent not affecting life or limb. 2 *Brevard's Dig.* 237 ; *Prince's Dig.* 452. In Maryland, thirty-nine stripes is the penalty for harbouring *one* hour. *Act of* 1748, *ch.* 19, § 4.

A slave for being on *horseback* without the *written* permission of his master incurs twenty-five lashes, (1 *Martin's Dig.* 622 ;) *for keeping a dog*, the like punishment, (1 *Rev. Code, Mississippi,* 379 ;) *for killing a deer*, though by the command of his master, overseer, &c., unless such command can be proved by a ticket in *writing*, twenty lashes, (2 *Brevard's Dig.* 246 ;) and in *Florida*, for *fire-hunting*, or *keeping a horse*, a *boat* or *canoe*, thirty-nine lashes, (*Thompson's Dig.* 541 ;) "*for being guilty of rambling, riding or going abroad in the night, or riding horses in the daytime without leave, a*

1751. The *endeavour* on the part of a slave to entice another to run away is, in both laws, regarded as a *crime worthy of death.* What shall constitute the *evidence* of this *endeavour* is defined in the amendment,—namely, "the preparing provisions, &c. *whereby the intention shall be manifested.*" And this is the only melioration of a law which it is acknowledged, in the same breath, imposed a punishment too severe for the offence ! ! And such is still the law, after the lapse of a century.

slave may be whipped, *cropped*, or branded on the cheek with the letter R, or otherwise punished, *not extending to life* or so as to render him unfit for labour." *Act of Maryland of* 1751, *ch.* 14, § 8. If a slave *beat the Patuxent River,* (which is sometimes done for the purpose of taking fish,) ten lashes. *Maryland Laws, act of* 1796, *ch.* 32, § 3. And if he *place a seine* across the Transquakin and Chickwiccomico Creeks, a justice of the peace may order him to receive *thirty-nine lashes. Ibid. (act of* 1805,) *ch.* 31, § 3.

In conclusion of this branch of the present section may be added an act of Assembly of the state of Mississippi, of great cruelty, relating to runaway slaves. It is entitled an act to *amend* an act entitled "An act to reduce into one the several acts concerning slaves, free negroes and mulattoes," and may be found among the laws of the session of 1824. The first section is in these words :—"When any slave or slaves shall be committed to any jail in this state, as a runaway or runaways, it shall be the duty of the jailer of said county to interrogate him, her or them as to his, her or their owner's or owners' name or names and place of residence ; and the account thus received, together with a description of the slave or slaves, the jailer shall forthwith transmit *by mail* to the owner or owners named by the slave ; and if the statement made by said slave or slaves shall prove to be false, it shall be the duty of the jailer, without delay, to give the said slave or each of them twenty-five lashes, well laid on, and interrogate him, her or them anew, and transmit the intelligence obtained, together with a description as aforesaid, to the owner or owners again named, and whip as before directed, if a second false account is given; *and so on, for the space of six months*, it shall be the duty of the jailer alternately to interrogate and whip as aforesaid, whenever the said slave or slaves may give a false account of his, her or their owner's or owners' name and place of residence."

To appreciate fully the cruelty of this law, it should be noticed that its entire administration, inquisitorial and punitive, is confined to a single person,—the jailer,—who, from the nature of his office, must have the slave wholly within his power; and yet for the abuse of this power, in a case within the meaning of the act, he may be regarded as altogether irresponsible to any one. Without any design on the part of the slave either to pervert or to conceal the truth, it is highly probable that his statement will, in many instances, be false, and in many more *appear* to be so. For the state of Mississippi is, as to the greater part of it, uncultivated and uninhabited; it is divided into but few counties; the number of post-offices which have been established there is very small, and the names of the *proper post-town* must be frequently unknown even to *white* inhabitants, whose means of information are vastly superior to what the slave possesses. The master's place of residence, which is mentioned in the act, may be very remote from the post-office, and, should *it* be known to the slave, would afford but little assistance to the jailer as to the *endorsement* of his letter to the master. As overseers are usually employed on plantations, it will not be thought strange that the ignorant slave should not be acquainted with his master's name, especially his *Christian* name. Proper names, both of men and places, are frequently spelled very differently from what the pronunciation would teach; and jailers are not ordinarily selected for good scholarship or extensive information. Added to the whole, it should be recollected that miscarriages of letters, even when carefully and correctly endorsed, occur not seldom, from the ignorance or inattention of postmasters. Notwithstanding all these considerations, the jailer may, *in his discretion*, determine when the slave's statement is false, and, having inflicted the legal measure of flagellation, may repeat the same punishment, again and again, for the space of six months,—or, to use the language of the act, so characteristic of that callousness to the slave's sufferings which familiarity with cruelty begets,—"and so on, for the space of six months, it shall be the duty of the jailer alternately to interrogate and whip as aforesaid."

I come now to the exemplification of the second branch of this chapter, which may be stated in the following proposition:—THE PENAL CODE OF THE SLAVE-HOLDING STATES INFLICTS PUNISHMENTS OF MUCH GREATER SEVERITY UPON SLAVES THAN UPON WHITE PERSONS CONVICTED OF SIMILAR OFFENCES.

In treating of this proposition, I place before the reader at the outset synopses of the penal codes of two of the states,— *Virginia* and *Mississippi*,—so far

15

as may be requisite to comprise the offences which are punishable by *death* in regard to any class of perpetrators.

Virginia, it will be seen, discriminates in punishments not only in respect to *whites* and *slaves*, but between *free* coloured persons and *slaves*. In this state, *whites* are punishable with *death* for four offences:—1. *Treason;* 2. *Murder* of the *first* degree; 3. *Maliciously burning* IN THE NIGHT *the dwelling-house* of another, or *a jail*, INHABITED AT THE TIME BY ANY PERSON; 4. *Maliciously setting fire to* ANY THING, *whereby a dwelling-house. of another, or a jail, shall be burnt* IN THE NIGHT-TIME, AND BEING THEN INHABITED BY ANY PERSON.

Treason is a crime of which a slave, as such, cannot be guilty. The following table is restricted to crimes which, when committed by *whites*, are *not* punished by *death*, nor even when committed by *free* coloured persons is this the *fixed* punishment *without alternative* in any one of these offences, whilst in the major part a term of *imprisonment* only is imposed. But DEATH *is the penalty to* SLAVES *in every case enumerated.*

VIRGINIA.

No.	CRIME.	PUNISHMENT OF WHITES.	Code of Virginia.	PUNISHMENT OF FREE NEGROES.	Code of Virginia.	PUNISHMENT OF SLAVES.	Code of Virginia.
1	Murder of the first degree	Death	p. 722	Death	p. 723	Death	p. 723
2	" second degree	5 to 18 yrs	723	5 to 18 years	723	"	753
3	Voluntary manslaughter	1 to 5 "	723	1 to 5 "	723	" (second offence)	753
4	Involuntary manslaughter						
5	Administering poison, &c. with intent to kill or injure any person						
6	Attempting to administer poison	3 to 5	723	3 to 5 "	723	"	753
7	Poisoning a spring, well or reservoir of water	3 to 5	723	3 to 5 "	723	"	753
8	Administering to a woman any drug, &c. to destroy unborn child: if child destroyed	3 to 5	723	3 to 5 "	723	"	753
9	Administering to a woman any drug, &c. to produce abortion or miscarriage: if abortion or miscarriage produced	1 to 5 "	724	1 to 5	724	" (second offence)	753
10	MALICIOUSLY shooting, stabbing, &c., with intent to maim	1 to 5	724	1 to 5 "	724	"	753
11	" " disfigure	1 to 10 "	724	1 to 10 "	724	"	753
12	" " disfigure	1 to 10 "	724	1 to 10 "	724	"	753
13	" " kill	1 to 10 "	724	1 to 10 "	724	"	753
13	Unlawfully but not maliciously shooting, &c., but with intent to maim	1 to 5 "	724	1 to 5 "	724	"	753
14	Unlawfully but not maliciously shooting, &c., but with intent to disfigure	1 to 5 "	724	1 to 5 "	724	"	753
15	Unlawfully but not maliciously shooting, &c., but with intent to kill	1 to 5 "	724	1 to 5 "	724	"	753
16	Unlawfully shooting, stabbing, &c. in the commission of a felony	1 to 5 "	724	1 to 5 "	724	"	753
17	Unlawfully shooting, stabbing, &c. in the attempt to commit a felony	1 to 5 "	724	1 to 5 "	724	"	753
18	Committing a robbery,—if armed with a dangerous weapon	5 to 10 "	724	5 to 10 "	724	"	753
19	" if not so armed	3 to 10 "	724	3 to 10 "	724	"	753
20	Threatening injury to the person of another, thereby extorting money	1 to 5	724	1 to 5 "	724	" (second offence)	754
21	" property	1 to 5	724	1 to 5 "	724	"	754
22	Seizing a child with intent to extort money	1 to 5	724	1 to 5 "	724	"	754

VIRGINIA—continued.

No.	CRIME	PUNISHMENT OF WHITES.	Code of Virginia.	PUNISHMENT OF FREE NEGROES.	Code of Virginia.	PUNISHMENT OF SLAVES.	Code of Virginia.
23	Committing a rape on a female of 12 years and upwards...........	10 to 20 yrs.	p.725	(Without regard to colour of female,) Death; or from 5 to 20 yrs., at the discretion of the jury......	p.753	Death......	p.753
24	Having carnal knowledge of a female child under 12 years......	10 to 20 "	725	Death, or from 5 to 20 yrs., &c.....	753	"	753
25	Attempting, by force or fraud, to have carnal knowledge of a white female	Not provided for.		" "	753	"	753
26	Taking away, against her will, a white female, with intent to marry her.......	3 to 10 yrs.	p.725	" "	753	"	753
27	Detaining, against her will, a white female, with intent to defile her.........	3 to 10 "	725	" "	753	"	753
28	Taking away, against her will, a white female, with intent to cause her to be married TO ANOTHER......	3 to 10 "	725	" "	753	"	753
29	Detaining, against her will, a white female, with intent to cause her to be defiled by another...........	3 to 10 "	725	" "	753	"	753
30	Taking a female child, under 12 years of age, from any one having lawful custody of her, for prostitution...........	3 to 10 "	725	" "	753	"	753
31	Taking a female child, under 12 years of age, from any one having lawful custody of her, for concubinage............	3 to 10 "	725	" "	753	"	753
32	Selling a free person as a slave............	3 to 10 "	725	3 to 10 years.......	753	"	753
33	Kidnapping a free person with intent to sell as a slave............	3 to 10 "	725	3 to 10 "	753	"	753
34	Burning in the night, a dwelling-house of another, when no person is within such house.............	5 to 10 "	727	5 to 10 "	727	"	727
35	Burning a jail................	5 to 10 "	727	5 to 10 "	727	"	727
36	Maliciously setting fire to any thing, by the burning whereof such dwelling-house (not inhabited) shall be burnt in the night.........	5 to 10 "	727	5 to 10 "	727	"	727
37	Maliciously setting fire to any thing, by the burning whereof such jail shall be burnt in the night.........	5 to 10 "	727	5 to 10 "	727	"	727

No.	Offence	Conf.	p.	Conf.	p.	p.	Acts
38	Maliciously burning, in the daytime, a dwelling-house	3 to 10	727	3 to 10	727	727	753
39	" " a jail	3 to 10	727	3 to 10	727	727	753
40	Maliciously setting fire, in the daytime, to any thing by the burning whereof a dwelling-house shall be burnt	3 to 10	727	3 to 10	727	727	753
41	Maliciously setting fire, in the daytime, to any thing by the burning whereof a jail shall be burnt	3 to 10	727	3 to 10	727	727	753
42	Maliciously burning a meeting-house, court-house, town-house, college, academy, or other building erected for public use, (except jail or prison,) or any banking-house, warehouse, storehouse, manufactory or mill of another person, not usually occupied by persons lodging therein at night, if either of such buildings, with the property therein, be worth $1000						753
43	" " if worth less than $1000. Maliciously SETTING FIRE to any thing whereby any such last-mentioned building, worth $1000, shall be burnt	3 to 10 / 3 to 5	727 / 727	3 to 10 / 3 to 5	727 / 727	727	753 / 753
44	" " worth less than $1000, shall be burnt	3 to 10	727	3 to 10	727	727	753
45	Maliciously burning any pile or parcel of wood, boards, or other lumber, or any barn, stable, cow-house, tobacco-house, stack of wheat or other grain, or of fodder, straw or hay,—if the thing burnt, with the property therein, be worth $100	3 to 5	727	3 to 5	727	727	753
46	Same offence,—if the thing burnt, with the property therein, be not worth $100	3 to 5	728	3 to 5	728	728	753
47	Maliciously burning any building, not before mentioned, if, with the property therein, worth $100 or more	1 to 3	728	1 to 3	728	728	753
48	Same offence, but value less than $100	3 to 10	728	3 to 10	728	728	753 (second offence)
49	Maliciously burning any bridge, lock, dam, or any ship, boat or other vessel, worth $100 or more	1 to 3	728	1 to 3	728	728	753
50	Wilfully burning any building, or any goods, &c., which shall at the time be insured, &c., with intent to injure the owner, whether such person be the owner of the property or not	3 to 10	728	3 to 10	728	728	753
51	Burglary	1 to 10	728	1 to 10	728	728	753 (second offence)
52	Breaking and entering into a dwelling-house, in the night-time, with intent to commit a larceny, although the thing intended to be stolen be worth less than $20	5 to 10	728	5 to 10	728	728	753
53	Entering, without breaking, in the night, a dwelling-house with intent to commit murder	5 to 10	728-9	3 to 10	728-9	728-9	753

VIRGINIA—continued.

No.	CRIME	PUNISHMENT OF WHITES	Code of Virginia	PUNISHMENT OF FREE NEGROES	Code of Virginia	PUNISHMENT OF SLAVES	Code of Virginia
54	Breaking and entering, in the *daytime*, such house, with like intent	3 to 10 yrs.	p.729	5 to 10 years	p.728-9	Death	p.753
55	Entering in *the night time*, without breaking, any *office, shop, storehouse, warehouse, banking-house*, or other house not adjoining to or occupied as a dwelling-house, or *any ship or vessel, with intent to commit murder*						
56	Same offence, with intent to commit a *rape*	3 to 10 "	729	5 to 10	728-9	"	753
57	Same offence, with intent to commit a *robbery*	3 to 10 "	729	5 to 10	728-9	"	753
58	*Breaking and entering* into any of the structures mentioned in No. 55, either in the *daytime or night*, with *intent to commit a murder*	3 to 10 "	729	5 to 10	728-9	"	753
59	Same offence, with *intent to commit a rape*	3 to 10 "	729	5 to 10	728-9	"	753
60	Same offence, with *intent to commit a robbery*	3 to 10 "	729	5 to 10	729	"	753
61	Same offence, with intent to commit *larceny*, or any other felony	1 to 10 "	729	1 to 10	729	" (second offence)	753
62	*Simple larceny of goods or chattels*, of the value of $20 or more	1 to 5 "	729	1 to 5	729	"	753
63	Stealing a *bank-note, check, &c. &c.* of the value of $20 or more	1 to 5 "	729	1 to 5	729	"	753
64	Administering poison to a horse, &c.	1 to 5 "	729	1 to 5	729	"	753
65	*Maliciously obstructing, removing or injuring any part of a canal*, or *railroad*, or any bridge or fixture thereof, &c. &c., to the endangering the life of a traveller	1 to 5 "	732	1 to 5	732	"	753
66	Counterfeiting coin	3 to 5 "	732	3 to 10	732	" (second offence)	753
67	*Having in his possession*, at one time, ten pieces of base coin, &c., knowing them to be base, " with intent to employ them as true "	2 to 10 "	734-5	2 to 10	734-5	"	753
68	*Crime against nature*	1 to 10 "	735	1 to 10	735	"	753
		1 to 5 "	740	1 to 5	740	"	753

I insert on the following page a table, which was contained in the former edition of this work, exhibiting the *inequality* of punishment, in the state of *Mississippi*, between *white* and *slave* convicts. Whether any change in this respect has been made since that time, I have assiduously endeavoured to ascertain, but without success. I have been unable to procure an edition of the laws of that state later in date than the *Revised Code* from which this table was originally formed.

The following crimes* are in that state punished with death, whether the perpetrators are slaves, free negroes, or white persons:—1. Murder; 2. Robbery; 3. Rape; 4. Burglary; 5. Wilfully burning a dwelling-house, a store, a cotton-house or gin-house, or any other out-house or building, adjoining to a dwelling-house or store; 6. Horse-stealing, *second* offence; 7. Forgery; 8. Being accessory *before* the fact to Rape; 9. Being accessory before the fact to Arson, (as before defined;) 10. Being accessory before the fact to Robbery; 11. Being accessory before the fact to Burglary; 12. For rescuing a person convicted of a capital offence.

But with respect to a large catalogue of other offences, it will be seen by the subjoined table that a wide difference is made according as the offender is a slave or free white person.

---

* The crime of High Treason, being inapplicable to the condition of a slave, is purposely omitted.

MISSISSIPPI.

CRIME.	Punishment of a Slave.	Punishment of White Persons.
1. Wilfully burning { a barn.	1. Death,* *R. C.* 381.	1. Imprisonment not exceeding six months and paying damages. *Rev. Code,* 298.
2. a stable.	2. Death, *ibid.*	2. Same punishment as No. 1. *Ibid.*
3. Murder.	3. Death, *ibid.*	3. A fine, at the discretion of the court, and imprisonment for not exceeding one year, and the exaction of surety of the peace.† *R. C.* 297.
Attempting to commit 4. Rape.	4. Death, *ibid.*	4. Same as No. 3. *R. C.* 297.
5. Burglary.	5. Death, *ibid.*	5. Same as No. 3. *Ibid.*
6. Robbery.	6. Death, *ibid.*	6.
Attempting to burn 7. a dwelling-house.	7. Death, *ibid.*	7.
8. a store.	8. Death, *ibid.*	8.
9. a cotton-house } adjoining a dwelling-house or store.	9. Death, *ibid.*	9. Not crimes either at common law, or by statute.
10. a gin-house	10. Death, *ibid.*	10.
11. any other out-house or building	11. Death, *ibid.*	11.
12. Horse-stealing, *second offence.*	12. Death, *ibid.*	12.
13. Attempting to commit } Forgery.	13. Death, *ibid.*	13.
14. Forgery.	14. Death, *ibid.*	14.
15. Being accessory *before the fact* to stealing { a freeman.	15. Death, *ibid.*	15. Not provided for by statute.
16. a slave.	16. Death, *ibid.*	16.
17. a horse, *second offence.*	17. Death, *ibid.*	17.

* The Benefit of Clergy is abolished by express law of this state, in all cases. *Revised Code,* 308.

† This is, in fact, the punishment of an offence better defined,—*i. e.* an *assault* with intent to commit murder.

No.	Offence	No.	Punishment
18. 19.	Being accessory before the fact to the burning of { a barn. a stable.	18. 19.	Same punishment as No. 1.
20.	Murder.	20.	A fine not exceeding $300, and may, at the discretion of the court, receive thirty-nine lashes. R. C. 304.
21.	Rape.	21.	
22.	Robbery.	22.	
23.	Burglary.	23.	
24.	Forgery.	24.	Not provided for by statute.
25.	Horse-stealing, *second* offence.	25.	
26. 27.	Being accessory after the fact to stealing { a free person. a slave.	26. 27.	Same as Nos. 20, 21, 22 and 23. *Rev. Code*, 304.
28.	a dwelling-house.	28.	
29.	a store.	29.	
30.	a cotton-house.	30.	
31.	burning { a gin-house.	31.	Death. *R. C.* 381.
32.	any out-house or building.	32.	
33.	a barn.	33.	
34.	a stable.	34.	
35.	Manslaughter of any free person.	35.	Fine and imprisonment at the discretion of the court, and being branded on the hand with the letter M.
36.	Maiming a free white person.	36.	Fine not exceeding one thousand dollars — standing in the pillory for two hours per day, for a term not exceeding three days.
37.	Preparing for, or administering any medicine to, any person with an intent to kill.	37.	Not provided for by statute.
38.	The perpetration of a second* offence, in all felonies not punishable with death for the first offence.	38.	No distinction is in general made in the punishment of this class of offences, when committed by white persons, between the first and second offences.

* This definition comprehends several offences,—as grand larceny, petit larceny, &c.

One of the provisions in the Constitution of *Alabama* is, "It shall be the duty of the General Assembly, as soon as circumstances will permit, to form *a penal code*, founded on principles of reformation and not of vindictive justice."

The penal code which has been adopted, so far as respects *free white persons*, conforms generally to this requirement. There are no crimes, when committed by white persons, for which *death* is affixed as the proper and positive sentence of the law. There are six which *may* be so punished, but none which *must* be. The alternative, "*confinement in the penitentiary for life*," may be granted in these cases by the *jury* by whom the *accused* has been found *convict*. These are—*treason; murder* in the *first* degree; *aiding a slave or slaves* in an *actual* or *meditated rebellion* or *insurrection* against the *white inhabitants; aiding the same against the laws and government of the state;* or *advising, consulting* or *plotting with any slave or slaves,* for the purpose of *encouraging, exciting, aiding* or *assisting* in any *such rebellion or insurrection,* either *actual or meditated;* for causing, *with malice aforethought, the death of a slave, by cruel, barbarous or inhuman whipping,* or *by any cruel or inhuman treatment,* or *by the use of any instrument in its nature calculated to produce death. Clay's Digest,* 411–13.

It is manifest, however, that the legislators of this state have not considered *slaves,* when convicted of crime, to be comprehended within the benignant spirit of the Constitution. For the catalogue of crimes for which they are subjected to the penalty of *death,* as the fixed and sole punishment without any alternative, is extensive and hideous. They are, —*consulting* or *conspiring* to *rebel,* or be *in any wise concerned in an insurrection or rebellion of the slaves against the white inhabitants of the state,* or the *laws and government thereof ;* or *conspiring to murder any white person;* for *murder ;* for *an assault* with *an intent to kill* any white person ; for the *voluntary manslaughter* of a *white* person ; for the *involuntary manslaughter* of a *white* person in the prosecution of an *unlawful act; rape* on a *white* female ; for an *attempt* to commit such *rape ;* for *burglary ;* for *robbery ;* for an *assault* and *battery* with intent to *rob* a white person ; for *wilfully maiming ;* for *cutting or biting off a lip ;* for *the cutting or biting off an ear ;* for *the cutting or biting off* the *nose* of a *white* person ; for an *attempt* to poison or deprive any white person of life by any means not amounting to assault ; for *wilfully and maliciously setting fire to or burning* any *dwelling-house,* or out-house appurtenant thereto ; or the like offence as to *a storehouse,* or *office,* or *back-house,* or *warehouse,* or *other edifice public or private,* or *corn-crib,* or *gin-house,* or *cotton-house,* or *stable,* or *barn,* or *cotton in the heap* of the value of $100, or *in bale,* or *any ship* or *steamboat,* or other *water-craft* used in navigating the waters of the state.

And to this large list are to be added nearly as many more *capital* offences by *slaves,* by force of the following section :—" All *accessories* BEFORE the *fact* to any of the crimes heretofore enumerated shall be *deemed* PRINCIPALS, and may be tried, though the principal offenders be not taken or convicted." *Clay's Digest,* 472.

And whilst offences by slaves to the persons and property of the *white* population are thus severely vindicated, the very next section to that which has been just quoted is in these words:—"Every *slave* who shall be guilty of the *manslaughter* of a SLAVE, FREE NEGRO or MULATTO, and be thereof convicted, shall be punished by any number of *stripes* not exceeding *thirty-nine*, or be branded in the hand, or both, at the discretion of the jury." *Ibid.*

The existing code of *Florida* enumerates distinctly twenty-three offences for which, as to *slaves*, the punishment is *death;* three others which *may* be so punished, or by whipping not exceeding thirty-nine stripes, having the ears nailed to posts, and in this condition standing one hour, or having the hand burnt with a heated iron in open court, at the discretion of the court. *Thompson's Digest,* 490, 537–8. So, *attempting* to commit any capital offence, by a slave, and being an *accessory* thereto, are subject to the same alternatives of *death* or *stripes, nailing the ears to posts,* or *branding in the hand.* Altogether, the offences in this state which *may* be punished *capitally* number nearly seventy.

It would enlarge this chapter beyond its proper limits, to furnish *in extenso* a similar view of the punishment of offences in each of the slave-holding states. I shall content myself, therefore, by indicating the difference which is made in the remaining states as to the severity of the punishments to which slaves and white persons are severally subjected, in a more general manner.

The penal code of *Georgia* has within the last

twenty-five years become exceedingly sanguinary. At the present time there are not less than *thirteen* offences for which *white* persons are punished *capitally*. See 2 *Cobb's Digest*, 782–3, 786, 789–90, 804–6, 811. And *slaves* are so punished for *twenty*. See 2 *Ibid.* 786, 806, 976, 987, 995–6, 1002.

Besides this punishment, *slaves* may be subjected to very severe punishment, in virtue of the following provision:—"All other offences committed by a slave or free person of colour, either against persons or property, or against another slave or person of colour, shall be punished at the discretion of the court, such court having in view the principles of humanity in passing sentence ; and in no case shall the same extend to life or limb." *Act of* 1816, § 2, 2 *Cobb's Digest*, 987.

In *Tennessee, whites* are punished by death for *two* offences:—1. Murder of the first degree; 2. Being an accessory to such murder *before* the fact. *Capital* offences by *slaves* are *eight:*—1. Murder; 2. Arson; 3. Burglary; 4. Robbery; 5. Rape, (*act of* 1819; *Carruthers & Nicholson*, p. 679 ;) 6. Assault on a white woman, with intent to commit a rape, (*act of* 1833, *ib.* 683 ;) 7. A conspiracy by *three* or more slaves to *rebel ;* 8. A conspiracy of like numbers to murder any person, (*act of* 1741, *ib.* p. 674.) But in regard to the *two* last offences, by act of 1831, the judges may, at their discretion, substitute for the *death*-penalty *stripes,* and *standing in the pillory,* and confinement in the county jail. *Ib.* 682.

The penal code of *Missouri* inflicts *death* upon *whites* for *four* offences: — 1. *Treason ;* 2. *Murder ;*

16

3. *Raising* a rebellion of slaves; 4. *Aiding* such rebellion, by furnishing arms, or doing any other *overt*
act in furtherance of such rebellion. *Missouri Digest*,
341-2. And on *slaves* for—1. *Murder;* 2. *Raising* a
rebellion; 3. *Entering into an agreement to rebel;* 4.
Conspiring the death of any person, or to commit
arson in furtherance of such conspiracy, if any *overt*
act in furtherance of such conspiracy be done.

In *Kentucky*, whites forfeit life for four crimes
only,* viz.:—1. Murder; 2. Wilfully burning the penitentiary; 3. Being accessory thereto *before* the fact;
4. The carnal abuse of a female child under ten
years of age. 2 *Litt. & Swi.* 1006-9. Slaves meet a
similar punishment for *eleven* crimes. These are:—
1. Murder; 2. Arson; 3. Rape on a white woman;
4. Robbery; 5. Burglary; 6. Conspiracy to rebel;
7. Administering poison with an intent to kill;
8. Manslaughter; 9. *Attempting* to commit a rape
on a white woman; 10. Shooting at a *white* person
with an intent to kill; 11. Wounding a white
person with an intent to kill. See 2 *Litt. & Swi.*
1060-6-4.

There is a difference in the punishment of *white*
offenders and *slaves* in this particular:—

For *voluntary* manslaughter, a *white* person is
punishable by imprisonment at hard labour not
less than *two* nor more than *four* years. *Act of*

---

* In this state, the benefit of clergy is taken away *entirely* as to
white persons. 2 *Litt. & Swi.* 985. Blacks and mulattoes, whether
bond or free, are allowed a privilege *somewhat* resembling it, *i. e.* a
commutation of capital punishment for "such corporal punishment,
short of life, as the court may direct." 2 *Litt. & Swi.* 1154.

1825, 2 *Morehead & Brown's Digest*, 1294. But a slave, for the same offence, is punished with *death;* and the same punishment is inflicted on a slave for shooting *at* a white person *with intent to kill.* 2 *Morehead & Brown*, 1291.

For *maliciously* blowing up, or *attempting* to blow up, with gunpowder, &c. any of the *locks* of the *Louisville* and *Portland Canal*, the punishment of a *white* offender is confinement in the penitentiary for not less than *two* nor more than *four* years. And for a similar offence, in regard to the *bridge* over the same canal, committed by a *white* person, a similar penitentiary punishment; whilst in regard to both of these offences by a *slave*, the punishment is *death.* 2 *Morehead & Brown*, 1304, (*act of* 1833.)

All other offences, when perpetrated by slaves, are punishable with whipping only, not exceeding thirty-nine lashes, *except ,for advising the murder* of any person : for this offence one hundred lashes are authorized to be given. 2 *Litt. & Swi.* 1161–2.

Capital felonies abound in *South Carolina.* White persons suffer death there for *twenty-seven* offences, in *twenty-three* of which the benefit of clergy is not allowed. Slaves incur a similar fate for *thirty-six* offences. From most of these, also, the benefit of clergy has been taken away. Simple larceny, to the value of one dollar and seven cents, whether perpetrated by a white person or by a slave, is a *capital* felony, without the benefit of clergy ! !* See *James' Digest, title Crimes and Misdemeanours.*

---

* A distinction is made by *express law* in South Carolina between males and females convicted of *clergyable* offences. Both are to be

The *capital* offences in *North Carolina*, according to her *Revised Statutes* of 1836–7, exceed in number those even of *South Carolina*. *Whites*, as well as *slaves*, suffer death for *at least* thirty-four offences; and *slaves* suffer for *six* more. See *Revised Statutes*, 191–5, 580–1. Besides these offences which can be so punished after a judicial conviction, a slave for resisting his master by force, (2 *Haywood's Rep.* 54,) or OUTLAWED for *running away, lurking in swamps*, &c., and *not returning home immediately*, may be killed by anybody, "by such means as he shall think fit, without accusation or impeachment of any crime for the same." *Revised Statutes*, 577–8.

Of the spirit which *once* breathed in Maryland against negroes, the reader will be instructed by an act passed in 1729, (*ch.* 4,) in the following words:—"Whereas several petit treasons and cruel and horrid murders have been lately committed by negroes; which cruelties they were instigated to commit, and hereafter may be instigated to commit, with the like inhumanity, because they have no sense of shame, or apprehension of future rewards or punishments; and that the manner of executing offenders, prescribed by the laws of England, is not sufficient to deter a people from committing the

---

marked in the hand, upon the brawn of the left thumb, with a *burning-hot* iron, having a Roman M or T upon it, according to the nature of the crime. But a *male* is discharged *without further* punishment: a *female* may be *whipped, placed in the stocks, or imprisoned for the space of a year afterwards*, at the discretion of the court. *James' Digest*, 97–9.

greatest cruelties, who only consider the rigour and severity of punishment; Be it enacted, &c. that when any negro or other slave shall be convicted, by confession or verdict of a jury, of any petit treason or murder, or burning of dwelling-houses, it shall and may be lawful for the justices before whom such convictions shall be, to give judgment against such negro or other slave, *to have the right hand cut off, to be hanged in the usual manner, the head severed from the body, the body divided into four quarters, and the head and quarters set up in the most public places of the county where such fact was committed*" *! !* The barbarous provisions of this law, it will be seen, were not made *compulsory* with the justices before whom the conviction might take place, but were intrusted to their *discretion.* And, as "the declaration of rights" prefixed to the Constitution of Maryland contains the following, among other just principles, "That sanguinary laws ought to be avoided, as far as is consistent with the safety of the state, and no law to inflict *cruel* and unusual pains and penalties ought to be made, in any case or at any time hereafter," no justice, I presume, would venture, in the exercise of his *discretion,* to give in his sentence full scope to the savage power confided to him. Yet it cannot but move our wonder that the act itself has not been annulled. The last AUTHORIZED edition of the laws of this state which I have examined comprises it among the laws still in force.

It is apparent, from the views given in this chapter, that slaves offending against the laws are subjected *chiefly* to two species of punishment,—*whipping and death.* Cropping and the pillory are seldom directed, unless in *conjunction* with whipping. In several of ᐧthe states, *transportation* is authorized, upon certain conditions, as a commutation for the sentence of death. See 1 *Virginia Revised Code*, 430 ; *Haywood's Manual*, 544 ; *Maryland Laws*, (*act of* 1809,) *ch.* 138, § 9, and *act of* 1819, *ch.* 159. *Putting in irons,* and while so made to labour for his master, is practised in Louisiana. 1 *Martin's Dig.* 688. As a mode of SECURING the person of a slave labouring under an accusation of crime *previous to his trial,* from necessity, *imprisonment** is resorted to. But as a *punishment after conviction,* except in the state of *Louisiana,* where the laws have in *some* measure recognised its adoption, it appears to be almost unknown. In an act of Assembly of this last-mentioned state, juries convoked for the trial of a slave on a charge *not capital* may direct the slave to be imprisoned *not*

---

* The following provision is contained in an act of the legislature of *Virginia:*—"*Whenever the master or owner of any slave shall desire to confine him in the jail of any county or corporation within this commonwealth,* it shall be lawful for any justice of the peace, in such county or corporation, upon application of such master or owner or his agent, to grant a warrant to the jailer, authorizing him to receive such slave into custody and to confine him in said jail; *provided,* such justice be of opinion that such slave may be so confined without public inconvenience," &c. The duration of this confinement is made to depend on the master's will, unless the public convenience should require the slave's discharge. *Act of Assembly of February 25th,* 1824, ₴ 4, entitled "An act concerning servants and slaves." A law of *Missouri,* nearly similar to this, though *less exceptionable,* I have noticed in a previous page. The remarks there made may, with equal appositeness, be repeated here. *See supra,* p. 70.

exceeding eight days. 1 *Martin's Dig.* 688, (*act of March 19th,* 1816.) *Imprisonment for life* is mentioned several times in the laws of the same state, as a known punishment for slaves; yet for what offences and under what circumstances it is authorized I have not been able to ascertain. See *ibid.* An act of Assembly, posterior in point of time to the publication of the work just cited, vests the power in the governor and senate to *commute* the punishment of *death* into a *lesser* punishment in favour of slaves, upon the recommendation of the judge and jury by whom the offender has been tried, if the circumstances of the case shall be such as may be thought to entitle him to such commutation; and among these *lesser* punishments perpetual *imprisonment* is named. *Act of March 5th,* 1822.

This exclusion generally of imprisonment as a mode of punishment for slaves has led, it is believed, to the multiplication of *capital* offences as to this class of people. *Dismemberment,* as it would in general diminish the value of the slave, and partakes so largely of savage ferocity, has probably at no period been *much* tolerated. For a solitary offence, however, it is authorized in Missouri. 1 *Missouri Laws,* 312.

Corporal punishment not extending to life or limb, (which is another name for excessive whipping,) though sanctioned in several cases, must be open, in a great degree, to the objections which apply to *dismemberment.* It is presumable, on this account, that it is not frequent in practice. In general, therefore, death has been resorted to as the only punishment, according to the sentiments of slave-holders, adapted to a state of slavery, for all offences except those of a trivial nature.

VII.—TRIAL OF SLAVES UPON CRIMINAL ACCUSATIONS IS IN MOST OF THE SLAVE STATES DIFFERENT FROM THAT WHICH IS OBSERVED IN RESPECT TO FREE WHITE PERSONS; AND THE DIFFERENCE IS INJURIOUS TO THE SLAVE AND INCONSISTENT WITH THE RIGHTS OF HUMANITY.

Trial by jury has been frequently and justly extolled as the palladium of civil liberty. As it existed in full vigour in England when the settlement of this country began, by the principles of colonization it was imported by our ancestors as part of the laws and customs of the mother-country applicable to their new situation. But African slavery having originated in the foulest iniquity, it was natural that it should be sustained and perpetuated by consentaneous means. Accordingly, in but few, if in any, of the colonies, was trial by jury allowed to the slave. And thus it happens that, though the Constitution of the United States, as well as most of the Constitutions of the individual members of the confederacy, secure to the citizen, impeached of crime, the benefit of this institution, yet, as this has been done through the medium of language which does not embrace the case of the slave, *but has reference to precedent usage*, he is left, in this particular, in the like condition of exclusion in which he stood under the colonial government.

A considerable diversity, however, obtains on this subject in the different states. In *Kentucky*, a slave charged with an offence punishable *with death* is entitled to the benefit as well of the *grand* as of the *petit* jury. He is to be "tried and prosecuted in the circuit courts only, and in the same manner, and under the same-forms of trial, as are by law pre-scribed in the cases of free persons." *Act of Feb.* 10*th*, 1819, 2 *Litt. & Swi.* 1164; 2 *Morehead & B.* 1291. And the law is equally favourable in *Tennessee*, (*Nich. & Caru.* 683.) In *Georgia*, on *capital* charges no provision is made for the interposition of the *grand* jury; yet the right of trial by a *petit* jury, with the privilege to the *master* of challenging seven persons on behalf of the slave, is expressly directed and sanctioned. *Prince's Dig.* 459. By the Constitution of *Mississippi* it is declared, "In the prosecution of slaves for crimes, no inquest by a *grand* jury shall be necessary; but the proceedings in such cases shall be regulated by law, except that in *capital* cases the general assembly *shall have no power* to deprive them of an impartial trial by a *petit* jury." The act of Assembly which has been passed to carry into effect this article of the Constitution grants to the slave, on his trial for a *capital* offence, nearly all the advantages of a petit jury (except as to witnesses) which are possessed by whites. *Mississippi Rev. Code*, 382. *Art.* 3, § 27, *of the Constitution of Missouri*, is in these words:—"In prosecutions for crimes, slaves shall not be deprived of an impartial trial by jury; and a slave convicted of a *capital* offence shall suffer the same degree of punishment, and no other, that would be inflicted on a free white person for a like offence; and courts of justice before whom slaves shall be tried shall assign them counsel for their defence." *Similar in Arkansas; art. 4, § 25.* In the Constitution of *Alabama* a provision is inserted, denying to the General Assembly power to deprive slaves of an impartial trial by a *petit* jury, when prosecuted for a crime "*of a higher grade than petit larceny.*" *See Constitution, title Slaves, § 2.* A declaration is comprised in the bill of rights which forms a part of the Constitution of *Maryland,* (and also in the Constitutions of several of the other states,) of the following tenor:—" That in all criminal prosecutions *every man* hath a right to be informed of the accusation against him; to have a copy of the indictment or charge in due time (if required) to prepare for his defence; to be allowed counsel; to be confronted with the witnesses against him; to have process for his witnesses; to examine the witnesses for and against him, on oath; and *to a speedy trial* BY AN IMPARTIAL JURY, *without whose unanimous consent he ought not to be found guilty.*" *Decl. of Rights,* 19; *and see Const. of Alabama, title Decl. of Rights,* 10; *ibid. of Mississippi, tit. ibid.* 10; *ibid. of Missouri, ibid.* 9, *&c. &c.* A citizen of one of the free states would unhesitatingly construe this declaration to be a constitutional guarantee to the slave of the *trial by jury* upon every criminal accusation. In the slave-holding states, however, it has no such meaning. By reference to the Constitutions of Alabama, Mississippi and Missouri, as above noted, the same provision will be found embodied there, in terms

equally strong and explicit;—indeed, in nearly the
same as those contained in the Constitution of Maryland as above cited. And yet quotations taken
from the *same* instruments, and already transcribed
into this chapter, evidence in the clearest manner
that slaves are not considered as embraced by such
provision. And in relation to the state of Maryland, the following *law* compels us to the like conclusion :—"Whensoever any negro, Indian or mulatto slave shall hereafter be charged with any
pilfering or stealing, or any other crime or misdemeanour whereof the county court might have cogni-
zance, it shall and may be lawful for any of the
justices of the provincial or county courts, upon
complaint made before him, to cause such negro,
Indian or mulatto slave so offending to be brought
immediately before him or any other justice of the
peace for the county where such offence is committed, who, upon due proof made against any such
negro or (Indian) or mulatto slave of any of the
crimes as aforesaid, *such justice is hereby authorized
and empowered to award and cause to be inflicted, according to the nature of the crime, such punishment by
whipping as he shall think fit, not exceeding forty lashes.*"
Act of 1717, *ch.* 13, § 6. This law, notwithstanding
that it abrogates the right of trial by jury in the
case of slaves accused of the offences enumerated
in it, is given as *in force*, in an edition of the laws
of the state, published under the express sanction
of the legislature in 1799, (twenty-three years *after*
the adoption of the Constitution,) and in other more
recent editions. But wherever the life of the slave

is the penalty of crime, no exception can be taken
to the tribunal which decides upon his fate in this
state; *trial by jury* is then allowed. *Maryland Laws,*
(*act of* 1751,) *ch.* 14.

The Constitution of *North Carolina* guarantees
trial by jury to *freemen* only. It declares "That *no
freeman* shall be put to answer any criminal charge
but *by indictment, presentment or impeachment.* That
no *freeman* shall be convicted of any crime *but by
the unanimous verdict of a jury of good and lawful men,*
in open court, as heretofore used." See *Bill of Rights,*
§§ 8 and 9. But by *statute,* except in petty offences,
of which a single justice of the peace has jurisdiction, trial of *slaves* for offences not capital takes
place before courts of Pleas and Quarter Sessions,
and is "to be conducted under the same rules, regulations and restrictions as the trials of *freemen;*" and
generally, in cases in which a slave is charged with
the commission of an offence the punishment of
which may extend to *life,* the *superior* courts of law
have *exclusive* jurisdiction, and the mode of trial is
the same as obtains in respect to *whites;* and it is
humanely provided that the judge of the court, on
an application for the purpose, on behalf of the
slave, by his master or his counsel, founded on an
affidavit that a fair trial cannot be had in the
county wherein the offence is charged to have been
committed, may order the removal of the case to
an adjacent court for trial. *Rev. Statutes, ch.* 111,
§§ 42–4; and "in all cases where the county or
superior courts shall have jurisdiction of offences
committed by *slaves,* the slave charged shall be

entitled *to a trial by a jury* of good and lawful men, owners of slaves," (§ 45;) and "a slave shall not be tried for a *capital* offence, but on presentment or indictment of the GRAND JURY; and the same right to challenge jurors is accorded *to him*, his *master* or *counsel*, where the offence is *capital*, as a freeman is entitled to." § 46. In *Tennessee* (by *act of* 1835, *ch.* 19) the law on this subject is much the same as that of *North Carolina*, with an additional advantage to the slave, in *capital* cases, of counsel to be assigned by the court, should the master neglect to employ any; and the master is bound to pay such a *fee* to counsel as the court may direct. *C. & N.* 683.

But trial by jury is utterly denied to the slave, *even in criminal accusations which may affect his life*, in the states of SOUTH CAROLINA, VIRGINIA and LOUISIANA; and the tribunal which is made to serve as its substitute can boast of none of its excellences. This tribunal is usually styled "the Justices and Freeholders' Court." Its constitution, and the manner in which its proceedings are conducted, will be best conveyed to the reader by a transcript of the act of South Carolina:—"*All crimes and offences* committed by slaves in this state, for which *capital* punishment may lawfully be inflicted, shall be heard, examined, tried and adjudged, and finally determined, by any two justices of the peace, and any number of freeholders not less than three nor more than five, in the district where the offence shall be committed, and at a place where they can be most conveniently assembled; either of which justices, on complaint made on information received of any such offence

17

committed by a slave, shall commit the offender to
the safe custody of some constable of the district,
and shall without delay, by warrant under his hand
and seal, call to his assistance and request any one
of the nearest justices of the peace to associate with
him; and shall by the same warrant summon the
number of freeholders aforesaid from the neighbour-
hood to assemble and meet together with the said
justices, at a certain day and place, *not exceeding six
days* after the apprehending of such slave or slaves, &c. ;
and the justices and freeholders, being so assembled,
shall cause the slave accused or charged to be brought
before them, and shall hear the accusation that shall
be brought against such slave or slaves, and his, her
or their defence, and shall proceed to the examination of witnesses and other evidence, and finally
hear and determine the matter brought before them
in the most summary and expeditious manner; and, in
case the accused shall be convicted of any crime for
which by law the punishment would be death, the
said justices shall give judgment and award *such
manner** of death* as the said justices with the consent of said freeholders shall direct, and which they
shall judge will be most effectual to deter others
from offending in the like manner." *James' Dig.*
392–3.   By the last revision of the laws of *Virginia,*
"The county and corporation courts, consisting of

---

* Under the authority here given to the justices and freeholders
"*to award such manner of death* as they may think fit," horrid spec-
tacles are sometimes exhibited to public gaze.   An account of one of
these—i. e. *the burning of a negro woman to death*—may be found in the
daily prints of 1820.

five justices thereof at least, shall be courts of *Oyer and Terminer* for the trial of negroes charged with felony, except in the case of free negroes charged with felonious homicide or an offence punishable with death. Such trial shall be on a charge entered of record stating the offence, BUT WITHOUT JURY *or a presentment, information or indictment.* The court, on the trial of a *slave* for felony, shall assign him counsel, and allow such counsel a fee not exceeding twenty-five dollars, which shall be paid by the owner of the slave. No *slave* shall be condemned *to death,* nor a free *negro* to the penitentiary, unless *all* the justices sitting on his trial shall agree in the sentence." *Code of Virginia, ch.* 212, § 2, 4 *&* 5, *p.* 787. In *Louisiana,* except in the parish of New Orleans, *two justices of the peace* and *ten* owners of slaves, resident in the parish where the crime has been committed, must be summoned as a tribunal for the trial of slaves accused of *capital* offences; but *one justice* and *nine* such persons constitute *a quorum. Statutes of Louisiana of* 1852, *p.* 541. A concurrence of all the members of this tribunal is now necessary to authorize a *conviction or acquittal. Ib.* § 92. "In case such court shall not *convict* or *acquit* the accused of an offence *punishable with death,* it shall have the power to decree the infliction of *such corporal punishment* as it may consider deserved by the prisoner." *Ib.* This last provision is entirely anomalous, and, as it seems to me, highly unjust. Any number less than the whole of which the tribunal consists may consider the accused *innocent* of the charge against him, and be therefore in favour of his *acquittal;* yet, for want of unanimity, (*a single juror dissenting* is enough,) the prisoner is regarded as measurably guilty; or he may perhaps, from the private knowledge of some of the jurors, have committed *some other* offence, or his general character may be bad; and, as a *compromise*, he is directed to be *corporally* punished and let go. The precedent for this seems to be *Acts of the Apostles, ch. 5, verse 40.*

In the best-constituted courts,—where skilful counsel aid the prisoner in his defence,—where a jury of twelve men impartially selected, against whom he has no ground for even the suspicion of an unfavourable bias, must concur in the verdict,—*and with the judge as his legal adviser*, (for such the humanity of the common law considers him,)—it is not to be doubted that innocent persons have in some instances, from the fallibility of human judgment, been condemned to death. At times when the passions of men are highly inflamed, when the offence charged is loudly reprobated by the public voice, or when, in monarchical governments, the strong arm of power is exerted to crush an obnoxious individual, even trial by jury, with all its guards against oppression, is not seldom an inadequate security to the accused. Yet a conviction in such cases can be obtained only through the concurrent decisions of *two distinct* tribunals, each composed of at least twelve men, all of whom act under the most solemn responsibility. What chance of justice, then, has an ignorant slave, under accusation, for example, of exciting an insurrection, before a tribunal chosen by his accuser, suddenly convoked, consisting of but five persons, (a majority of whom in South Carolina may convict,) without any one to countenance or advise him in the conduct of his defence?

The court of justices, &c., it would *appear*, is to continue in session for the trial of *all* slaves against whom complaint has been made. I speak in reference to the law of South Carolina and Louisiana, as not being *entirely* certain on this point; for, as respects Virginia, there can be no doubt that such is the case, inasmuch as the ordinary justices of the county courts make up this extraordinary tribunal for the trial of the slave. Those who are to determine upon the guilt or innocence of another accused of a criminal offence, ought, if possible, to be uninformed, except through the medium of witnesses examined in the particular trial, of the facts alleged against him as grounds for conviction. A permanent tribunal in cases of extensive conspiracies—in insurrections especially—cannot possess this essential qualification. One of the many advantages which appertain to the trial by jury is that each prisoner may, if he so elect, have a separate body to hear and decide between him and his accusers.

The foregoing remarks have an especial bearing on the *constitution* of the justices and freeholders' courts. A law made for the regulation of these courts in the *conduct* of the slave's trial is also obnoxious to severe reprehension. Holding the slave (as indeed all persons who are not white) to be unworthy of belief in a controversy which concerns even the property of a white man, the lawmakers of most of the slave-holding states have neverthe-

less directed the testimony of the slave, without
oath* or solemn affirmation, to be received for or
against a fellow-slave arraigned as the perpetrator of
any criminal offence; and at the same time, in several
of these states, the precious boon of freedom is never
conferred, except for what is termed "*meritorious
services;*" *an important part of which, is, giving information of crimes committed by a slave.* The admission of slave testimony *upon such conditions* can hardly
result beneficially to the accused. In truth, it would
seem, by the preamble of the law of South Carolina
on this head, that *convictions* only were sought for by
the legislature who enacted it. The whole section
reads thus:—"*And for the preventing the concealment of
crimes and offences committed by slaves, and for the more
effectual discovery and bringing slaves to condign punishment,*† Be it enacted, That not only the evidence of
all free Indians without oath, but the evidence of
any slave without oath, shall be allowed and admitted
in all causes whatsoever for or against another slave
accused of any crime or offence whatsoever, the
weight of which evidence, being seriously considered
and compared with all other circumstances attending
the case, shall be left to the conscience of the justices

---

* *Louisiana* and *Georgia* are exceptions to this. In the *former*, on the
trial of *slaves*, free Indians and *slaves* may be examined on *oath*,
(*Statutes of Louisiana*, 543, § 103;) and in the latter, on the trial of
a *slave* or free person of colour, any witness shall be *sworn* who believes in God and a future state of rewards and punishments. *Prince's
Dig.* 461; 2 *Cobb*, 988.

† In Virginia an act was passed in 1705, a part of the title of which
was, "for the *speedy* and *easy* prosecution of slaves committing capital
crimes." See 2 *Tucker's Blackstone, appendix*, 59.

and freeholders." 2 *Brev. Dig.* 232; *James' Dig.* 394. In Virginia, (1 *Rev. Code*, 422 and 431,) in North Carolina and Tennessee, (*Haywood's Manual*, 522,) in Kentucky, (2 *Litt. & Swi.* 1150 and 1153–4,) in Mississippi, (*Rev. Code*, 382,) laws of a similar character may be found, though the meaning is left somewhat to implication.

Hitherto our attention has been *chiefly* confined to the consideration of the trial of the slave when accused of a *capital* offence. Another species of punishment, scarcely less severe, is sometimes imposed. I allude to " *corporal punishment, not extending to life or limb,*"* as it is usually denominated in the acts of Assembly, but which may be more accurately defined as *any torture on the body of a slave which can be practised without producing death or dismemberment. Cutting off the ears*, and *the pillory*, are in considerable favour with the legislatures of Georgia and Delaware. Confinement in *stocks* and the *tread-mill* are author-

---

* This barbarous punishment is not in *terms* licensed in Kentucky. Yet, in point of fact, I fear it may occur there, and yet challenge the sanction of law.   A very high crime—" *advising or consulting to commit murder*"—is punishable, if a *jury* so direct, with one hundred lashes! (2 *Litt. & Swi.* 1161;) "and when any *negro, mulatto* or *Indian* whatsoever shall be convicted of any offence within the benefit of clergy, judgment of death shall not be given against him or her upon such conviction, but he or she shall be burnt in the hand by the jailer in open court, and suffer *such other corporal* punishment as the court shall see fit to inflict." *Act of* 1798, § 20 ; 2 *Morehead & Brown*, 1475. In Georgia and South Carolina, it will be recollected that, terrible as this punishment is, *in one case* at least the slave incurs it, for what in the estimation of no rational being can be accounted a crime or any thing resembling it,—i. e. *the want of success in a trial for freedom before a judicial tribunal!!*   See *supra*, p. 123.

ized in *South Carolina. Act of December 19th,* 1833.
But neither the *pillory* nor *cutting off the ears* is now
allowed. *Ib.* But the punishment of universal prevalence and of perpetual occurrence is *whipping.* The
infliction of this punishment to the *extent* of "twenty
lashes on the bare back, well laid on," is deemed in
a great variety of cases of insufficient moment to
claim the intervention even of a single magistrate.
Any white person—a drunken patrol, an absconding felon, or a vagabond mendicant—is supposed to
possess discretion enough to interpret the laws, and
to wield the cowskin or cart-whip for their infraction;
and, should death ensue by *accident* while the slave
is thus receiving *moderate* correction, the Constitution
of Georgia kindly denominates the offence *justifiable*
homicide!!

In Kentucky, offences by slaves which are not
capital are, with the solitary exception indicated in
the last act, punished with whipping not exceeding
thirty-nine lashes, (2 *Litt. & Swi.* 1160;) and one
justice* of the peace, without the intervention of
a jury, may inquire into and decide upon the guilt
or innocence of the slave charged with the commission of the same. *Ibid.* 1161. The like authority
is vested in a justice of the peace by the laws of
North Carolina, in cases where the punishment cannot exceed the number of forty stripes. *Haywood's
Manual,* 526–7; *Revised Statutes,* 581–2. So, in Vir-

---

* "No jurisdiction ever did exist which is liable to more abuse than
that exercised by magistrates over slaves." Per *O'Neall,* J., in *Ex-parte
Boyleston,* 2 *Strobhart's Rep.* 47.

ginia and Mississippi, many of the breaches of the law, for which the. allotted expiation is whipping, must undergo the examination of a justice of the peace before punishment can be lawfully inflicted. The decision of the justice is, however, final, and the sentence is carried into execution *immediately*.

But in most of the slave-holding states* the ordinary tribunal for the trial of slaves charged with the perpetration of *inferior crimes*, for which the punishment of death is not awarded, is composed of justices and freeholders, or justices only. The number of these varies in a small degree in the different states, being in Virginia *five justices*, (1 *Rev. Code*, 428;) in Georgia, *three*, (*Prince's Dig.* 459;) in Louisiana, one justice and three freeholders, (1 *Martin's Dig.* 645–6;) in South Carolina, one justice and *two* freeholders, (*James' Dig.* 393;) in Mississippi, one justice and two *slave*-holders, (*Miss. Rev. Code*, 391;) in Louisiana, ONE-HALF OF THE COURT MAY CONVICT, ALTHOUGH THE OTHER HALF BE IN FAVOUR OF ACQUITTAL,† (1 *Martin's Dig.* 646;) in South Carolina, a majority (*i. e.* two, one of which must be the justice) is necessary to a conviction; and, except in Virginia, where, as it has been before stated,

---

* In Kentucky the Justices and Freeholders' Court is, I believe, unknown. The Constitution of Missouri, by the extract from it given in this chapter, secures to the slave trial by jury under *every* criminal accusation. A similar provision exists in that of Alabama, for all offences *higher* than petit larceny.

† *I. e.* the *justice* and one freeholder may convict.

unanimity is always required for this purpose, I take it to be the proper construction of the law that a majority constitutes a quorum, and is competent to render judgment either for or against the slave.

CHAPTER IV.

ON THE DISSOLUTION OF SLAVERY.

SECTION 1.—OF THE LAWS FOR THE ABOLITION OF SLAVERY.

The laws which regulate the *voluntary* emancipation of slaves by their masters will form the principal subject of this chapter. But, before entering upon the consideration of these, I purpose furnishing, with but little deviation from chronological order, some notice of the measures by which slavery has been abolished in many of the states.

It is well known that negro slavery was intro· duced into this country by means of the African slave trade prosecuted during the period of our colonial subjection to Great Britain. At the time of our separation from the mother-country, this evil, which had taken deep root at a much earlier date, prevailed more or less in all the British American colonies. It was protected by the laws of each of these, and continued so to be, even after the *Declaration of Independence*, and until the *first day of March*, A. D. 1780, when the first glorious effort for its abolition was made by the COMMONWEALTH OF PENNSYLVANIA. That day gave birth to an act of Assembly, in its consequences second only to the

Declaration of Independence. Its title distinctly proclaimed its object, in words few but of large import:—" AN ACT FOR THE GRADUAL ABOLITION OF SLAVERY."

The preamble to this act contains such just and generous sentiments, depicts with so much force of truth and language the *sorrows* of slavery, and places the arguments for its abolition so concisely and yet so advantageously before the mind, that I cannot refuse myself the pleasure of transcribing it at length:—" When we contemplate our abhorrence of that condition to which the arms and tyranny of Great Britain were exerted to reduce us,—when we look back on the variety of dangers to which we have been exposed, and how miraculously our wants in many instances have been supplied, and our deliverance wrought, when even hope and human fortitude have become unequal to the conflict,—we are unavoidably led to a serious and grateful sense of the manifold blessings which we have undeservedly received from the hand of that Being from whom every good and perfect gift cometh. Impressed with these ideas, we conceive that it is our duty, and we rejoice that it is in our power, to extend a portion of that freedom to others which hath been extended to us, and release from that state of thraldom to which we ourselves were tyrannically doomed, and from which we have now every prospect of being delivered. It is not for us to inquire why, in the creation of mankind, the inhabitants of the several parts of the earth were distinguished by a difference in feature or complexion. It is sufficient to know that all are the work of an Almighty hand. We find, in the distribution of the human species, that the most fertile as well as the most barren parts of the earth are inhabited by men of complexions different from ours and from each other; from whence we may reasonably as well as religiously infer that He who placed them in their various situations hath extended equally his care and protection to all, and that it becometh not us to counteract his mercies. We esteem it a peculiar blessing granted to us, that we are enabled this day to add one more step to universal civilization, by removing as much as possible the sorrows of those who have lived in undeserved bondage, and from which, by the assumed authority* of the kings of Great Britain, no effectual relief could be obtained. Weaned by a long course of experience from those narrow prejudices and partialities we had imbibed, we find our hearts enlarged with kindness and benevolence towards men of all conditions and nations; and we conceive ourselves at this particular

---

* The most signal effort here alluded to on the part of the General Assembly of Pennsylvania, when a colony, to prevent the importation of slaves, was by an act which bears the title, "*An act to prevent the importation of negroes and Indians into this province*," passed June 7th, 1712, but disallowed and accordingly repealed by Queen Anne, on the 20th February, 1713. This act, though repealed, may be found on record in the office of the Secretary of the commonwealth, at Harrisburg, *Book A, vol. 2, page 50*. I am induced to be thus minute in this reference, since the same act is mentioned, in the *Memoirs of the Historical Society of Pennsylvania, vol.* 1, *page* 370, to have been lost. The date there assigned to it is 1711,—an error which has probably misled the person by whom the search was made.

18

period extraordinarily called upon, by the blessings
which we have received, to manifest the sincerity
of our profession, and to give a substantial proof of
our gratitude.

"And whereas the condition of those persons
who have heretofore been denominated negro and
mulatto slaves has been attended with circumstances which not only deprived them of the
common blessings that they were by nature entitled
to, but has cast them into the deepest afflictions by
an unnatural separation and sale of husband and
wife from each other and from their children,—an
injury the greatness of which can only be conceived
by supposing that we were in the same unhappy
case,—in justice, therefore, to persons so unhappily
circumstanced, and who, having no prospect before
them whereon they may rest their sorrows and their
hopes, have no reasonable inducement to render
their service to society, which they otherwise might,
and also in grateful commemoration of our own
happy deliverance from that state of unconditional
submission to which we were doomed by the tyranny of Britain, *Be it enacted,* That all persons, as
well negroes and mulattoes as others, who shall be
born within this state from and after the passing of
this act, shall not be deemed and considered as
servants for life or slaves ; and that all servitude for
life or slavery of children in consequence of the
slavery of their mothers, in the case of all children
born within this state from and after the passing
of this act as aforesaid, shall be and hereby is

UTTERLY TAKEN AWAY, EXTINGUISHED, AND FOREVER
ABOLISHED."
The *fourth* and next section of the act relates to
the children of the slaves which, according to the
foregoing provisions, would be born free. It will
be more properly introduced hereafter.

The *fifth* section made it the duty of the owner
of any slave for life, &c. to cause him or her to be
registered* at a place particularly designated, (the
registry to contain the name, age, and sex of such
slave, and the name, surname, occupation or profession of the master, and the name of the county,
&c. wherein the master resided,) on or before the
first day of November next ensuing the date of
this act, "in order to ascertain and distinguish
the slaves, &c. within this state, who should be
such on the said first day of November, from all
other persons;" and declared that, with certain
exceptions mentioned in other sections of the act,
no negro or mulatto then within the state should,
from and after the said first day of November, be
deemed a slave, &c. unless his or her name, &c.
should be registered as aforesaid; and in the *tenth*
section the latter provision of the *fifth* was in
substance repeated, the language of which being

---

* Many suits have been brought under this act, chiefly in consequence of an omission by the master to register his slaves in due
time, or from some defect in the statement furnished by the master
to the officer by whom the registry was directed to be made. None
of them, however, possess general interest, nor are deemed of sufficient practical value, so much time having elapsed since the passing
of the act, to require particular reference.

as follows:—"No man or woman of any nation or colour, except the negroes and mulattoes who shall be registered as aforesaid, shall at any time hereafter be deemed, adjudged or holden, within the territories of this commonwealth, as slaves or servants for life, but as free men and free women, except the domestic slaves attending upon delegates in Congress from the other American states, foreign ministers and consuls, and persons passing through or sojourning in this state and not becoming resident therein, and seamen employed in ships not belonging to any inhabitant of this state, nor employed in any ship owned by any such inhabitant; *provided*, such domestic slaves be not alienated or sold to any inhabitant, nor (except in the case of members of Congress, foreign ministers and consuls) *retained in this state longer than six months.*"*

---

* It has been decided in Pennsylvania that where the owner of slaves, in Maryland, leased a farm, together with his slaves, to cultivate it, the consent of such lessee that one of the slaves should be removed to Pennsylvania, and his being brought there, would not entitle him to freedom. *Butler and others vs. Delaplaine, 7 Serg. & Rawle's Rep.* 378. Had the *owner* himself consented to such removal the decision would have been different, unless he had been within the *excepted cases* mentioned in this tenth section. It was also decided at the same time that "the sojourning of a master, a citizen of another state, with his slave, in the state of Pennsylvania, would not entitle such slave to freedom, unless there was at some time a continued retaining of the slave here for six months, except perhaps in a case of *fraudulent* removal backwards and forwards."

A decision of JUDGE WASHINGTON, given at Philadelphia, in 1806, at the October term of the *Circuit Court of the United States for the third circuit, &c.,* inasmuch as it recognises the validity of the tenth

But by act of Assembly of 3d March, 1847, "so
much of the act of the General Assembly, entitled

---

section of the abolition act of 1780, may be here introduced. It is
thus reported *in the first volume of Washington's Circuit Court Reports,
page 500, et seq. ; case of Butler vs. Hopper:*—"This case comes before
the court on a special verdict, the material parts of which find that
the plaintiff formerly lived in the state of South Carolina, where, as
well as in Georgia, he had a valuable plantation which he cultivated,
and still cultivates, by his overseers and slaves, and on which he had,
and still has, a furnished house and servants. That from the year 1794 to
the present time, with the exception of an annual visit to his plantations
at the southward, continuing from October in each year till May or June
following, he has kept a dwelling-house in the city of Philadelphia,
and has *resided* in it with his family, consisting of several children and
domestic servants, and among the latter *Ben*, the subject of the present suit, who was his property, as a slave, at the time of his coming
into this city, and who continued with him, claimed as such, until
September, 1805, when he was discharged from his service under a
habeas corpus issued from the Court of Common Pleas of this state.
Whilst on his plantation in South Carolina, during these annual visits,
the plaintiff kept house, always having *Ben* with him. From the
year 1794 until the 4th of January, 1805, the plaintiff represented
the state of South Carolina in Congress, except for two years, between
1796 and 1800, when he was a member of the legislature of that state.
Upon these facts," said Judge Washington, "the question is, whether
Ben became free by virtue of a law of this state, (Pennsylvania,)
passed on the first of March, 1780." (The Judge then quoted the tenth
section of this act.)

After disposing of an objection which had been suggested by the
plaintiff's counsel to the validity of the law, by reason of the ninth
section of article first of the Constitution of the United States, and
showing the inapplicability to the present case of the second section
of article fourth of the same instrument, he proceeded in the following words:—"We come then to the consideration of this law, (act of
1780, tenth section,) and of the facts found in the special verdict.
The plaintiff claims an exemption from the enacting part of the section above stated, upon two grounds:—first, as a member of Congress,
and, *secondly*, as a sojourner. The first will not answer his purpose,

18*

' An act for the gradual abolition of slavery,' passed the 1st day of March, 1780, as authorizes the masters or owners of slaves to bring and retain such slaves within the commonwealth for the period of six months in involuntary servitude, or *for any period of time whatsoever*, is repealed."

The Common Pleas of Philadelphia county has decided that a slave voluntarily brought into this state by his master, since March 3d, 1847, becomes thereby immediately free. *Pierce's case;* 1 *Western Legal Observer*, 14.

The *judge* of the District Court of the *United States* for the Eastern District of Pennsylvania issued a writ of *habeas corpus* on Wednesday, July 18th, 1855, late in the evening, when the court was not in session, against *Williamson*, commanding him to produce the bodies of certain alleged slaves, &c. Proceedings took place afterwards, growing out of the issuing of this writ, the particulars of which

because for two years he ceased to be a member of Congress, and, therefore, lost the privilege which that character might otherwise have conferred upon him under the exception in the law.

" The next question then is, Can the plaintiff be considered as within the other exception of the law,—a sojourner during the period when he ceased to be a member of Congress? But the verdict precludes all inquiry into this point, by finding that the plaintiff, from the year 1794 to the present time, has *resided* with his family in Philadelphia, except at those times when he visited his plantations in the Southern States. No person is entitled to the protection of the exception who is a resident in the state, unless he be a member of Congress, a minister or consul. But the jury find that the plaintiff was a *resident*, and was not either a member of Congress, a minister or consul. The conclusion is inevitable, &c. I am, therefore, of opinion that upon this verdict the law is with *the defendant* "

need not here be stated. In the course of these proceedings an opinion was given by the JUDGE of this court, in which he maintained that the proper construction of the act of March 3d, 1847, did not affect the case of slaves who were landed in Philadelphia not for the purpose of retaining them here, but solely with the view of transporting them to another country. He denied also the constitutionality of this act, on the ground that slaves were articles of property, and therefore that their transportation from one place to another fell within the jurisdiction of the Federal Government exclusively, in virtue of the power in the Constitution given to Congress " to regulate commerce with foreign nations *and among the several states.*"

On this question no case has ever yet been brought *directly* before the *Supreme Court* of the United States. But *incidentally* it has arisen there and been somewhat discussed. I allude particularly to the case of *Groves vs. Slaughter,* 15 *Peter's Reports,* 449.

Two of the judges gave decided opinions, denying that *slaves* were comprehended in this clause of the Constitution and were to be regarded as articles of commerce by the Federal Government.

CHIEF-JUSTICE TANEY uses this language:—" In my judgment, the power over this subject is EXCLUSIVELY *with the several states:* and each of them has a right to decide for itself whether it will or will not *allow persons of this description* to be brought within its limits from another state, either for sale or for any other purpose ; and also to prescribe the manner and mode in which they may be introduced, and to determine their condition and treatment within their respective territories; and the action of the several states upon this subject *cannot be controlled by Congress, either by virtue of its power to regulate commerce, or by virtue of any other power conferred by the Constitution of the United States.*" *Ibid.* 508.

JUDGE McLEAN discussed the same question briefly, and expressed a decided opinion adverse to the existence of this power in Congress. *Ibid,* p. 503.

JUDGE BALDWIN'S views were different, and were given at considerable length. *Ibid.* p. 514.

The subject has, *in the slave states*, been treated as clearly within the jurisdiction of each particular state and over which the Federal Government had no control. And Congress has, again and again, impliedly acquiesced in this construction. For, as has been shown, (*ante,* p. 87, *et seq.*,) several of the older states have passed laws *forbidding* slaves, except under certain circumstances, from being introduced into those states; and in the Constitutions of most of the *new* states a similar prohibition is incorporated. In regard to these new states, Congress, by their admission, has given its sanction to this assumed right of the states.

The *unvarying exposition* of the Constitution on this subject has been consonant with the opinions of CHIEF-JUSTICE TANEY and JUDGE McLEAN.

The import of the fifth and tenth sections could not have been mistaken, had not the legislature inserted between the two, under the name of a *sixth* section, this obscure proviso to the *fifth*,— "Provided always, that any person in whom the ownership or right of service of any negro, &c. shall be vested at the passing of this act, other than such as are hereinbefore excepted, his or her heirs, executors, administrators and assigns, &c. severally shall be liable to the overseers of the poor of the city, township, &c. to which any such negro, &c. shall become chargeable, for such necessary expense, with costs of suits thereon, as such overseers may be put to, through the neglect of the owner, master or mistress of such negro, &c., notwithstanding the same and other descriptions of such negro, &c. shall *not* be entered and recorded as aforesaid, unless his or her master or owner shall, before such slave, &c. attain *his or her twenty-eighth year*, execute and record in the proper county a deed or instrument securing to such slave, &c. his or her freedom."

The introduction of the particle "*not*," which is *italicized* in the above quotation, was supposed to limit the generality and unequivocal meaning of the fifth and tenth sections, as applied to the *absolute* emancipation of persons born as slaves, and who had *not attained the age of twenty-eight years at the date of the act*, and whose masters had omitted to register them according to the direction of the fifth section; and a case of this kind was accordingly brought before the Supreme Court in the year 1789:—"Negro Betsy and two others, Cato and Isaac, who were brought before the court by *habeas corpus* at the same time, were born before the first day of March, 1780, of parents who were held as slaves for life when these children were born; but neither the parents nor the children had been registered by the master agreeably to the directions of the fifth section of the act. The parents, being more than twenty-eight years of age, were admitted to be free; but their former master claimed to retain the children, not as slaves for life, *but as servants until they should severally attain the age of twenty-eight years.*" The case was twice argued; yet ultimately a difference of opinion existed in the court. A majority of the judges, however, decided against the construction contended for on behalf of the master, and thus was established the important principle, "That in Pennsylvania no person born before the first of March, 1780, although born a slave, unless registered before the first day of November of that year, could be held by his or her former master, either as a slave or as a servant for years, but was absolutely free." *See the case, Respublica vs. Negro Betsy et al.* 1 *Dallas' Reports*, 469, *et seq.*

It was deemed inconsistent with the duty which, as a member of the *Union*, Pennsylvania owed to her sister states, to interfere with what in those states were regarded as *rights of property;* and on this account it was expressly provided that nothing contained in the act should give protection to any slave, &c. *absconding** from his or her owner, &c.

---

* Several very important cases have arisen under this section of the act. One of these, reported in the *second volume of Sergeant &*

residing in any other state, and coming into this
state. See 1 *Smith's Laws of Pennsylvania*, 492, *et seq*.
Such were the leading provisions of the first act
which was passed in the United States of America
for the abolition of slavery. Its plain intent was to
diminish gradually the number of slaves among us,
and eventually to destroy the institution itself. By
the positive terms of its enactments none could
thereafter be born as slaves; and from its whole
scope and spirit it was evidently opposed to the
introduction of any of this denomination of persons
from the neighbouring states. On the 29th of
March, 1788, it was, however, found necessary for
further legislative aid in the grand cause which had
been so nobly entered upon in 1780; and an act was
passed on that day, which recites, "For preventing
many evils and abuses, arising from ill-disposed
persons availing themselves of certain defects in the
act for the gradual abolition of slavery, passed on
the first day of March, in the year of our LORD one
thousand seven hundred and eighty, *Be it enacted,*

Rawle's Reports, p. 305, *et seq.,* was of this kind:—"*Mary,* a negro
woman, the slave of *James Corse,* of *Maryland,* absconded from her
master, and came into the state of *Pennsylvania,* in which, after a
residence of about two years, she became the mother of a female
child. The owner of the mother claimed the child as his slave, and,
having obtained possession of her person, committed her to the prison
of the city and county of *Philadelphia.* She was afterwards brought
before the Judges of the Supreme Court, by writ of *habeas corpus.*
The sole question before the court was, whether *birth in Pennsylvania*
gave freedom to the child of a slave who had absconded from another
state *before she became pregnant.* The court decided in the affirmative,—that Eliza (the child) was not a slave,—and she was accordingly
set at liberty.

That the *exception* contained in the *tenth* section of the act of first March, 1780, relative to domestic slaves attending upon persons passing through or sojourning in this state, and not becoming resident therein, shall not be deemed or taken to extend to the slaves of such persons as are inhabitants of or residents in this state, or who shall come here with an intention to settle and reside; but all and every slave and slaves who shall be brought into this state, by persons inhabiting or residing therein, or intending to inhabit or reside therein, shall be immediately considered, deemed and taken to be free, to all intents and purposes." 2 *Smith's Laws of Pennsylvania*, 443.

The abolition of slavery in *Massachusetts* takes its date *one day* LATER than the date of the abolition law of *Pennsylvania*. It was not effected there by a *direct and intentionally specific act* of the legislature, but resulted as a consequence of the primary article in the *bill of rights* prefixed to the *Constitution* of the state,—the language of which article is, "All men are born free and equal, and have certain natural, essential and unalienable rights, among which may be reckoned the right of enjoying and defending their lives and liberties; that of acquiring, possessing and protecting property; in fine, that of seeking and obtaining their safety and happiness."

This declaration, embodied as it was in the Constitution, became at once the paramount law of the land; and, though so totally repugnant to its *spirit* as well as to its *letter* was the enslavement of one part of the human family by another, that, as it appears to me, but one opinion could, with the least show of reason, be entertained on the subject, yet it was not till after a solemn adjudication of the courts *that slavery was by this means forever abolished* in Massachusetts,—that in *practice* it was considered so to be. See *Winchenden vs. Hatfield*, 4 *Massachusetts Reports*, 129.

Connecticut appears to have been the earliest among her sister states to follow the precedent of Pennsylvania. At a special session held in January, 1784, for the purpose of revising and amending her code of laws, the legislature agreed to incorporate this section:—"No negro or mulatto child, that shall after the first day of March, 1784, be born within this state, shall be held in servitude longer than until they arrive to the age of twenty-five years, notwithstanding the mother or parent of such child was held in servitude at the time of its birth, but such child, at the age aforesaid, shall be free," &c. See *Statutes of Connecticut*, 625.

Probably about the same time (the *precise* date is not mentioned in the work which is in my possession) the legislature of *Rhode Island* enacted a law on the same subject, varying in a slight degree from that of Connecticut, yet fixing the same day as the period at which hereditary servitude should cease, as the subjoined extract will show:—"No person born within this state on or after the *first day of March*, A.D. 1784, shall be deemed or considered a servant for life or a slave ; and all servitude for life or slavery of children to be born as aforesaid, in consequence of the condition of their mothers, shall be

19

and the same is hereby taken away, extinguished and forever abolished." *Laws of Rhode Island*, 443; (*"An act relative to slaves, and their manumission and support,"* § 8.)

The importation of slaves into the state of Connecticut having been prohibited in October, 1774, and in Rhode Island, it is believed, at a period equally remote, the *entire* abolition of slavery in these states, as well as in Pennsylvania, may be now considered as virtually accomplished.

New Hampshire having in her Constitution, which was finally ratified on the eighth day of February, 1792, inserted a provision of similar import, and comprised indeed in nearly the same words with that already cited from the Constitution of Massachusetts, has by *implication* also abolished slavery within her territory.

The same important doctrine previously promulgated, as it is well known to have been, in the memorable Declaration of our Independence on Great Britain, has served the like glorious purpose in the state of *Vermont*. The citizens of *Vermont*, however, were not content with *implication* on such a momentous article of their political faith, but wisely established, by *distinct enunciation*, the *inference* as well as the *principle* which they so justly revered. I give the whole article, notwithstanding it enters more into detail than is altogether necessary:—

"That all men are born equally free and independent, and have certain natural, inherent and unalienable rights, among which are the enjoying and defending life and liberty, acquiring, possessing and protecting property, and pursuing and obtaining happiness and safety; THEREFORE, no male person born in this country or brought from over the sea ought to be holden by law to serve any person as a servant, slave or apprentice, after he arrives to the age of twenty-one years, nor female, in like manner, after she arrives to the age of eighteen years, unless they are bound by their own consent after they arrive at such age, or bound by law, for the payment of debts, damages, fines, costs or the like." *See the Constitution of Vermont, ch.* 1, *art.* 1. The date of the Constitution is *July 4th,* 1793.

The first act of the state of *New York* on this subject was designed to work a *gradual* abolition of slavery in that state. It bears date the 29*th day of March,* 1799, and provides that all children born of slaves after the 4*th of July,* 1799, should be held by the owner of the mothers of the same only until they should respectively attain to the age of twenty-eight years, if males; and, if females, until the age of twenty-five years. Another act, of similar import so far as respects the point under examination, was passed *April 8th,* 1801. But by an act of the 31*st of March, one thousand eight hundred and seventeen,* a final blow was given in that state to the dominion of the slave-holder. The fourth section of this act is as follows:—"Every child born of a slave within this state, after the fourth day of July, in the year of our LORD one thousand seven hundred and ninety-nine, shall be free, but shall remain the servant of the owner of his or her mother and the executors, administrators or assigns of such owner, in the same manner as if such child had been bound to service by the overseers of the poor, and shall continue in such service, if a male, until the age of twenty-eight years; and, if a female, until the age of twenty-five years; and every child born of a slave within this state, after the passing of this act, shall remain a servant as aforesaid until the age of twenty-one years, and no longer." And by the thirty-second section of the same act it was declared that "Every negro, mulatto or mustee, within this state, born before the fourth day of July, 1799, should, from and after *the fourth day of July,* 1827, BE FREE." This auspicious day has gone by; and there is, therefore, at this moment, not a slave within the wide-spread territory of this prosperous state.

After several ineffectual* efforts on the part of the advocates of human rights, an act was at length obtained, on the 14th day of February, 1804, from the legislature of *New Jersey*, entitled "An act for the gradual abolition of slavery." It differs in nothing material to the present inquiry from the law of *Rhode Island,* except that white male children born of slaves, after the 4*th day of July*, 1804, may be retained *as servants* by the owners of their mothers, until the age of twenty-five years only, and female children in like manner, until the age of twenty-one years only. See *Revised Laws of New Jersey*, 679.

The six non-slave-holding states,—*Ohio, Indiana,*

---

* One of these efforts was frustrated by a *single* vote in the House of Assembly. This was six years before the passing of the law in the text.

Illinois, Michigan, Wisconsin and *Iowa*, it is well known, derive this important characteristic from the "ordinance for the government of the territory of the United States northwest of the river Ohio," which was ratified by Congress July 13th, 1787. The ordinance recites and adopts certain articles, previously agreed upon by the states of Massachusetts, Connecticut, New York and Virginia, in the compact* by which these states ceded the Northwestern Territory to the Federal Government. The articles alluded to are styled "Articles of compact between the original states and the people and states within the said territory, *forever to remain unalterable, unless by common consent,*" the sixth of which provides, "There shall be neither slavery nor involuntary servitude in said territory, otherwise than in the punishment of crimes whereof the party shall have been duly convicted."

Six states have been formed out of the Northwestern Territory,—namely, *Ohio, Indiana, Illinois, Michigan, Wisconsin* and *Iowa.* In the Constitution of each of these, a prohibition of slavery, in language nearly the same as that which was used in the ordinance of the Northwestern Territory, is contained. *Constitution of Ohio,* of 1802, *art.* 8, § 2 ; and of 1851, *art.* 1, § 6. *Constitution of Indiana,* of 1816,

---

* Notwithstanding the solemnity with which this compact was originally entered into and afterwards ratified by the Congress of the United States, and notwithstanding, also, the plain and strong prohibition of slavery contained in the sixth article, a violent endeavour was made several years since, in *Illinois,* to obtain a convention of delegates, in order to expunge the prohibition inserted in the Constitution of that state!

19*

art. 11, § 7 ; and of 1851, *art.* 1, § 37. *Constitution of Illinois*, of 1818, *art.* 6, § 1 ; and of 1847, *art.* 13, § 16. *Constitution of Michigan*, of 1850, *art.* 18, § 11. *Constitution of Wisconsin*, of 1848, *art.* 1, § 2. *Constitution of Iowa*, of 1846, *art.* 2, § 23. *California*, in which, happily, *Mexico* had abolished slavery while its territory constituted an integral part of that republic, wisely elected to prevent its restoration there, and accordingly in its Constitution inserted an absolute prohibition. *Art.* 1, § 18.

The state of *Maine* is the only remaining non-slave-holding state. As the territory of which it is composed was a part of the state of Massachusetts until, within a few years since, *Maine*, as a distinct sovereignty, has never been contaminated with slavery. Her Constitution, moreover, adopted October 29th, 1819, by a convention chosen for the purpose by the freemen within the limits of her territory, and ratified by Congress on March 2d, 1821, contains the same grand declaration of unalienable rights which gave unconditional freedom to all slaves within the parent state. See *Const. of Maine, art.* 1, § 1.

It will be observed, from the notices here given, that the abolition of slavery in the states above mentioned has been of two kinds, — *gradual* and *immediate.* In those states in which it has been *gradual*, prejudice, the effect of long-established practice, and the spirit of gain which so frequently overpowers the sense of justice, have usually made a difference in the condition of the white population and of such of the coloured as have been exempted from slavery for life, unfavourable to the rights and happiness of the latter. Thus in Pennsylvania, by the fourth section of the abolition act, it is enacted "That every negro or mulatto child born within this state after the passing of this act, &c. (who would, in case this act had not been made, have been born a servant for years or life, or a slave) shall be deemed to be, and shall be, by virtue of this act, the servant of such person or his or her assigns, who would in such case have been entitled to the service of such child until such child shall attain unto the age of *twenty-eight* years, in the manner and on the conditions whereon servants bound by indenture for four years are or may be retained and holden, &c. &c."*

So in Connecticut, according to the section already extracted, the same class of persons might be held, not as servants bound by indenture, but as slaves,

---

* The want of precision in the phraseology used in this section seems to have induced an opinion, with some persons, that *the servitude for twenty-eight years* which is authorized by this section was not confined to the *immediate offspring* of those who were slaves at the date of the abolition act, but was designed to be extended to their DESCENDANTS, *if duly registered*, to the remotest generation. The case of *The Commonwealth vs. Barker*, 11 *Sergt. & Rawle's Rep.* 360, presented this point for the decision of the court; but, as the registry was defective, the court, on the ground of this *defect* alone, ordered the person claimed as such servant to be discharged, declaring at the same time that the former was a point of great importance, upon which no opinion was intimated. But in a later case, in which the *evaded* point came again before the same court, it was decided that the species of servitude alluded to did not extend beyond the immediate offspring of *slaves;* that the children of coloured *servants* were, in this particular, on the same footing with the children of white persons. 14 *Sergt. & Rawle's Rep.* 442, *Miller vs. Dwilling*.

until they should arrive at *twenty-five* years of age.
At the present time the law there is somewhat different, it having been enacted in May, 1797, that
"no negro or mulatto child born within this state
after the first day of August, 1797, shall be held in
servitude longer than until he arrives to the age of
twenty-one years, &c., but that such child, at the age
aforesaid, shall be free." *Statutes of Connecticut*, 626.
Accordant with this latter section of the laws of
Connecticut is the law of Rhode Island. See *Laws
of Rhode Island*, 443, *section 9th of the act relative to
slaves, &c.*

In New York, by the acts of 1799 and of 1801,
every child born of a slave within the state, after
the 4th of July, 1799, was declared to be free, but
might be retained by the owner of the mother, &c.
as a servant, in the same manner as if bound to
service by the overseers of the poor; if a male,
until he should arrive to the age of *twenty-eight* years
of age, and if a female until *twenty-five* years of age.
This section was re-enacted by the act of 31st of
March, 1817, with this important supplement, that
every such child born after the passing of the last
act should "remain a servant as aforesaid until the
age of *twenty-one* years and *no longer*." So that the
only distinction which now exists on this subject in
the state of New York between the condition of the
white population and the children born of slaves
since the 31st March, 1817, is, that *females* as well as
males may be held as servants till they attain the
age of *twenty-one* years, instead of being freed at the
age of *eighteen* years.

The abolition act of New Jersey conforms to the precedent of Pennsylvania with respect to the general principle here adverted to, yet humanely diminishes the period of servitude to *twenty-five* years in the case of *males*, and to *twenty-one* in the case of *females*.

The term *gradual*, in its usual acceptation as applied to the abolition of slavery, and as it is to be understood in the acts of Assembly before quoted, as also in the remarks which I have made upon them, is restricted in its signification to the extinction of slavery, by depriving it of its *hereditary* quality. A *gradual* abolition act operates *to prevent* the enslavement of the unborn, while it leaves unaffected the condition of those already in being. Such were the abolition acts of Pennsylvania, Connecticut, Rhode Island, New Jersey, and the *first two* abolition acts of the state of New York. But a measure which communicates freedom to those previous to and at the time of its adoption held as slaves is here called *immediate*, whether such freedom be conferred instantaneously, or whether it be postponed to a point of time future in relation to the date of the measure. This distinction comprehends the *last* abolition act of New York, as also the *constitutional* provisions of Massachusetts, New Hampshire and Vermont, and the sixth article of the ordinance of Congress of 1787 for the government of the territory northwest of the Ohio.

Slaves being considered *property*, it has been said an immediate abolition act like that of New York would be *unconstitutional,* unless compensation should be made to their former owners to the extent of their value. But men, *as such,* by nature are equally free; it is impossible, therefore, that one can acquire a right over the person of another unless by his consent. Involuntary servitude, unless inflicted by society as the punishment of crime, is a usurpation of power; and it would be strange if society at its pleasure might not put an end to its own wrong. On a theme so hackneyed, however, it is unnecessary to waste argument; and happily, in the state of New York, a new Constitution has been adopted since the passing of the abolition act, and the acts of the legislature in force at the adoption of the Constitution have been expressly declared in that instrument to be valid. The abolition act, therefore, may be regarded as a part of the present Constitution itself.

The abolition of slavery in Massachusetts and New Hampshire was effected, as has been stated, by force of the first article of the declaration of rights prefixed to their respective Constitutions. In Massachusetts, an express decision of the Supreme Court of that state has established this construction. No unprejudiced intelligence can, I believe, find fault with this decision. The language of the article must be wrested from its proper and obvious signification to give countenance to any other conclusion. And yet, in *Pennsylvania,* the birthplace of efficient hostility to negro bondage, the highest judicial tribunal of the state has pronounced, as the result of its solemn deliberation on *a similar article of her*

Constitution, that slavery was not inconsistent with it.* This mockery of justice took place on the twenty-third day of January, in the year of our Lord one thousand eight hundred and two. It took

---

* This case is not to be found in the books of reports. It may, therefore, be proper to give some further notice of it. It was instituted in the Supreme Court, to January term, 1795, by a writ *de homine replegiando,* and is entitled, on the docket, *Negro Flora vs. Joseph Graisberry.* The defendant having died, his executors, John Reed and James Glentworth, were substituted, agreeably to an act of Assembly providing for such contingencies. On the 15th of December, 1797, the trial came on, when a special verdict was found by the jury, on the suggestion and by the consent of counsel, and at March term, 1798, judgment was entered for the defendant, "for the purpose," as it stated in the record, "of an appeal to the High Court of Errors and Appeals, and that the justices of this court may there assist in hearing and determining it." On the 20th of January, 1802, the hearing took place before the High Court of Errors and Appeals. *Jared Ingersoll, William Rawle,* and *William Lewis, Esquires,* were of counsel with the plaintiff; and, from the known character of these gentlemen, it is to be inferred that, during the four days which were occupied in the hearing, no argument which ingenuity and learning could supply was wanting. The judges, with a reserve more convenient to themselves than convincing to their hearers, were content with the brief declaration, announced through their president, "that it was their unanimous opinion slavery was not inconsistent with any clause of the Constitution of Pennsylvania;" in conformity with which, judgment was entered on the record:—"court unanimously of opinion that negro Flora is a slave, and that she is the property of the defendants in error, and the judgment of the Supreme Court is affirmed."

I believe that the decision just referred to is the only one upon the construction of any part of the Constitution of Pennsylvania of 1790 which was made *prior* to *Hobbs vs. Fogg,* 6 *Watts,* 553, in the year 1838; and, consequently, that *Hobbs vs. Fogg* had no such support as was vouched for it on that occasion.

The point decided in *Hobbs vs. Fogg* was that, by the Constitution of 1790, the right of suffrage was confined to *whites;* and the late

place after the most able and ample discussion by counsel. It was not suddenly cast forth in the hurry of a *nisi prius* trial and by a single judge, but the record is stamped with the *unanimous* sanction of seven men claiming to be in the full possession of intellectual faculties of no common order, and acting upon mature consideration. Such are the deplorable effects of long familiarity with injustice and oppression.

General principles of political government, militating against the existence of slavery, are asserted in the Constitutions of most of the slave-holding states; yet care has been taken to qualify their bearing by some express declaration, importing that the rights of *freemen* only were designed to be pro-

---

James Gibson, Esq., was said to have remembered that this very point had arisen "about the year 1795," and was determined by the *High Court of Errors and Appeals* in favour of such restriction.

Mr. Gibson was unable to remember any thing about the case, except that it had arisen and been decided in the way mentioned by him; that he had been *invited* to take part in the *argument* before the court, but had declined to do so. He could not remember *the names of the parties, nor of any of the counsel*, nor any other concomitant circumstance. No trace of such a case can be found in the records of the court. This was accounted for on the ground "that the papers of the court had fallen into disorder." This *I know* to be a *mistake.* In 1826 or 1827 I examined them, and found them in a state of excellent preservation and in perfect order. I have, since the decision of *Hobbs vs. Fogg*, re-examined them, and feel warranted in saying I believe that the minutes of the court were so well kept and remain so perfect that every proceeding of the court during the fifteen years of its existence may be satisfactorily traced out and ascertained. *Negro Flora vs. Graisberry*, it will be seen, had its origin in the year 1795,—the very year which Mr. Gibson names for the decision which he remembered; but he mistook the point in controversy.

tected. The Constitution of the state of *Delaware*, though a slave-holding state, seems to have been framed with somewhat less caution on this subject. It sets forth, that, "Through divine goodness, *all men* have, by nature, the rights of worshipping and serving their Creator according to the dictates of their consciences ; OF ENJOYING AND DEFENDING LIFE AND LIBERTY ; *of acquiring and protecting reputation and property;* and, in general, *of attaining objects suitable to their condition* WITHOUT INJURY BY ONE TO ANOTHER." Here we have a charter of liberty of sufficient amplitude. How far it may be considered as annihilated by what follows in connection—"and, as these rights are essential to their welfare for the due exercise thereof, power is inherent in them; and *therefore* all just authority in the institutions of a political society is derived from the· people, and established with their consent to advance their happiness, and they may, for this end, as circumstances require, from time to time, alter their constitution of government"—will depend very much on the moral sentiments of those who pass judgment upon the question.

Section II.—ON THE LAWS REGULATING THE EMAN-CIPATION OF SLAVES.

Slavery, being *hereditary*, may, of consequence, be rendered *perpetual*, if such be the will of the master of the slave. From a just consideration of the rights of *property*, it would seem equally plain that the master might, at his pleasure, relinquish his dominion over the slave. But society, in our slave-

holding states, has decreed otherwise. Having degraded a rational and immortal being into a *chattel*,
—a thing of bargain and sale,—it has been discovered that certain incidents result from this degradation which it concerns the welfare of the
community vigorously to exact and preserve. One
of these is, that the master's benevolence to his
unhappy bondman is not to be exercised, by
emancipation, *without the consent of his creditor*. This
is a principle of law which pervades nearly every
code in the slave-holding states.

In Virginia and Mississippi, Alabama and Arkansas, an emancipated slave may be taken in execution to satisfy *any debt* contracted by the person
emancipating him previous to such emancipation.
1 *Rev.* (*Vir.*) *Code*, 434; *Mississippi Rev. Code*, 386;
Clay's Dig. 542; *Digest of* (*Arkansas*) *Statutes*, 476.
In Kentucky, the act which authorizes emancipation and directs the mode by which it may be
effected contains a *saving* of the rights of creditors,
&c. 2 *Litt. & Swi.* 1155, § 27, (*act of* 1798.)

By the new civil code of Louisiana it is declared:—"Any enfranchisement made in *fraud of
creditors*, or of the portion reserved by law to forced
heirs, is null and void; *and such fraud shall be considered as* PROVED, *when it shall appear that, at the moment of executing the enfranchisement*, THE PERSON
GRANTING IT HAD NOT SUFFICIENT PROPERTY TO PAY
HIS DEBTS." *Art.* 190.

But in addition to the obstacle to emancipation
which is created by the *saving* in favour of creditors,
a very extraordinary one is opposed on behalf of

the *widows* of deceased slave-holders. For where a widow is entitled by law to one-third of her deceased husband's personal estate, unless he shall have left sufficient other personal estate, after payment of his debts, to satisfy her claim of one-third, his slaves, though declared to be free by his last will, shall nevertheless *not* be free, but shall be held liable for the *third* to which the widow is entitled. 1 *Vir. Rev. Code*, 435 ; *Mississippi Rev. Code*, 386 ; 2 *Litt & Swi.* (*Kentucky*) 1246.

But it is in the mode by which emancipation is to be effected that the most formidable difficulties arise. In South Carolina,* Georgia, Alabama and Mississippi, it is only *by authority of the legislature specially granted* that a valid emancipation can be made. It is not enough that a penalty is imposed upon the benevolence of a master who may permit his slave to work for himself; a slave-owner must continue a slave-owner, (unless he dispose of his *chattels* by *sale*,) until he can induce the legislature

---

* In South Carolina, before the passing of the act of 1820, here referred to, the law stood thus :—"No emancipation of any slave shall be valid, except it be by deed, and according to the regulations above described, (which regulations made it necessary for the person intending to emancipate a slave to obtain the approbation of a justice of the quorum and five freeholders,) and accompanied by the above certificate," (*i. e.* the certificate of the justice and freeholders.) 2 *Brevard's Dig.* 256. With such strictness was this law construed, that where a testator made a bequest of slaves to a trustee, *with directions to liberate them*, it was held by the Court of Chancery to be a void bequest, and that therefore the slaves might be retained in perpetual servitude. *See the case of Byrnum vs. Bostwick ; 4 Dessaussure's Chancery Reports*, 266.

to indulge him in the wish to set the captives free. *Prince's Dig.* 456, (*act of Dec.* 5, 1801;) *James' Dig.* 398, (*act of* 1820;) *Toulmin's Dig.* 632; *Mississippi Rev. Code,* 386.

In Georgia, the *attempt* to set free a slave by any other mode than by an application to the legislature is visited with severe penalties, as will appear from the following act:—"If any person or persons shall (after the passing of this act, 1801) set free any slave or slaves, in any other manner and form than the one prescribed herein, (*i. e.* by special legislative act,) he shall forfeit for every such *offence two hundred dollars,* to be recovered by action of debt, or *indictment,* the one-half to be applied to the use of the county in which the *offence* may have been committed, the other half to the use of the informer; and the said slave or slaves so manumitted and set free *shall be still to all intents and purposes as much in a state of slavery as before they were manumitted and set free* by the party or parties so offending." *Prince's Dig.* 457; 2 *Cobb's Dig.* 982. By a subsequent act, the penalty *for this offence* is increased to *five hundred dollars.* 2 *Cobb's Digest,* 990. Notwithstanding the punishment thus imposed for this *new* crime which the Christian people of the republic of Georgia have seen fit to create in the nineteenth century, some refractory heretic, it is presumed, must have been found within her borders; for in the year 1818 the following act was added to her code:—"All and every will and testament, deed, whether by way of trust or otherwise, contract or agreement or stipulation, or other instrument in writing, or by parole,

made and executed for the purpose of effecting or
endeavouring to effect the manumission of any slave
or slaves, either directly by conferring or attempting to confer freedom on such slave or slaves,
indirectly or virtually by allowing and securing or
attempting to allow and secure to such slave or
slaves the right or privilege of working for his, her
or themselves, free from the control of the master
or owner of such slave or slaves, or of enjoying the
profits of his, her or their labour or skill, shall be
and the same are hereby declared to be utterly null
and void; and the person or persons so making,
&c. any such deed, &c. &c., and all and every person
or persons concerned in giving or attempting to
give effect thereto, whether by accepting the trust
thereby created or attempted to be created, or in any
other way or manner whatsoever, shall be severally
liable to a penalty not exceeding *one thousand dollars*, to be recovered, &c. &c.; and each and every
slave or slaves in whose behalf such will or testament, &c. &c. shall have been made shall be liable
to be arrested by warrant under the hand and seal
of any magistrate of this state, and, being thereof
convicted, &c., shall be liable to be sold as a slave or
slaves, by public outcry, and the proceeds of such
sales shall be appropriated, &c. &c." *Prince's Dig.*
466; 2 *Cobb*, 991.

Formerly, in *North Carolina*, a slave could not be
manumitted *except for meritorious services*, to be adjudged of and allowed by the county court, (*Haywood's Manual*, 525;) but by the *Rev. Statutes* of 1836–7,
the court on the petition in writing of the master,

and his entering into a bond with two sufficient securities, in the sum of one thousand dollars, conditioned that the slave so to be emancipated shall honestly and correctly demean himself while he shall remain within the state, and that he will, within ninety days after granting the prayer of the petitioner to emancipate him, *leave the state and never afterwards come within the same*, may permit such emancipation. The rights of creditors are expressly saved.

The same end may be attained by a compliance essentially with the same terms on the part of executors of a last will, in which the testator has authorized his executors to emancipate a slave. *Rev. Statutes*, 585.

The law of *Tennessee* on this subject requires the presentation of a petition to the county court, "setting forth the intention and motives for such emancipation;" and these must be consistent, *in the opinion of the court*, with the interest and policy of the state to authorize its reception. The emancipator must give a bond with sufficient security conditioned that the emancipated slave shall *forthwith* remove from the state. *Laws of Tennessee*, 277-9; (*act of* 1801, *ch.* 27, and *of* 1831, *ch.* 102.)

Mississippi has combined in one act all the obstacles to emancipation which are to be met with in the laws of the other slave-holding states. Thus, the emancipation must be by an *instrument in writing*, a last will or deed, &c. *under seal, attested by at least two credible witnesses, or acknowledged in the court of the county or corporation* where the emancipator resides;

*and proof satisfactory to the General Assembly must be
adduced that the slave has done some meritorious act for
the benefit of his master, or rendered some distinguished
service to the state;* all which circumstances are but
prerequisites, and are of no efficacy until a *special act
of Assembly* sanctions the emancipation ;—to which
may be added, as has been already stated, *a saving
of the rights of creditors* and the protection of *the
widow's third. Mississippi Rev. Code,* 385–6, (*act of
June 18th,* 1822.)

In Kentucky, Missouri, Virginia, Maryland, and
Arkansas, greater facility is afforded to emancipation. The first-named of these states enacted in
1798 the following law, which continues still in
force :—" It shall be lawful for any person, by his or
her last will and testament, or by any other instrument in writing, under his or her hand and seal,
attested and proved in the county court by two
witnesses or acknowledged by the party in the
court of the county where he or she resides, to
emancipate or set free his or her slave or slaves,
who shall thereupon be entirely and fully discharged from the performance of any contract
entered into during their servitude, and enjoy their
full freedom as if they had been born free. And
the said court shall have full power to demand bond
and sufficient security of the emancipator, his or her
executors, &c. for the maintenance of any slave or
slaves that may *be aged or infirm* either of body or
mind, to prevent him, her or them becoming
chargeable to the county; and every slave so emancipated shall have a certificate of his freedom from

the clerk of such court on parchment, with the county seal affixed thereto, &c., *saving, however, the rights of creditors*, &c. &c." 2 *Litt. & Swi.* 1155. And in 1800, in consequence of a humane law particularly noticed in a previous page* of this sketch, by which slaves were constituted *real estate*, and therefore, so far as concerns *the law of descents*, not subject to disposition by the will of a *minor* or by a deed executed by him, an act was passed to remove this impediment, declaring "That any person of the age of *eighteen* years, being possessed of or having a right to any slave or slaves, may, by his last will and testament, or by an instrument in writing, emancipate such slave or slaves." *Ibid.* 1247.

The law of Missouri on this subject bears so close an analogy to the law of Kentucky of 1798 as not to call for a particular recital. See 2 *Missouri Laws*, 744.

In Virginia the law of emancipation has undergone many changes since the year 1699, when the first legislative interposition happened. By an act of that year the emancipation of any negro or mulatto slave was rendered nugatory unless the emancipator *should send his freedman out of the country within six months* from the time of his emancipation; and, in default of so doing, the church-wardens were authorized to apprehend and sell him. 3 *Henning's Statutes*, 87. Another act was passed in 1723, forbidding emancipation, except for *meritorious* services, to be adjudged of by the governor and council.

---

* See *supra, note* †, p. 35.

4 *Ibid.* 132. In 1782 this restraint on the power of the master to emancipate his slave was removed, and since that time the master may emancipate by *his last will or deed.* By the *Code of Virginia* of 1848–9, "Any person may emancipate any of his slaves *by last will in writing* or *by deed recorded* in the court of his county or corporation:" p. 458. The usual saving of the rights of *creditors* is retained; but some modification was made in the harsh provision noticed on page 27 of this sketch, by which emancipated slaves were compelled to abandon the state after twelve months from the time at which they became free. *Ibid.* 466. But, by the last *Constitution* of the state, (of 1851–2,) this inhuman policy has been restored, as is shown by the following provision:—"Slaves hereafter emancipated shall FORFEIT *their freedom* by remaining in the commonwealth more than twelve months after they became *actually* free, and SHALL BE REDUCED TO SLAVERY under such regulations as may be prescribed by law."

The existing law of Maryland on this subject takes its date from the act of 1796, *ch.* 67,—the 29th section of which is in these words:—"Where any person or persons possessed of any slave or slaves within this state, who are or shall be of *healthy constitutions* and sound in mind and body, capable by labour to procure to him or them sufficient food and raiment, with the requisite necessaries of life, and not exceeding forty-five years of age, and* such person or persons possessing such

---

* The word *and*, though in the law, should be stricken out.

slave or slaves as aforesaid may by writing, under
his, her or their hand and seal, evidenced by two
good and sufficient witnesses at least, grant to such
slave or slaves his, her or their freedom; and any
deed or writing whereby freedom shall be given or
granted to any such slave, which shall be intended
to take place in future,* shall be good to all intents,
constructions and purposes whatsoever, from the
time that such freedom or manumission is intended

---

* In a case of this kind, where a future point of time is fixed at
which the slave is to be free, it is plain he ought to be regarded not
as an absolute slave, but merely as bound to a servitude *for years*.
According to the maxim that the condition of the *issue* depends upon
the condition of the *mother*, it would, therefore, follow that the issue
born of female slaves *so circumstanced*, during the period of *their
mother's servitude for years*, should not be considered slaves for life.
Whether such issue should be held as *slaves for life*, or should be
regarded as *free*, seems not to have been well settled by the courts.
To remove all doubt on this subject, as on some other nearly similar
cases, it was enacted "That from and after the first day of February,
1810, if any negro or mulatto female slave, by testament, or last will,
or deed of manumission, shall be declared to be free after any given
period of service, or at any stipulated age, or upon the performance
of any condition, or on the event of any contingency, it shall be lawful for the person making such last will, &c. &c. to fix and determine in the same the state and condition of the issue that may be
born of such negro or mulatto female slave during their period of
service." So far the act is judicious; but in the next section it is
provided that, in the event that the testator, &c. shall not determine
the condition of the issue so born, they shall be esteemed *slaves for
life! ! Maryland Laws*, (act of *Nov.* 1809, *ch.* 171.). In *Virginia*, by
the Code of 1849, the *increase* of any female emancipated by *deed* or
will thereafter made, born between the death of the testator or the
record of the deed and the time when her right to the enjoyment of
her freedom arrives, *shall also be free* at that time, *unless the deed or
will otherwise provides.* pp. 458–9.

to commence by the said deed or writing, so that such deed and writing be not in *prejudice of creditors*, and that such slave, at the time such freedom or manumission shall take place or commence, be not above the age aforesaid, and be able to work and gain a sufficient livelihood and maintenance, according to the true intent and meaning of this act, which instrument of writing shall be acknowledged before one justice of the peace of the county wherein the person or persons so granting such freedom shall reside, which justice shall endorse on the back of such instrument the time of the acknowledgment, and the party making the same, which he or they, or the parties concerned, shall cause to be entered among the records of the county court where the person or persons granting such freedom shall reside, within six months after the date of such instrument of writing; and the clerk of the respective county courts within the state shall, immediately upon the receipt of such instrument, endorse the time of his receiving the same, and shall well and truly enroll such deed or instrument in a good and sufficient book, in folio, to be regularly alphabeted in the names of both parties, and to remain in the custody of the said clerk, for the time being, among the records of the respective county courts; and that the said clerk shall on the back of every such instrument, in a full, legible hand, make an endorsement of such enrollment, and also of the folio of the book in which the same shall be enrolled, and to such endorsement set his hand, the person or persons requiring such entry paying the usual and legal fees for the same." Emancipation is also authorized by the same act, to be made by *last will and testament*, subject to the same restrictions which are imposed in case the emancipation is effected by deed, &c. agreeably to the above section. *Ibid.* § 13.*

The state of Louisiana directs emancipation to be made in the manner set forth in the following articles of her new Civil Code:—"A master may manumit his slave in this state, either by an act *inter vivos*, or by a disposition made in prospect of death, provided such manumission be made with the forms and under the conditions prescribed by law; but an enfranchisement, when made by a last will, must be express and formal, and shall not be implied by any other circumstances of the testament, such as a legacy, an institution of heir, testamentary executorship, or other dispositions of this nature, which in such case shall be considered as if they had not been made." *Art.* 184. The manner to be observed by the emancipator (when the emancipation is not by a last will) is thus delineated:— " The master who wishes to emancipate his slave is bound to make a declaration of his intention to the

---

* In this state, a slave may be manumitted by *implication* contained in a last will and testament,—as by a devise of real or a bequest of personal property to a slave by his owner. See *Hall vs. Mullin,* 5 *Harris & Johnson's Reports,* 190. In North and South Carolina, it will be recollected, such a devise or bequest, so far from entitling the slave to freedom, is held to be *utterly void.* The decision in Maryland is, however, in conformity with the law of villanage, as well as to the civil law. See *Coke, Litt. title Villanage,* § 205.

judge of the parish where he resides; the judge must order notice of it to be published during forty days by advertisement posted at the door of the court-house; and if, at the expiration of this delay, no opposition be made, he shall authorize the master to pass the act of emancipation." *Art.* 187. The general powers thus conferred are subject nevertheless to these limitations: — "No one can emancipate his slave unless the slave has attained the age of *thirty years,** and has behaved well at least for four years preceding his emancipation," (*art.* 185,) except "*a slave who has saved the life of his master, his master's wife or one of his children;" for such a one "may be emancipated at any age." Art.* 186.

It was a part of the law of this state, adopted in 1806, that a slave, as a reward for discovering a *plot, rebellion, rising in arms,* or *mutinous assembly,* or *any other crime tending to subvert or endanger the public*

---

* The bearing of this law has given rise to a private act of the Assembly of Louisiana, which, to one accustomed to consider freedom as among the imprescriptible rights of rational creatures, may seem inexplicable. The act alluded to is entitled "An act to authorize the manumission of certain slaves," and contains the following recital and enactment:—"Whereas Maria Martha, a free woman of colour, of the parish of West Baton Rouge, has presented a petition to the legislature, praying *to be authorized to manumit two of her children,* one named Terence, of *twenty-six years of age,* and the other Valery, of *twenty-four years of age,* both being *her own property,* and begotten whilst the said Maria Martha was in the bonds of slavery; and whereas, in conformity of the existing laws of this state, slaves cannot be manumitted until they have attained a certain age, therefore, be it enacted, &c. that the said Maria Martha, &c. be and she is hereby authorized to manumit her two children, &c. &c." See *Acts of Assembly of Louisiana in the year* 1823, p. 36.

21

tranquillity or safety, might obtain his liberty, besides
such further recompense as the legislature might
think adequate to the service rendered. This continues to be the law. *Revised Statutes*, 546.

Since 1825, when the *Civil Code* of Louisiana,
prepared by Mr. Livingston, came into effect,
several changes and additions have been made on
this subject. The chief of these is a mode by
which slaves *under* thirty years of age may be
emancipated by their masters. The principle is
much the same as the law of *Tennessee* requiring
a petition from the master "in which he shall ex-
plain the motives which induce him to wish the
emancipation of the slave." The tribunal to act
upon this petition consists, in *New Orleans*, of the
recorder and council of the municipality, and in the
other portions of the state of a *police jury*, composed of a *president* and *eight* or *twelve* members,
who hold their offices for two years and are elected
by ballot. *Three-fourths* of either of these tribunals,
in addition to the respective presiding officer, determine upon the merits of the claim set forth in the
petition. If they allow the slave to be emancipated, they have the power to permit him to remain
in the state, or to depart within one month and not
return. In the latter case, the master must give
a bond, with security, for compliance with the decision of the tribunal. *Revised Statutes*, 548-9.

The restraints on the power of the master to
emancipate his slave produce occasionally effects
which shock the native sensibility and sense of justice of every one. Within the last few years, a case

of this description occurred in *North Carolina*. A free coloured man was so industrious and thrifty that he was enabled to purchase, and did purchase, his wife, who was a slave, and the children which had been up to that time born to them. They had several other children subsequently born. By the law of the state *the wife and all these children* were HIS *slaves*, and not, as he himself was, *free*. For a considerable number of years he continued prosperous, and was induced to extend his business; but, in the end, he was involved in debt beyond his ability to pay. His creditors obtained judgments against him, and under these *his wife* and *children* were sold into perpetual slavery! Whether the family was actually separated in this way I do not know. The law would permit it to be, and the probability is that the different members were at once torn from each other.

There is another case which, if possible, is a greater outrage on humanity. This is evidenced in the most indisputable way. It is reported in 2 *Howard's Mississippi Reports*, 840, *Hinds vs. Brazealle*.

A citizen of Mississippi, named *Elisha Brazealle*, held a coloured woman as a slave. She had a son called *John Monroe Brazealle*, of whom her master, Elisha Brazealle, was the acknowledged father.

Elisha Brazealle left Mississippi and took with him to the state of Ohio this negro woman and her son, for the purpose of emancipating them, and with the intention of then bringing them back to Mississippi. He accordingly executed the deed of emancipation while in Ohio, and returned with the woman and her son to his residence in Jefferson county, Mississippi, where he continued to reside until his death. By his will, executed after the deed, he recited the fact that such a deed had been executed, and declared his intention to ratify it, and devised his property to the said *John Munroe Brazealle,* ACKNOWLEDGING HIM TO BE HIS SON.

His executors proved the will and took charge of the estate, and continued to hold it and receive the profits.

Persons claiming to be *the heirs*-at-law of *Elisha Brazealle,* the deceased, filed a bill in chancery, claiming all the estate which had belonged to him in his lifetime, " on the ground *that the deed of emancipation* was void, as being contrary to the laws and policy of Mississippi, and that, being so, the said John Munroe Brazealle was still a slave, and incapable of taking by devise or holding property."

The decision of the inferior court in which the bill of chancery was filed was in favour of the HEIRS of *Elisha Brazealle.* An appeal from this decision was taken to the highest court in the state, and, on hearing there, *the decision of the inferior court was affirmed.*

The main question in the case was, whether *the deed of emancipation executed in Ohio* was valid. And it was held *not* to be so.

Chief-Justice Starkey, by whom the opinion of the court was given, said, "Upon principles of natural comity, contracts are to be construed *according to the laws of the country or state* WHERE THEY ARE MADE, and the respective rights and duties of parties are to be defined and enforced accordingly. As these laws derive their force entirely from comity, they are not to be adopted to the exclusion of state laws by which the great and fundamental policy of the state is fixed and regulated."

He then argues that it was the intention of *Elisha Brazealle* to evade the laws of Mississippi, by going to Ohio and there executing the deed of manumission, and says this attempt to evade the laws of that state rendered the deed fraudulent and inoperative; and he concludes in these words:—"As we think the validity of the deed must depend upon the laws of this state, it becomes unnecessary to inquire whether it could have any force by the laws of Ohio. If it were valid there, it would have no force here. *The consequence is, that the negroes John Munroe and his mother* ARE STILL SLAVES, AND A PART OF THE ESTATE OF ELISHA BRAZEALLE.

"John Munroe, being *a slave*, cannot *take property* as devisee; and I apprehend it is equally clear that it cannot be held in trust for him. 4 *Desaussure*, 266.

"It follows, therefore, that *the heirs* are entitled to the property."

Of the *injustice and cruelty* of this decision I shall say nothing. But was it consonant with *strict law*?

Supposing, as is asserted, that it was the *intention* of *Elisha Brazealle* to evade the law of Mississippi in regard to the emancipation of slaves, by taking the slaves with him to Ohio and there executing the deed of emancipation: could he, if alive, set up this *his own* fraudulent intention, for his

21*

own benefit, on a trial of freedom brought by *the mother and son?* Certainly not; for it is a principle of the common law, universally received, that a party cannot thus avail himself of *his own wrong;* that the deed, though fraudulent as to creditors, is *good between the parties.* And the same rule holds in respect to those who *claim through and under him.* His HEIRS, as well as himself, were *estopped* from denying the validity of the deed.

What then was the proper conclusion on the facts of this case? The alleged fraud, according to *Chief-Justice Starkey,* consisted in an effort to contravene the *law and policy of Mississippi* which forbade free negroes to continue in the state, &c. This policy could have been satisfied by enforcing this law and compelling both the mother and the son to remove from the state. But, being free, the devise of the property to the son was good.

While treating on the subject of emancipation, with reference to the laws of Louisiana, it is due to the framers of the new Civil Code, as well as to the legislature and people by whom it has been adopted, to notice distinctly several provisions in this code, which evidence greater benevolence to the slave than is usually exhibited in slave-holding countries. Thus, to meet a case which may frequently occur, it is an article of the code that "the child born of a woman after she has acquired the *right* of being free at a *future time* follows the condition of the mother, *and becomes free* AT THE TIME FIXED *for her enfranchisement, even though the mother should die before that time."* Art. 196. Again, "The slave who has acquired the right of being free at a future time is, from that time, (*i. e.* the period when the *right* is acquired,) capable of receiving by testament or donation. Property given or devised to him must be preserved for him, in order to be delivered to him in kind when his emancipation shall take place. In the mean time it must be administered by a curator." *Art.* 193.

CHAPTER V.

ENCROACHMENTS INDUCED BY SLAVERY ON FREEDOM OF SPEECH AND OF THE PRESS.

BESIDES the laws which affect *slaves only*, the statute-books of the slave-holding states exhibit degrading and despotic enactments growing out of the institution of slavery, which bear directly upon the *free white* population.

Those to which I particularly allude are restraints upon freedom of speech and of the press.

I pass over all statutable efforts to prevent the circulation of publications designed to excite insurrection among the slaves. I regard the distribution of all such publications as utterly indefensible.

In the *Revised Statutes* of *Louisiana* are these enactments:—"If any white person shall be convicted of being the author, printer or publisher of any written or printed paper or papers within this state, or shall use any language with the intent to disturb the peace or security of the same, in relation to the slaves of the people of this state, or TO DIMINISH THAT RESPECT *which is commanded to free people of colour for the whites* by law, or *to destroy that line of distinction which the law has established between the several classes of this community*, such person shall be adjudged guilty of high misdemeanour, and shall *be fined* in a sum not less than three hundred dollars nor exceeding one thousand dollars, and, moreover, *imprisoned* for a term not less than *six months* nor exceeding *three years.*" *Statutes of Louisiana,* (1852,) *p.* 554.

"Whosoever shall write, print, publish or distribute any thing having a TENDENCY to produce *discontent* among the *free coloured population* of the state, shall, on conviction thereof before any court of competent jurisdiction, be sentenced to IMPRISONMENT AT HARD LABOUR FOR LIFE, or SUFFER DEATH, at the discretion of the court." *Ibid.* 208.

"Whoever shall make use of language in any public discourse from the bar, the bench, the stage, the pulpit, or in any place whatsoever, or whoever shall make use of language in private discourses or conversations, or shall make use of signs or actions *having a tendency to produce discontent* among the *free coloured* population of this state, or to excite insubordination among the slaves, or whosoever shall knowingly be instrumental in bringing into this state any paper, pamphlet or book having such tendency as aforesaid, shall, on conviction thereof before any court of competent jurisdiction, suffer *imprisonment at hard labour* not less *than three years nor more than twenty-one years,* or DEATH, at the discretion of the court." *Ibid.*

Passing over the heartless despotism which only could have dictated such enactments,—the intolerance,—the want of all charity for human infirmity,— the utter disregard of the plainest rights of man,— were there ever crimes of so loose and indeterminate a character?—"*to diminish the respect which is commanded to free people of colour for the whites by law"?* or *"to destroy that line of distinction which the law has established between the several classes of this community"?* or *"writing any thing or using in discourse language or signs or actions having a tendency to produce discontent among the free coloured population"?*

In what code of laws can the counterpart of these, in ferocity of punishments, be found? In none certainly on which the light of Christianity has dawned. *Imprisonment at hard labour* FOR LIFE, or the infliction of DEATH itself, for *writing any thing having a* TENDENCY *to produce discontent* in the breast of a *nominally*-free but greatly-oppressed people; or *"imprisonment at hard labour* for TWENTY-ONE years, or DEATH, for using *language* or *signs* or *actions* having such TENDENCY."

When human life is the forfeiture of such offences, it is quite a descent to speak of *"a fine of one thousand dollars* AND *imprisonment of three years"* for *printing* a paper or *uttering any language* with the *"intent* to DIMINISH *the respect which is commanded to free people of colour for the whites by law,"* or *"to destroy that line of distinction* which the law has established *between the several classes of the community."*

Which of these *crimes* is of the deepest dye—that *"which has a tendency to produce discontent,"* or *"to diminish respect,"* &c., or *"to destroy the line of distinction between the several classes of the community"*—would require a very minute knowledge of the state of society in Louisiana to determine.

The first of these laws requires a criminal *intent,* which is certainly an aggravation of the offence;

and yet the punishment is less severe that that which is imposed for the perpetration of the other offences mentioned, which are nevertheless *crimes* in the language of the statutes, although no criminal intent existed. They may be committed through sheer ignorance or inadvertence; but these considerations are no palliation of the imputed guilt.

It is quite obvious that particular parts, if not the whole, of the *Declaration of Independence* are proscribed by these statutes. What words can be named more likely " *to produce discontent,*" or "*diminish the respect,*" &c., or "*destroy the line of distinction between the several classes of the community,*" than—"ALL MEN ARE BORN FREE AND EQUAL," which this imperishable document declares is a *self-evident truth?* It says too that "*life,* LIBERTY, and *the pursuit of happiness,* are *inalienable rights* of man;" and it denominates this declaration also a *self-evident truth.*

But to utter these sentiments or any thing equivalent, even in *private conversation,* within the territorial boundaries of *Louisiana,* is punishable with "*imprisonment at hard labour* not less than *three* years," and it may be with *twenty-one years* or DEATH, at the discretion of the court; while for the more deliberate criminality of *printing or publishing* the same, nothing will expiate but *such imprisonment* FOR LIFE, or the infliction of DEATH!

The *clergy* and the *bar* will find it very difficult to discharge their duties conscientiously and fearlessly with these terrific penalties before their eyes. How large a part of the Holy Scriptures must be thus placed under the ban will be obvious upon a little

reflection. And should any one be indicted under
these statutes, how could his counsel sustain the
proper character of an advocate, if he dare not *repeat*
for the purpose of explanation or palliation the language which is charged against his client as a crime?
But it is unnecessary to dilate on such a subject.
It speaks its own condemnation.

In *Alabama* there are kindred laws, but less exceptionable, because in these a guilty *intent* is requisite to constitute crime. As, however, *intent* is
always a question for a jury, this tribunal, composed
of the same people who make the laws, will have no
difficulty in imagining an intent wherever a *distaste-
ful* publication is charged upon a prisoner. See
Clay's Dig. 412.

The Code of *Virginia* of 1849 contains the following:—"If a free person by speaking or writing
maintain that owners have not right of property in
their slaves, he shall be confined in jail not more
than one year and fined not exceeding five hundred
dollars. He may be arrested and carried before a
justice by any white person." *Ch.* 198, § 22, 745
–46. Under an act a little earlier in date to this,
expressed in nearly the same language, a *Methodist
clergyman* was indicted in 1849, tried, and *convicted.*
According to the report of the case to be found in
7 *Grattan's Reports,* 602, "it was charged in the indictment that the defendant, on the 26th of March, 1849,
preached a sermon from the text in the New Testament, '*Ye are the salt of the earth,*' or, '*Ye are the light
of the world.*' [The witnesses differed as to which of
these was the real text.] Towards the conclusion of

his discourse the defendant cited a passage of Scripture which related to the overthrow of the tables of the money-changers in the temple, and said, 'Those persons [alluding to the money-changers] were pronounced, by our Saviour, *thieves and robbers*, and there are thieves and robbers in the church at this day. If I go to my neighbour's crib and steal his corn, you would call me *a thief;*' *but that it was worse to take a human being and keep him all his life, and give him nothing for his labour except once in a while a whipping or a few stripes.*"

The jury, as before stated, found the defendant *guilty* upon this indictment, and, according to the practice in that state, assessed as a fine upon him forty-nine dollars sixty-two-and-a-half cents.

The record was taken to the Supreme Court, when the judgment which had been entered below was *reversed*, the court being of opinion that the language imputed to the defendant did not amount to a denial in any one of a right of property in a slave.

I make no remark on this *proceeding* except this:— that it furnishes another example of the injustice of charging any one *criminally* upon the memory of witnesses of words *spoken* by him. Here the witnesses were unable to agree as to which of two texts was the one announced from the pulpit. Certainly as to the *criminal charge* this disagreement was unimportant. But what confidence could be placed in their recollection as to what was spoken in the less noticeable part of the discourse?

The Constitution of *Virginia* of 1830, which was in force at the date of the statute above cited, denies

22

to the General Assembly power to pass "ANY LAW
ABRIDGING THE FREEDOM OF SPEECH OR OF THE PRESS."
Art. 3. § 11. The Constitution of 1776 contained
a similar restriction, and it has been preserved in *the
last Constitution* of 1851. I am unable to reconcile
the statute with this constitutional provision. They
are, it seems to me, in direct conflict.

With respect to *Louisiana* and *Alabama,* despotic
and tyrannical as their laws are, the terms of their
Constitutions *on the freedom of speech and of the press,*
although very broad in the declarative part, are so
qualified by the proviso which follows that in effect
these invaluable rights can scarcely be said to be
protected at all. The language is the same in each.
It is this:—"Every citizen may freely speak, write
and publish his sentiments on all subjects, *being
responsible for the abuse of that liberty.*" *Const. of
Louisiana, art.* 110; *Const. of Alabama, art.* 1, § 8.

This qualification, which is not confined to these
states, but is found in several others, (and among
these is *Pennsylvania,*) leaves the *freedom both of speech
and of the press* at the *mercy of the legislature.* I do
not mean to be understood that there may not be a
conceivable encroachment by the legislature which
the courts would be bound to declare unconstitutional. But a tyrannical legislature may for all
practical purposes utterly destroy these cherished
rights, as is done by the statutes of *Louisiana* and
Alabama. It is a curious fact that the *first amendment*
to the Constitution of the United States which was
proposed and adopted forbids CONGRESS to pass any
law "*abridging the freedom of speech or of the press*" at

all. And yet the very *states*, or rather many of them, have incorporated in their own Constitutions a similar qualification to that which exists in *Louisiana* and *Alabama*. The distinction between such states as *Pennsylvania* and *Louisiana* and *Alabama* is, that in *Pennsylvania* the legislature has regarded the Constitution as a *shield*, while *Louisiana* and *Alabama* have used it as a *sword*.

Before leaving this subject, some notice ought, perhaps, to be taken of the legislation of the *territorial* government of *Kansas*, so far as it falls within the meaning of the present chapter.

The government of this territory is but pupilary,—subject to the will of the Federal Government wholly and absolutely. The Constitution of the United States must control all its action. Now, as has just been stated, the Constitution of the United States forbids, in the most unqualified manner, any ABRIDGMENT OF THE FREEDOM OF SPEECH AND OF THE PRESS.

Without entering into the question whether slavery can be sustained at all by *Kansas* during her pupilage, it is too plain to admit of controversy that the territorial government can pass no laws of the kind which it has undertaken to do in the 11th and 12th sections of an act entitled "*An act to punish offences against slave property.*" These sections read thus:—

"*Section* 11.—If any person print, write, introduce into, publish or circulate, or cause to be brought into, printed, written, published or circulated, or shall knowingly aid or assist in bringing into, printing, publishing or circulating within this territory any book, paper, pamphlet, magazine, handbill or circular containing any statements, arguments, opinions, sentiment, doctrine, advice or inuendo calculated to produce a disorderly, dangerous or rebellious disaffection among the slaves in this territory, or to induce such slaves to escape from the service of their masters or to resist their authority, he shall be guilty of felony, and be punished by imprisonment and hard labour for a term not less than five years.

"*Section* 12.—If any free person, by speaking or by writing, assert or maintain that persons have not the right to hold slaves in this territory, or shall introduce into this territory, print, publish, write, circulate, or cause to be introduced into this territory, written, printed, published or circulated in this territory, any book, paper, magazine, pamphlet or circular containing any denial of the right of persons to hold slaves in this territory, such person shall be deemed guilty of felony and be punished by imprisonment at hard labour for a term of not less than two years."

Of the *paternity* of these sections no one will doubt who peruses the extracts which I have given in this chapter from the statutes of *Louisiana and Virginia*. That the courts of *Virginia* must and will pronounce the act of Assembly in that state *unconstitutional* so soon as the question shall be *forced* upon them I entertain no doubt. The language of the Constitution of *Virginia* and of the Constitution of *the United States* in regard *to the freedom of speech and of the press is the same*, and no language could be selected more plain, forcible and positive. There is no room for subterfuge; nothing is left to construction: it has but one meaning.

APPENDIX.

OF THE LAWS OF THE UNITED STATES RELATING TO SLAVERY.

CHAPTER I.

ON THE APPORTIONMENT OF REPRESENTATIVES TO CONGRESS, ETC.

THE introduction of negro slavery into this country was, as has been already stated, a part of the colonial policy of Great Britain. It has been also stated that long before and at the era of our independence it existed to some extent in each of the original states of the Union. It was an institution, the evils of which, at this latter period in particular, were severely felt, while its incompatibility with the principles of a republican government was too palpable not to be generally perceived and acknowledged. Prevailing, however, as was the case, in *some* states *much more* than in *others*, it was the dictate of sound policy, on the part of the FIRST *Con-*

22*   257

gress, to leave the whole subject unaffected by any national measure. Accordingly, when the *original* draught of the Declaration of Independence was presented to that body, a portion of this instrument, which reprobated in strong language the conduct of the mother-country in relation to the slave population, was entirely stricken out. And afterwards, in 1778, when the articles of confederation between the several states were adopted, the topic of slavery was again carefully excluded. But when the perils of the revolutionary conflict were over, and peace invited the exercise of patriotism, philanthropy and religion, in the formation of a more stable and more perfect system of government, by which were to be reconciled the jarring elements incident to a wide-spread country, peopled by inhabitants whose education, whose interests, and whose religious creeds, were different, the consideration of slavery was *forced* upon the convention. Politically speaking, a majority of the states would have been benefited had the *same caution* been observed with respect to the *Constitution* which had been pursued in reference to the *Declaration of Independence* and the *Articles of Confederation*. The apportionment of representatives among the several states was, however, a subject of such prominence as to claim the earliest attention of the convention. In an evil hour the important advantage was conceded to the slave-holding states of including within the enumeration of inhabitants by which the ratio of representation was to be ascertained, *three-fifths of those who were held in slavery*.

For the surrender of right involved in this anomalous arrangement the *large non*-slave-holding
states, such as New York and Pennsylvania, obtained not even a nominal equivalent. The provision relative to *direct taxes*, when viewed in all its
bearings, is beneficial to the slave-holding rather
than to the *non*-slave-holding states.* It will not
be pretended that the equal representation of the
states in the Senate confers undue power upon the
LARGE *non-slave-holding states*. On the contrary, this
is known to have been the result of a compromise
in which the interest of the *small* states only was
consulted. It was deemed necessary in order to
preserve the federative system; and believing, as I
do, that for this purpose it was indispensable, great
as was the sacrifice on the part of the large states,

---

* The late Honourable William Paterson, who was a member of
the convention by which the Constitution of the United States was
formed, speaking of the mode which is prescribed by that instrument
for the regulation of *direct taxes*, says, "The provision was made
in favour of the Southern States. They possessed *a large number of
slaves;* they had extensive tracts of territory, thinly settled and not
very productive. A majority of the states had but few slaves, and
several of them a limited territory, well settled and in a high state
of cultivation. The Southern States, if no provision had been introduced in the Constitution, would have been wholly at the mercy of the
other states. Congress, in such case, might tax slaves at discretion
or arbitrarily, and land in every part of the Union after the same
rule and measure,—so much a head in the first instance, and so much
an acre in the second. To guard them against imposition in these
particulars *was the reason of introducing the clause in the Constitution*
which directs that representatives and *direct taxes* shall be appor-
tioned among the states according to their respective numbers." See
3 *Dallas' Reports*, 177.

nevertheless, it ought, I concede, to have been made.

This latter principle of equal representation of the several states in the Senate induced the consent of the *small non-slave-holding states* to the monstrous anomaly in a republican government of the legislative representation of *slaves* by their *masters*. No argument can be advanced to give plausibility to this article of the Constitution. It has been already the cause of incalculable detriment to the nation. It has secured the recognition of slavery in Missouri; it may operate the like effect in other territories equally enriched by the bounty of heaven,—the like fit abodes of the children of freemen.

CHAPTER II.

At the adoption of the Constitution, *a majority of the states* had but few slaves. In several, acts for the abolition of slavery had been passed. These states were politically interested to oppose the further importation of slaves. The *ninth section of article second* was accordingly incorporated in the Constitution. It is in these words:—" The migration or importation of such persons as any of the states now existing shall think proper to admit shall not be prohibited by the Congress prior to the year one thousand eight hundred and eight; but a tax may be imposed on such importation, not exceeding ten dollars for each person."*

---

* By the article of the Constitution just quoted, Congress was prevented from passing any law to prohibit, *prior to the year* 1808, the importation of slaves *into the United States;* yet no restraint was imposed upon its power to prevent her citizens from engaging in the slave-trade for the supply of *foreign* countries. And *a convention of delegates from the Abolition Societies established in the States of Connecticut, New York, New Jersey, Pennsylvania, Delaware, and Maryland*, having assembled on the first day of January, A.D. 1794, at Philadelphia, addressed a memorial to Congress, requesting *"that a law might be passed, prohibiting the traffic carried on by citizens of the United States for the supply of slaves to foreign nations, and preventing*

261

As this article concerns the *slave-trade*, and not
the condition of slaves after their introduction into
our country, *in itself* it has no immediate connection

---

*foreigners from fitting out vessels for the slave-trade in the ports of the
United States.*" This memorial was acted upon by Congress with
great promptness; and, on the 22d day of March of the same year, an
act of this body was passed, which prohibited, under the penalty of
the forfeiture of the ship and a fine of two thousand dollars for each
person concerned, any citizen of the United States, or any foreigner
resident here, for himself, or for any other person whatsoever, either
as master, factor or owner, from building, equipping, &c. any vessel
within any port or place in the United States, or causing, &c. for the
purpose of carrying on any trade or traffic in slaves to any FOREIGN
COUNTRY. *Ingersoll's Abridgment*, 670. And afterwards (May 10th,
1800) it was made unlawful for any citizen of the United States, or
other person residing within the same, directly or indirectly to hold
any right or property in a vessel employed in the transportation of
slaves from *one foreign country to another;* and a penalty was incurred,
by a violation of this act, of a forfeiture of such share or right as he
might hold, &c. and a fine of double the value of such share or right,
&c. in the vessel, and also a fine equal to twice the value of his interest
in any slave which, at any time, might have been transported in any
such vessel, &c. Citizens of the United States were, by the same act,
forbidden to serve on board any vessel employed in the slave-trade,
under the penalty of a fine not exceeding two thousand dollars and
of imprisonment not exceeding two years. *Ibid.* 672–3.

My purpose, in introducing the subject of this note, is, to evidence
the sentiments of, at least, a majority of the people of the United
States in regard to the *slave-trade*. Additional authority on the same
point may be derived from another act of Congress, which was passed
February 28th, 1803, entitled, "An act to prevent the importation of
certain persons into certain states, where, by the laws thereof, their
admission is prohibited." This law, the purport of which is but
obscurely intimated by the title, was designed as a co-operation on
behalf of the Federal Government in carrying into effect laws which
had been enacted by our Atlantic states (both the *slave-holding* and
the non-slave-holding) to prohibit the importation of slaves from
foreign dominions into their respective territories.

with the subject in hand. But certain laws have
been enacted by Congress, under the sanction of it,
from which consequences have ensued of such a
nature as to require more than a passing notice,
particularly in regard to the subject treated of in
the first part* of this sketch. To illustrate this
point satisfactorily will require a minute detail of
the provisions contained in the acts of Congress
alluded to, as also a careful examination of several
acts of the Assemblies of some of the individual
states of the Union.

The time fixed by law for the annual meeting of
Congress is, it will be recollected, the first Monday
in December. The interval between this date in
the year 1807 and that at which, by the terms of
the Constitution, the importation of slaves *might* be
interdicted, was so brief that it was obviously the
dictate of wisdom to begin with legislation on so
momentous a subject before the expiration of the
preceding session. Accordingly, on *the second of
March*, 1807, an act was passed by which such importation *from abroad* was utterly prohibited after
the first day of January, one thousand eight hundred and eight.

The *date* of this leading act evinces, in an unequivocal manner, the strong and general repugnance
felt by the people of the United States to the slave-
trade. But, while a firm persuasion of the truth of
this remark compels me to offer it, I cannot forbear
to add that, viewed as a whole, the act is so *dis-*

---

* See *supra*, p. 28.

cordant as to involve in no little obscurity the character of its supporters for perspicacious foresight. An analysis of its provisions will sufficiently elucidate my meaning.

The *first* section is short, and, being the groundwork of what follows, I will extract it verbally:— "From and after the first day of January, one thousand eight hundred and eight, it shall not be lawful to import or bring into the United States or the territories thereof, from any foreign kingdom, place or country, any negro, mulatto or person of colour, with intent to hold, sell or dispose of such negro, mulatto or person of colour as a slave or to be held to service or labour." The *second* section prohibits any person, after the first day of January, 1808, for himself or for any other person, from being concerned in any way whatever in building, equipping, &c. a vessel, in any port, &c. of the United States, for the purpose of carrying on the slave-trade; and for a transgression of this prohibition authorizes a forfeiture of the vessel, her tackle, &c. The *third* section enforces the restriction in the *second*, by imposing a fine of twenty thousand dollars on each person who shall contravene the object of the preceding sections. The *fourth* section is specially directed against the actual *importation* of slaves. And it is in the provisions of this section that the discordancy I have spoken of is introduced. It may be given as follows:—"If any citizen of the United States, or any person resident within the jurisdiction of the same, shall, from and after the first day of January, 1808, take on board, receive or transport from any of the coasts or kingdoms of Africa, &c. &c. any negro, &c. &c. in any ship or vessel, for the purpose of selling them in any port, &c. within the jurisdiction of the United States, *as slaves*, &c., or shall be in any way aiding, &c. such citizen, &c., shall forfeit and pay five thousand dollars, &c. &c., and the ship, &c. shall be forfeited, &c. And neither the importer, nor any person or persons claiming from or under him, shall hold any right or title whatsoever to any negro, &c. who may be imported, &c. within the United States, &c. in violation of this law; *but the same shall remain subject to any regulations, not contravening the provisions of this act, which the legislature of the several states or territories at any time hereafter may make, for* DISPOSING *of any such negro, mulatto or person of colour.*"

Had the act stopped here, though the meaning would have been obscure as to what was to be understood by the authority given to the different state and territorial legislatures to make "regulations *not contravening the provisions of the act* FOR DISPOSING of any such negro, &c.," yet I conceive it would have been held as the proper construction that the *imported* negro could not be retained as a *slave*. But the *sixth* section removes the obscurity of the fourth, and explains the intention of Congress to have been that the negro, &c., though *illegally* imported, yet, if so directed by the state legislatures, he and his offspring should be regarded as *absolute slaves ! ! !*

The sixth section is long, but it is too important to be omitted. It is as follows:—"If any person or

23

persons whatever shall, from and after the first day
of January, 1808, purchase or sell any negro, mulatto or person of colour for a slave or to be held
to service or labour, who shall have been imported
or brought from any foreign kingdom, place or
country, or from the dominions of any foreign
state immediately adjoining to the United States,
into any port or place within the jurisdiction of the
United States, after the last day of December, 1807,
knowing at the time of such purchase or sale such
negro, mulatto or person of colour was so brought
within the jurisdiction of the United States as aforesaid, such purchaser and seller shall severally forfeit
and pay for every negro, mulatto or person of colour
so purchased, &c. as aforesaid, eight hundred dollars;
one moiety to the United States, &c.: *Provided, that
the aforesaid forfeiture shall not extend to* THE SELLER
OR PURCHASER *of any negro, &c. who may be sold or disposed of* IN VIRTUE OF ANY REGULATION WHICH MAY
HEREAFTER BE MADE BY ANY OF THE LEGISLATURES
of the several states in that respect, IN PURSUANCE OF
THIS ACT and the Constitution of the United States."
The legislature of Louisiana was not tardy in *im-
proving* the privileges thus preposterously conferred
by Congress. By an act of Assembly, passed March
20th, 1809, it was enacted that *every negro, mulatto or
person of colour,* who had been, posterior to the *first
day of January,* 1808, or who should be at any time
thereafter, imported into the *territory* of Louisiana
from any foreign kingdom, place or country, with
intent to be held, sold or disposed of for a slave or
to be held to service or labour either for life or for

a term of years, should *be sold* by virtue of a judgment to be rendered by the territorial courts, before whom proof of such importation should be made; and that the proceeds of such sale should be delivered into the hands of the treasurer of the territory, to be afterwards disposed of as the legislature might deem proper. 1 *Martin's Digest*, 664. North Carolina and Georgia respectively adopted a similar law, the former in 1816, (*Haywood's Manual*, 545, *et seq.*,) the latter* in 1817. *Prince's Digest*, 463.

Public attention had not yet been attracted to the inconsistency of the act of Congress which I have indicated. And, what may seem not a little surprising, on the 20th of April, 1818, another act of Congress was passed, imposing more severe penalties on the prosecution of the slave-trade, *but re-enacting the odious sixth section of the act of March 2d, 1807, and recognising the laws of the several state legisla-*

---

* The act of Georgia contains a provision equally just and humane, which is not to be found in the act of North Carolina or in that of Louisiana. Having authorized the governor to make sale of the unhappy captives, who, though *illegally* imported, were nevertheless subjected to the control of the state legislatures and might be by them consigned to interminable bondage, the subjoined section was added :—
"If, previous to any sale of such persons of colour, the society for the colonization of free persons of colour within the United States will undertake to transport them to Africa or any other foreign place which they may procure as a colony for free persons of colour at the sole expense of said society, and shall likewise pay to his excellency the governor all expenses incurred by the state since they have been captured and condemned, his excellency the governor is authorized and requested to aid in promoting the benevolent views of said society in such manner as he may deem expedient." *Prince's Digest*, 463.

tures on this subject which have just been commented upon! See *Ingersoll's Abridgment*, 680.

The evil, however, soon afterwards reached its crisis. The repetition of such monstrous injustice awaked the slumbering energies of the friends of injured Africa; and the *same* Congress by which the act of 1818 had been passed was induced to *resume* the consideration of the slave-trade; and, having done so, by a law of March 3d, 1819, authorized the President, at his discretion, to cause any of the public armed vessels of the United States to be employed to cruise on any of the coasts of the United States, &c., or on the coast of Africa, in order to suppress the slave-trade; and directed that when any vessels should be captured, having negroes, &c. on board, &c., they should be delivered to the marshal of the district into which the vessel might be brought, if the same should be a port of the United States, and, if brought in elsewhere, to an agent whom the President was empowered to appoint for such purpose, &c.; and authority was given to the President to make such arrangements as he should think expedient for the safe-keeping, support and *removal beyond the limits of the United States* of such negro, &c. And to meet the case of slave vessels which might escape seizure from the public armed vessels, it was enacted that when any citizen or other person should lodge information with the attorney-general for the district of any state, &c. that any negro, &c. had been imported, &c. contrary to the provisions of the acts for the suppression of the slave-trade, such attorney

' should be bound forthwith to commence a prosecution, &c., and process was to be issued against the person charged with holding such negro, &c.; and if, upon the verdict of a jury, it should be ascertained that any such negro, &c. had been imported contrary to the acts of Congress, &c. it was made the duty of the court to direct the marshal, &c. to take the said negroes, &c. into his custody for safe-keeping, subject to the orders of the President of the United States, &c. &c. The act also grants to the informer a bounty *of fifty dollars for each negro* thus delivered into the custody of the marshal. See *Ingersoll's Abridgment*, 683. And, lastly, *the sections of the former acts which conferred authority upon the state legislatures to dispose of the* ILLEGALLY-IMPORTED NEGROES WERE REPEALED.

Notwithstanding this repeal, I find in the *Revised Statutes of Louisiana*, compiled and adopted by the legislature as lately as 1852, an act of this state which recites the provisions of the act of Congress of 2d March, 1807, and authorizes the *captured* slaves to be sold as SLAVES FOR LIFE by the sheriff of the parish of Orleans. "The proceeds of such sale shall, after deducting all charges, be paid over by the said sheriff, one moiety to and for the use of the commanding officer of the capturing vessel, and the other moiety to the treasurer of the Charity Hospital of New Orleans, for the use and benefit of said hospital." *Rev. Stat. of Louisiana*, 536–7.

The only excuse for this disregard of the act of Congress is that the state law which is thus re-enacted was passed originally in 1818, *before* the act

23*

of Congress, the date of which is March 3d, 1819. But why is it re-enacted in 1852? Can it be that the legislature were ignorant of the act of Congress?

So in *Alabama,* two statutes, one passed in 1815, the other in 1823, the latter entitled *"An act to carry into effect the laws of the United States* prohibiting the slave-trade," are comprehended in *Clay's Digest* of the laws of the state *in force* in 1843. The provisions of these statutes are in direct repugnance to the act of Congress. *Clay's Dig.* 547–8.

CHAPTER III.

THE *Federal Government* being composed of thirteen distinct and independent sovereignties, in *four* of which, before the Constitution of the United States was formed, *slavery* had been *abolished*, it was deemed expedient to secure, by a stipulation to be inserted in the Constitution, a right in the citizens of one state, whose servants or slaves should *escape* from their masters and take refuge in another state, to reclaim such fugitives and subject them again to bondage.

This stipulation is comprised in *the third division of section 2, article 4*, and is in these words:—"No person held to service or labour in one state under the laws thereof, *escaping* into another, shall in consequence of any law or regulation therein be discharged from such service or labour, but shall be delivered up on claim of the party to whom such service or labour may be due."

The question has been, especially of late years, much agitated, whether the intent of this provision of the Constitution was to clothe Congress with the power of legislating in respect to the surrender of the persons who, being held to service or labour in

271

one state, have *escaped* into another, or whether it was intended to leave it to the several states to provide a mode for the investigation of *claims* which might be made, and, if found for the *claimants,* to deliver up the fugitives to them.

This question has been set at rest by the decision of the Supreme Court of the United States that the power belonged *exclusively* to the Federal Government. *Prigg vs. The Commonwealth of Pennsylvania,* 16 *Peters,* 539, 622.

A much more important question is, *In what mode* ought the power to be exercised?

The two acts of Congress on the subject — the *first* passed February 12th, 1793, the *second,* September 18th, 1850—have intrusted the entire execution of the power to the judgment of a *single person,* and that, too, without any regard to his qualifications for the proper performance of the duties of his office.

The principal section of the act of 1793, relating to fugitives *from labour,* is in these words:—"When a person held to labour in any of the United States, or in either of the territories on the northwest or south of the river Ohio, under the laws thereof, shall *escape* into any other of the said states or territories, *the person to whom such labour or service may be due,* his agent or attorney, is hereby empowered to seize or arrest such fugitive from labour, and to take him or her before any judge of the Circuit or District Courts of the United States, residing or being within the state, *or before any magistrate of a county, city or town corporate* wherein such seizure or arrest shall be made ; and, upon proof *to the satisfaction* of such judge or *magistrate*, either by oral testimony or *affidavit*, taken before and certified by a magistrate of any such state or territory, that the person so seized or arrested doth, under the laws of the state or territory from which he or she fled, owe service or labour to the person claiming him or her, it shall be the duty of such judge or magistrate to give a certificate thereof to such claimant, his agent or attorney, which shall be sufficient warrant for removing the said fugitive from labour to the state or territory from which he or she fled."

The act of 1850 vests the same powers in certain *commissioners*, holding their appointments from the several Circuit Courts of the United States. These commissioners were not originally selected from any supposed qualification for judicial functions. They were a species of inferior committing magistrates, who sought the appointment for its perquisites. The *judges* of the Circuit and District Courts of the United States may perform the same duties. But, as they are few in number and not easily accessible, and as the act gives to the *claimant the right to* SELECT out of the whole of the functionaries named *such a one as he may prefer*, in practice *the judges* are usually passed over. In fact, under the act of 1793, nearly all the cases fell into the hands of a few *justices of the peace* in each particular locality ; and these were men in whom the general community had no confidence.

But the strong objection to the *tribunal*—whether a *judge of a court*, or a *justice of the peace*, or a *commis-*

sioner—is, that a question affecting HUMAN LIBERTY, not for a *day* or a *year*, but for a LIFE TIME, is committed to *one person*, and THAT PERSON CHOSEN BY THE VERY MEN WHO WOULD TAKE AWAY *this inestimable gift* of the Great Author of our being!

An essential part of every case arising under these acts of Congress has respect to the *identity* of the alleged fugitive. And *identity of person* is very frequently a matter most difficult of ascertainment. In relation to *slave* cases this is eminently true. A slave escapes while yet a youth, and years elapse before the owner pursues him. During this interval the *boy* or *girl* may have reached middle life, and a marked change in personal appearance has taken place. Some one—the master or overseer or a neighbour—makes a visit to a Northern city, on some wholly different business from slave-hunting; but, knowing of the *escape*, he concludes to keep *a bright look-out* for the *runaway*. He descries an active waiter at a hotel. May not this be the runaway? He tries to recall his peculiarities,—his voice, his gait, and the like. He fancies a resemblance, and determines to make the experiment of arresting the unsuspecting victim. He has been furnished, probably before he left his home, with the names of the *proper* constable, the *proper* lawyer, and the *proper* justice of the peace or commissioner. If not himself the owner, he may be a *witness*,* and in a

* There is another highly important consideration which belongs to this topic. *Coloured persons* seized as slaves are, by the agents of their alleged owners, *compelled* by threats and stripes to admit themselves to be slaves,—slaves of whomsoever these agents may name as their

short hour or so the machinery is put in motion, and
the alleged fugitive finds himself in irons, after a
sham hearing, in which he has had no opportunity
to see a friend or adduce a witness, a prisoner in a
railway-car, which soon bears him beyond the pos-
sibility of successful pursuit by all who can sympa-
thize with his sufferings or assist him in a fair trial
for freedom.

A fair trial for freedom This is the answer which
is given to silence the objection to the *summary* proceeding which the act of Congress *permits*. The
decision of the *commissioner*—for nearly all this ne-
farious business is now transacted by this class of
arbiters—is, say the supporters of the law, merely

---

masters. The case of *Elizabeth Parker*, one of the sisters kidnapped
in December, 1851, from Chester county, furnishes a memorable example of this *extorted* confession. Even after she had been brought
back as far as *Baltimore*, in an interview with the respectable counsel
employed by the state of Pennsylvania in her behalf *she* AT THE FIRST
told them she was the slave of Mr. Schoolfield, her pretended owner. And
it was not until she was convinced by their assurances *that they were
her friends,* that she ventured to tell the truth and relate the story of
her kidnapping.

The relation of *Solomon Northup,* rescued after twelve years' captivity,
gives shocking details of the punishment to which he was subjected to
compel him to confess himself a slave.

These are not exceptional cases. It is well known to be a part of
the system of *kidnapping.*

Ought it to be permitted that any ONE man should have the power
of determining the value of such evidence? If there were *three* commissioners, and these not under the bias of the double fee, the thing
would be less objectionable. But there is no tribunal that ever has
been devised equal to the Constitutional one, — *a court and jury*
sitting with open doors, and assisted by able counsel accustomed to
the trial of causes.

initiative, and not final. So soon as the fugitive reaches the home of his master, he may demand a *trial for freedom*, and, if not a slave, he will be declared free.

Here lies the grand fallacy which has deceived *Northern* Congressmen and soothed the consciences of their constituents. *A fair trial for freedom* IN A SLAVE STATE, by a negro *born in a* FREE ONE is *impossible*. I refer to the laws on that subject, and to my remarks upon them, as abundant evidence to sustain this strong assertion. See *ante*, 122–6.

No reliance should be placed upon *any single person as a substitute for a court and jury where the arrest is made*. The Constitution fully sanctions a jury trial. It is the accustomed mode to determine all questions in which the ascertainment of *facts* is the principal duty.

Both acts of Congress authorize, as evidence *on the hearing* where the alleged fugitive is arrested, *ex parte* affidavits on behalf of the claimant. This is contrary to the practice of all well-constituted courts. In the act of 1850 this anomaly is carried so far as in express terms to justify such evidence to prove *identity*. How is this possible? Can a person in Alabama, or anywhere else, so describe the *personal appearance* of another that, by reading the description, a third person can certainly know to whom it applies? Will it be said he may be described by *scars* from *casualties* or from ARTIFICIAL *marks? A brand of a letter or letters of the alphabet* approximates most nearly to reliable evidence of this kind. But even this would give no certainty; and, at all events, unless the description *in all other particulars* could be made in the same affidavit, a single correspondence in artificial marks would prove nothing.

But, to a *willing* commissioner, *identity*, or any thing else, may be proved by *affidavit*. It must have been in this way, I presume, that a coloured man named *Gibson*, shortly after the passage of the act of 1850, was arrested in Philadelphia, taken before a *commissioner*, who gave to his captors a *certificate*, under the act of Congress, that *Gibson* was a fugitive from Maryland, where he owed service or labour to one *Mitchell*. ON SIGHT OF THE MAN, however, MITCHELL DECLARED HE DID NOT KNOW HIM, AND HAD NO CLAIM UPON HIM!

Happily for *Gibson*, the fear of a rescue induced the captors to ask the aid of the police to guard the prisoner, until, by being placed in a railway-car, it was supposed the apprehended danger would cease. The officers selected for this purpose, however, received, from the honest heart of their superior, directions that they should continue with the prisoner *until he should be delivered to Mitchell*, and *should bring him back if not claimed by him*. Faithful to their duty, faithful to the behests of humanity, the officers brought the captive freeman home again.

The injustice of the cardinal principle of these acts of Congress is, I trust, clearly shown.

The act of 1850 contains several other provisions of a most exceptionable and humiliating character in respect to *free white citizens*.

All marshals and deputy-marshals are bound to execute *the warrants* issued by *a commissioner* to

24

arrest an alleged fugitive; and they are made responsible to the claimant should he be taken and afterwards escape. This is not an unusual condition in regard to process against individuals arrested for debt or accused of crime; and the *officers*, having sought or at least voluntarily entered upon the office, have no right to complain.

But the *commissioner* may direct his warrant to any other person; and this person, or the commissioner himself, may " *summon and call to* their aid the *bystanders*, or *posse comitatus*, when necessary to insure a faithful observance of the clause of the Constitution referred to, in conformity with the provisions of this act; and *all good citizens are commanded* to aid and assist in the prompt and efficient execution of the law, whenever their services *may be required as aforesaid* for that purpose."

By the common law, and also by statute of *Hen. V.*, the high power of enforcing the assistance of all the king's subjects, over fifteen years of age and under the degree of peers, to suppress riots and arrest felons, &c., is undoubtedly conferred upon a *high-sheriff* and upon two *justices of the peace*. But the act of Congress intrusts an equally high power to the discretion of *the commissioner*, or to *a single delegate* of the commissioner. And this tyrannical exaction, from which no age or calling is exempt, is not for the purpose of *preserving the public peace* or to *arrest rioters and felons*, but to enable the alleged master of a slave to obtain or keep possession of him, in order that he may be carried away and subjected to bondage for life.

To assist with all his faculties *in preserving the public peace, in the suppression of riots, or even in the arrest of felons*, is a high duty, from which no good citizen will shrink. But to be converted into *catchpolls*, or, what is nearer the mark, compelled in the North, to be substitutes for bloodhounds in the South, in the ignoble chase of unfortunate negroes struggling for freedom, is insufferably degrading and revolting.

To obey the command of *known public functionaries* chosen by the people, may be reasonable and safe. But when the call is made by an unknown deputy of an unknown commissioner, who can tell whether he ought, in mere prudence, to act or refuse?

But there is yet another provision of the act of 1850, which throws in the shade even these indefensible and before unheard-of anomalies. "In all cases where the proceedings are before a *commissioner*, he shall be entitled to *a fee* of TEN dollars in full for his services in each case *upon the delivery of said certificate* TO THE CLAIMANT his or her agent or attorney; or *a fee* of FIVE dollars, in cases *where the proof* shall NOT, *in the opinion of such commissioner, warrant such certificate* and *delivery*, including all services incident to such arrest and examination, to be paid in either case by the claimant, his agent or attorney."

On giving the certificate to the claimant, the commissioner is to be paid "*a fee of* TEN *dollars;*" for *refusing* it, his fee is reduced to FIVE dollars. The only difference in the labour of the commissioner, in the one case and the other consists, in the *writing* of the *certificate*. Every thing to be done by him, up to this point, is *precisely the same*. The question then is, What is the *manual labour* of such a writing fairly worth?

The following is submitted as a form of the certificate, prepared in conformity with the directions of the statute:—"I hereby certify that negro Betsy owes service to John Jones, of Savannah, state of Georgia; that she escaped from said state into the state of Pennsylvania, where she was arrested; and I hereby authorize said John Jones to use such reasonable force and restraint as may be necessary to take and remove her to the said state of Georgia."

This certificate contains just *sixty* words; and, by the recording act of Pennsylvania, would entitle the recorder, were it an instrument requiring to be recorded, to the fee of *one cent* for every *ten* words. It is, therefore, worth *six cents*. An ordinary penman would execute it readily in three minutes.

Is it not demonstrable, therefore, that, in giving *five* dollars for these three minutes' labour, something more than *compensation* was intended to be offered? In a free state, an office whose chief duties are such as the act of Congress prescribes can never be regarded as a *post of honour*. It will be sought for or retained, solely, for the *emoluments*.

These remarks are but suggestive.

The remarks which have been made on the acts of Congress, if well founded, require radical changes in the legislation of Congress to carry out, in a proper manner, the constitutional provision in respect to *fugitives from labour.*

But if the present system of confiding the decision of so important a question as liberty or slavery to a *single arbiter* is to be retained, some restriction should at once be placed on the exercise of this tremendous power, to warrant the least hope that a fair trial will be had.

In an act of Assembly of *Pennsylvania,* passed March 25th, 1826, there were two provisions which experience has shown to be of great value in order to secure a fair trial.

I transcribe so much of the 5th and 10th sections of that act as may be necessary to disclose the *principle* of the legislation which I have in mind.

" Sect. 5.—That it shall be the duty of any judge, justice of the peace or alderman, when he grants or issues any warrant under the provisions of the third section of this act, to make a fair record on his docket of the same, in which he shall enter the name and place of residence of the person on whose oath or affirmation the said warrant may be granted, and also, if an affidavit shall have been produced under the provisions of the fourth section of this act, the name and place of residence of the person making such affidavit, and the age and description of the person of the alleged fugitive contained in such affidavit, and shall, within ten days thereafter, file a certified copy thereof in the office of the Clerk of the Court of General Quarter Sessions of the Peace, or Mayor's Court, of the proper city or county.

24*

" Sect. 10. That it shall be the duty of the judge
or recorder of any court of record of this commonwealth, when he grants or issues any certificate or
warrant of removal of any negro or mulatto, claimed
to be a fugitive from labour, to the state or territory
from which he or she fled, in pursuance of an act of
Congress passed on the twelfth day of February,
one thousand seven hundred and ninety-three,
entitled ' An act respecting fugitives from justice,
and persons escaping from the service of their masters,' and of this act to make a fair record of the
same, in which he shall enter the name, age, sex
and a general description of the person of the
negro or mulatto for whom he shall grant such
certificate or warrant of removal, together with the
evidence and the name of places of residence of
the witnesses and the party claiming such negro
or mulatto, and shall, within ten days thereafter, file
a certified copy thereof in the office of the Clerk of
the Court of General Quarter Sessions of the Peace,
or Mayor's Court, of the city or county in which he
may reside."

I will close my remarks upon the article of the
Constitution and the acts of Congress, by bringing
to notice decisions of the courts, fixing the construction of some of the most important provisions in
them.

The acts of Congress and the article of the Constitution of the United States above cited are so
essentially connected, that the judicial decisions to
which I have alluded have been made generally as
much in reference to the one as to the other. I

shall not, therefore, attempt a distinct classification.

The first case of an important character, as relates to the present chapter, was that of *Butler vs. Hopper*, already inserted at considerable length. It was there said, by *Judge Washington*, that "the second section of the fourth article, (*i. e.* of the Constitution of the United States,) which declares *that no person held to labour or service in one state under the laws thereof*, ESCAPING *into another, shall, in consequence of any law therein, be discharged from such service,* did not extend to the case of a slave *voluntarily* carried by his master into another state and there leaving him under the protection of some law declaring him free." 1 *Washington's Circ. Court Rep.* 501.

At October term, 1823, the principle of the decision in *Butler vs. Hopper* was again recognised by *Judge Washington*, on an application preferred by *J. W. Simmons*, agreeably to the act of Congress of February 12th, 1793, for a certificate that *James Mathist*, a black man, was his slave. It was proved in this case that *Simmons* was a citizen of *Charleston, South Carolina*, and had lived there generally till within a few years, when he came to the city of Philadelphia, took a house, and with his family had resided in the city ever since. *James* was admitted to have been his slave before and at the time of his leaving Charleston, and as such *to have been brought by him to Philadelphia* in June, 1822. Upon these facts the judge refused the certificate and dismissed the application, saying *that the act of Congress applied exclusively to fugitive slaves, and not to those whom their*

masters themselves brought from one state to another.
4 *Wash. C. C. R.* 396; *ac.* 1 *Morris' Rep.* 1.

A third case may be adduced, decided on the twentieth of February, 1826, by *Judge Barnes*, then President of the District Court for the city and county of Philadelphia, upon the following facts:—
"*Marshall Green*, a black man, was claimed as a slave by *Peter Buchell*, administrator, &c. of *John Buchell*, deceased, who for many years before and at the time of his decease was an inhabitant of *Cecil county, Maryland.* About four years previous to the hearing before *Judge Barnes*, and one year before the death of *John Buchell, Marshall* absconded from his master's residence, and continued absent until August, 1825, when he was arrested by *Peter Buchell* and carried back to *Maryland.* At the time when he *absconded* he took with him his three children, who were alleged also to be slaves. After *Marshall's* return to Maryland, in August, 1825, *Peter Buchell*, then his master, in order to obtain possession of these children, *gave him permission, and for that purpose furnished him with a* PASS, to come to *Pennsylvania*, upon his express promise that he would, within a certain period, if successful in the pursuit of his children, bring them to his master; if not successful, he would return himself. The time of absence granted by the master having expired, *Marshall* was again arrested, by virtue of a warrant issued by *Judge Barnes*, in compliance with the directions of the *act of Assembly* of the commonwealth of Pennsylvania, passed March 25th, 1826, and brought before him for a hearing. The judge, having taken time for delibe-

ration, refused the certificate applied for by the master under the act of Congress, upon the ground, which was ably supported in the opinion he pronounced, that the act of Congress did not embrace a case like that before him, inasmuch as *Marshall* was *not a fugitive* slave,—had *not* "escaped from one state into another,—*but, by his master's consent, had left Maryland and come into Pennsylvania.*

The Supreme Court of *Massachusetts* has expressed its concurrence with the foregoing decisions of *Judge Washington*, (*Commonwealth vs. Aves,* 18 *Pickering,* 219.)

A construction of considerable importance , has been placed upon another portion of the act of Congress by the Supreme Court of Pennsylvania, in a case brought before it in 1819. The following is the reporter's statement prefixed to the decision of the court:—" This was a writ *de homine replegiando,* sued out by the plaintiff, a coloured man, against the defendant, who was the keeper of the prison of the city and county of *Philadelphia;* and the defendant's counsel now moved to quash it, on the ground of its having issued *contrary to the Constitution and laws of the United States.* The facts were submitted to the court in a case stated, by which it appeared that the plaintiff, having been claimed by *Rasin Gale,* of *Kent county,* in the state of *Maryland,* as a fugitive from his service, was arrested by him in the county of *Philadelphia,* and carried before *Richard Renshaw, Esq.,* justice of the peace, who committed the plaintiff to prison, in order that inquiry might be made into the claim of the said

Gale. The plaintiff then sued out a *habeas corpus*, returnable before *Thomas Armstrong, Esq.*, an associate judge of the Court of Common Pleas. *Judge Armstrong*, having heard the parties, gave a certificate that it appeared to him, by *sufficient* testimony, that the plaintiff owed labour or service to said *Gale*, from whose service, in the state of *Maryland*, he had absconded; and the said judge, therefore, in pursuance of the act of the Congress of the United States, &c., delivered the said certificate to the said *Gale*, in order that the plaintiff might be removed to the state of *Maryland*." The court, having held the case under advisement for several days, directed *the writ to be quashed*, on the ground that, by the act of Congress, the certificate of the judge was conclusive evidence of the right of the master to remove the plaintiff to the state of Maryland, and, therefore, that no writ of a civil nature could be issued to interrupt the master in the exercise of the power conferred upon him by the certificate. *Wright (otherwise called Hall) vs. Deacon, 5 Sergeant & Rawle's Reports*, 62–4.

But the Constitution of the United States does not exempt runaway slaves from the penal laws of a state in which they may happen to flee upon escaping from their masters. As, where a slave had absconded from his master, living in the state of *Maryland*, and was afterwards confined in prison in the city of Philadelphia, upon the charge of fornication and bastardy, committed during his residence in Pennsylvania, the Supreme Court refused to deliver him to his master, but ordered him to be detained, to answer the charge which had been made against him. *Case of The Commonwealth (on the relation of Johnson, a negro) vs. Holloway, 3 Sergeant & Rawle's Reports,* 4–6. And see, for a similar opinion, 9 *Johnson's (N. Y.) Reports,* 70; *Glen vs. Hodges.*

But it was held in this latter case, by the Supreme Court of the state of *New York,* that where a slave had absconded from his master, living in the state of New York, and had taken refuge in Vermont, a citizen of the latter state, who had traded with him under the belief that he was free, and as such had given credit to him for goods, could not issue civil process to prevent the master from reclaiming him, inasmuch as a slave is, in law, incapable of making a contract.*

It has been decided in *Maryland, Virginia* and *Louisiana,* that if a master consent to his slave's being taken to a free state, whereby he becomes free THERE, he cannot, on a return to his master, be held as a slave, but is entitled to his freedom. *Bland vs. Negro Dowling,* 9 *Gill and Johnson's Rep.* 19; *Betty vs. Horton,* 5 *Leigh's Rep.* 615; *Josephine vs. Poultney,* 1 *Louisiana Annual Reports,* 329. The same point had been decided in *Louisiana* on several previous occasions. See 14 *Martin's Reports,* 403; 13 *Louisiana Reports,* 441. Yet the whole have been rendered nugatory *in this state* by an act of the legislature, in 1846, that "no slave shall be entitled to his or her freedom, *under the pretence* that he or she has been,

---

* See *supra,* p. 99.

with or without the consent of his or her owner, in a
country where slavery does not exist, or in any of
the states where slavery is prohibited." *Louisiana
Statutes*, 524.

A question in which this general doctrine is involved is *now pending* in the Supreme Court of the
United States. Having been free, by virtue of the
laws of the country or state to which he had been
voluntarily carried, I am at a loss to conjecture the
course of reasoning by which he is to be converted
into a slave.

CHAPTER IV.

OF THE JURISDICTION OF THE FEDERAL GOVERNMENT
OVER THE TERRITORIES NOT YET FORMED INTO
STATES.

By several treaties with foreign powers, and by
cessions from many of the original states of the
confederacy, the Federal Government has, at different times, acquired lawful and peaceable possession
of a vast extent of country, much of which is not
yet formed into states, but is known by the name of
territories. Over these territories the Federal Government is expressly authorized by the Constitution to exercise entire jurisdiction. The provision
alluded to, of the Constitution, is this :—" Congress
shall have power to dispose of and make all needful rules and regulations respecting the *territory* or
other property belonging to the United States." *Art.*
4, § 3. Unless, therefore, the treaties and acts of
cession impose conditions, the authority of the
Federal Government over the territories is without
limit. And such is not only the plain intent, but
has been the uniform construction, of this article of
the Constitution.

The territory *northwest of the river Ohio* was ceded,
happily, upon the condition* that slavery should not

---

* In the celebrated debate in the Senate of the United States, in
1830, *Mr. Webster* ascribed the merit of incorporating this important

be permitted there.   On the contrary, the *deed* of cession of the territory *south of the same* river, forming at this time the state of Tennessee, made it imperative on Congress to tolerate it within the limits of that cession.   The treaties by which the Federal Government derives title to *Louisiana* and the *Floridas* contain no provision on the subject.

With respect to Louisiana, previous to the formation of a state out of a part of its territory, it was

---

condition in the *ordinance for the government of the Northwestern Territory*, to *Nathan Dane*, who at the date of the ordinance was a member of Congress from *Massachusetts*.   It has been shown by *Edward Coles*, formerly Governor of the state of Illinois, in a paper read before the *Historical Society of Pennsylvania*, June 9th, 1856, entitled *"History of the Ordinance of* 1787," that the original effort on this subject was made by *Thomas Jefferson soon after* the cession of territory by *Virginia* on March 1st, 1784.   On the 19th of April, 1784, a motion was made in Congress, by which the *condition* was *rejected*.   On March 16th, 1785, *Rufus King*, then of *Massachusetts*, moved the *restoration of Mr. Jefferson's* proposition, and it was adopted, EIGHT states voting *for* and THREE *against* it.

Mr. Dane took his seat in Congress, November 17th, 1785, and was appointed *one* of a committee of *five* by whom an ordinance for the government of the territory was reported.   *The prohibition of slavery* as it now stands in the ordinance was part of this report, and the whole ordinance was adopted *unanimously* by Congress, July 13th, 1787.

That the great *conception* of prohibiting slavery in that territory belongs to *Mr. Jefferson* there can be no doubt.   The difference between his proposition and that which was finally adopted was, that *Mr. Jefferson* named *"after the year* 1800" as the time at which the prohibition was to take effect, whereas, as adopted, it was *contemporaneous* with the date of the ordinance.   The difference was of small importance, for the whole territory was little else than a wilderness.

It is worthy of remark that *Mr. Jefferson* drew up a *Constitution for Virginia*, in which all persons born after the same year—A.D. 1800—were to be *free*.

competent to the United States to have annihilated the institution of slavery within the *whole* of its extensive borders.   It is competent for her *now* to do so, as to those portions which are not comprised within the bounds of the two states which have been created out of it.   It is hardly necessary to apply this remark specifically to the Floridas; they are obviously in a similar predicament.

The *abolition* of slavery in her territories has not been attempted by the Federal Government.   But highly important regulations have been made by Congress, on a point not very remotely allied to that subject.   On the 7th of April, 1798, an act was passed by this body, "authorizing the establishment of a government in the Mississippi Territory;" the *seventh* section of which provides "That, after the establishment of the aforesaid government, it shall not be lawful for any person or persons to *import or bring into the said Mississippi Territory*, from any port or place without the limits of the United States, or to cause or procure to be so imported, &c., or knowingly to aid or assist in so importing, &c. *any slave or slaves;* and that every person so offending, &c., shall forfeit, &c. for each and every slave so imported, &c. the sum of three hundred dollars, &c.; and *that every slave so imported, &c. shall thereupon become entitled to and receive his or her freedom.*"   See *acts of the 2d session of the 5th Congress, ch.* 45.   This section is incorporated, without the least variation, except as to the name of the territory, into the act of Congress passed March 26th, 1804, entitled, "An act erecting Louisiana into two territories, and providing for the temporary government thereof," with supplementary regulations, prohibiting, in the first place, under an equal penalty, the introduction into Louisiana Territory, "from any port or place *within* the limits of the United States, &c., *any slave or slaves* which had been imported since the first of May, 1798, into any port or place within the limits of the United States, or which should be imported thereafter from any port or place without the limits of the United States," and concluding in this manner:—"And no slave or slaves shall directly or indirectly be introduced into said territory, except by a citizen of the United States *removing* into said territory *for actual settlement*, and being at the time of such removal *bona fide owner* of such slave or slaves; and every slave imported or brought into the said territory, contrary to the provisions of this act, shall thereupon be entitled to and receive his or her freedom." 2 *Story's Laws*, 937.

This act does honour to the illustrious body from which it proceeded. In practice, however, its benefits were of much less value than one not fully conversant with the mode in which the DOMESTIC *slave-trade* is prosecuted would be led to infer. A prohibition on this subject, to be *effectual*, should be ABSOLUTE AND WITHOUT ANY EXCEPTION. *Actual settlers and bona fide owners* may *protect* this traffic to an extent adequate to the demand, without incurring a risk at all commensurate with the probable gain.

But the act is of great moment, as a *precedent* to Congress in regard to the Missouri, the Arkansas and Florida Territories. The defects which have been suggested may be easily supplied. Let the introduction of slaves into these territories be, without delay, WHOLLY FORBIDDEN. Humanity and religion, the character of our country, the true interests as well of the slave-holding as of the non-slave-holding states, demand this to be done.

The foregoing is the text as it stood in the *first* edition of this sketch. It was written at a time when the *Missouri Compromise*, then recently settled, was in full force. That Compromise prohibited slavery beyond *thirty-six and a half degrees* of north latitude. The justice and wisdom of this arrangement remained unquestioned for more than *a third of a century*. *Arkansas*, falling *impliedly* within the scope and spirit of the Compromise, was admitted in 1836, without the slightest opposition from any quarter, as a *slave-holding* state. *California*, formed out of territory acquired long after the date of the Compromise, and therefore not in the view of Congress at the time, made her *own* election to insert a prohibition of slavery in her Constitution, and was in like manner received into the Union.

Suddenly, while the Indian title still remained intact, and neither propriety nor necessity required any action looking forward to the formation of a new state, a *Senator* from a *free* state announced the discovery that there was in the *slavery-prohibition* of the Missouri Compromise a *principle* at variance with the free and equal spirit of our republican government. A majority of both Houses of Congress and

25*

a President of the United States have ratified this discovery, and the Missouri Compromise has been annulled.

The author of the discovery has, within a short time, as chairman of the Committee on Territories, made a report to the Senate of the United States, in which he has undertaken to show that the provision of the *third* section of the *fourth* article of the Constitution of the United States gives no authority to Congress "to organize temporary governments for the territories" belonging to the Union. Since the adoption of the Constitution, no one else seems to have entertained a doubt upon this subject. National legislation has uniformly recognised it, from the first moment when the condition of the territories was supposed to *need* "*rules and regulations,*" until and *inclusive* of the *Nebraska-Kansas* act itself. The power is *expressly* given in the section and article referred to. There are two distinct grants contained in the same sentence. There is a power given "to *dispose* of the territory belonging to the United States," which has been exercised directly, perhaps, on several occasions, but *certainly* in one,—the act of Congress of June 7th, 1836, by which "the *Platte purchase*" was ceded to the state of *Missouri*, augmenting its territorial limits *one-seventh* more than were originally included within them.

The *second* grant of power in the third section of article fourth of the Constitution is, to "make *all needful rules and regulations* respecting the *territory.*" Can any language be more expressive, distinct,

apposite and plenary for the purpose of enabling
the establishment of a territorial government? And
can any be less suitable, and therefore more in-
eligible to declare such an intent, than the provision
in regard to the admission of *new* states?

The *Missouri Compromise* was emphatically *an act
of peace*. It calmed at once the stormy elements
which the subject of *slavery* invariably excites when
brought into the full view of the people of the free
states. The spirit of enterprise and adventure
which has so long distinguished the inhabitants of
the *North*, but which is scarcely known at all in the
South, had ample scope in the virgin soil of *Iowa*,
Wisconsin and *Minnesota*, and would have been content with this theatre of action until the extinction
of the Indian title should have prepared the way
for the peaceful extension of the arts of civilized life
in *Kansas* and *Nebraska*.

But the undisguised purpose in the *repeal* of this
compromise—namely, the introduction and ultimate
establishment of *slavery* in these fertile regions,
which *had been consecrated* to freedom by that Compromise—has waked up a spirit of strife which, if
appeased at all, can be done only by an honourable
restoration of the plighted faith of 1820.

Had the *Missouri Compromise* nothing else to re-
commend it than the recollection of the circumstances in which it originated, this alone would
have been a sufficient reason, with most minds, to
suffer it to remain undisturbed. But when the
inevitable effects of annulling it could be so readily
foreseen, what shall be said of the prescience, or

patriotism, or *mere statesmanship*, which could have suggested its repeal?

Looking at the subject of slavery in a national point of view, as in plain conflict with the Declaration of Independence and the genuine spirit of our republican government,—by the light of philanthropy, which is the proper heritage of man,—or by the teachings of political economy, resting on the basis of selfishness alone,—no better or wiser measure was ever conceived by the Congress of the United States than the Missouri Compromise.

NOTE A, pp. 34–35.

In the former edition of this work this language was used:—"Nevertheless, the cardinal principle of slavery, that the slave is not to be ranked among *sentient beings*, but among *things*, &c."

Professor Bledsoe, in his recent apology for slavery, takes exception to what, as it stood, was properly a mere *parenthetical* remark; *i. e.* that slaves are not ranked by the slave law among "*sentient beings.*" In *strictness*, his criticism is just; and I have, therefore, left out the words objected to. But the very pith and point of the sentence—that the slave is regarded by that law as A THING—he does not attempt to controvert. How *very near* the truth the original expression is the reader will see by a careful study of the quotation which I have given from the decision of the Supreme Court of North Carolina. *Ante* 33.

As further illustrations of the same approximation to truth in this particular,—the denial to the slave of the attributes of a *sentient being*,—I commend to the sober reflection of the learned professor the following adjudications of the highest courts of judicature in two of the Southern States. The *first* of these is a decision of the Supreme Court of *Georgia*.

A slave—a carpenter—was hired to the owner of a steamboat, which was under the management of an agent of the owner. Some perilous service—the precise character of which is not clearly stated— was exacted of the slave by the owner's agent, the captain. It would seem that in the performance of this service the captain, through ignorance or carelessness, subjected the slave to such peril that he lost his life. The *master* of the slave sued the *owner* of the boat to recover the value of the slave. The defence was, that the slave's life had been lost not through any act of the owner of the boat, but by the improper conduct of the captain; and that it was a rule of law that, for an injury occasioned to one *employee* by the negligence or improper conduct of another employee, the common superior of the two was not liable.

This rule having been relied upon by the defendant, its applicability where the *injured employee* was *a slave* was denied, on the ground that a *slave* had no will of his own, but was bound to surrender his own judgment, however correct, to the command of *any one* whom the law for the time being had constituted his master.

The plaintiff's counsel summed up his argument with this terrific proposition :—" Their (*slaves*') posi-

tion in our section of the country would not allow
them to direct or interfere; COMPLAIN they DARE
NOT, and LEAVE they CANNOT.''

Lumpkin, J., after adverting to this rule of law
and the grounds upon which it was established,
asks, '' Can any one of these considerations apply
to *slaves?* They dare not interfere with the busi
ness of others. They would be instantly chastised
for their impertinence. It is true that the owner
or *employer* of a slave is restrained by the penal
code from inflicting on him cruel, unnecessary and
excessive punishment, and that *all others* are forbidden to beat, whip or wound them *without sufficient
cause* or *provocation.* But can any one doubt that if
this unfortunate boy, although shipped as a *carpenter*, had been ordered by the captain to perform
the perilous service in which he lost his life, and
he had *refused* or REMONSTRATED, that he would
have received prompt correction? and that *on the
trial*, on a bill of indictment for a misdemeanour, his
conduct would have been deemed a *sufficient justification* for the supposed offence? No! *Slaves dare not
intermeddle with those around them, embarked in the
same enterprise with themselves. Neither can they testify
against their misconduct. Neither can they exercise the
salutary discretion left to free white agents, of quitting
the employment when matters are mismanaged or portend
evil.* Whether engaged as carpenters, bricklayers
or blacksmiths, as ferrymen, wagoners, patroons or
private hands, in boats or vessels, in the coasting or
river navigation, or railroads, or any other avocation,
THEY HAVE NOTHING TO DO BUT SILENTLY SERVE OUT
THEIR APPOINTED TIME, AND TAKE THEIR LOT IN THE

MEAN WHILE IN SUBMITTING TO WHATEVER RISKS AND DANGERS ARE INCIDENT TO THE EMPLOYMENT." *Scudder vs. Woodbridge*, 1 *Kelly's Rep.* 197–200.

This is the language of a court of *civil* jurisdiction. Take a case falling within the range of *criminal* jurisprudence.

In *Britain vs. The State*, (of Tennessee,) 3 *Humphrey's Rep.* 203, a master of a slave was held to be indictable for keeping his slave employed in *public* view in apparel so tattered and torn as indecently to expose her person.

This decision is rested entirely on the ground that the *feelings of the community* were outraged by such exposure of the slave by her master's neglect. The injury or wrong to the slave is not hinted at; and it is quite certain the law would not interfere in her behalf, no matter to what extent humanity in her feelings was affected. The principle of the decision is just the same as would be invoked against the owner of a horse who should turn out the animal to die on the commons while suffering from any loathsome disease,—the glanders, or the like. The owner would be punishable, not because the *animal* deserved better treatment, but because the community in its interests or its taste would be offended.

Do these decisions regard the *slave* as a *sentient* being, or as a *mere thing?*

I add a third case,—*Fairchild vs. Bell*, 2 *Brevard's* (*South Carolina*) *Reports*, 129,—and transcribe the very language of the reporter: —"The plaintiff was a physician, who, seeing, not far from his residence, a female negro slave, belonging to the defendant, *in the road,* in a miserable condition, *almost naked, shockingly beaten, and having an iron on her leg of fifteen pounds' weight,* was induced, from motives of humanity, to take her to his house, where she was carefully attended, clothed, nourished and cured.

"The action was to recover the amount of his account, for medicine and attendance expended on that occasion. The defendant avowed the beating and other ill-treatment of the wench, but utterly refused to satisfy the plaintiff for his services in the care and cure of her.

"It was clearly proved at the trial that the defendant had exercised towards the poor slave a continued series of cruelties, and *that she must have perished* but for the humane assistance of the plaintiff.

"The defendant was immediately applied to, to furnish the wench with clothes and necessaries; *but he refused to do so, was outrageously angry, and threatened to sue the plaintiff for harbouring his slave.* The jury found for the *defendant,* contrary to the judge's charge." The doctrine of the *court* in this last case is not open to the objection that it does not recognise a *slave* as a *sentient* being. But what a revolting picture do *the facts* present of injured humanity, *without an intimation from any quarter that there existed an effectual remedy!* The master admitted that he had perpetrated these maddening wrongs upon the slave, refused to bestow the slightest relief, and, with a shameless audacity not easily paralleled, "*threatened to sue the plaintiff for harbouring his slave.*" And, in the end, the jury by their verdict sanctioned his conduct!!

THE END.

A Select List of Black Classic Press Titles

The Negro
W. E. B. DuBois

Originally published in 1915, Dr. W. E. Burghardt Du Bois' "little book," as he called it, was one of the most important and seminal works on African and African American history. It was small in size but gigantic in purpose. In it Du Bois, unquestionably an eminent historian, brilliantly attempted to encapsulate the ten thousand-year record of the peoples of Africa, then referred to as "Negroes." Introduction by W. Burghardt Turner and Joyce Moore Turner. ISBN 1-58073-032-9. 1915*, 2005. 281 pp. Paper $14.95.

David Walker's Appeal
David Walker

Walker's Appeal represents one of the earliest African-centered discourses on an oppressed people's right to freedom. African American political philosophy has evolved from many of the themes that it articulates. ISBN 0-933121-38-5. 1929*, 1993. 108 pp. Paper $8.95.

A Tropical Dependency
Flora Shaw Lugard

When Lady Lugard sat down to write *A Tropical Dependency*, it was not her intention to inspire generations of Africans to regain the independence of their countries. Lugard writes of slavery as though it was a God-given right of Europeans to own Africans as slaves. Ironically, her text on Africa's place in history reaffirms the belief that "If Africa did it once, Africa can do it again!" Introduction by John Henrik Clarke. ISBN 0-933121-92-X. 1906*, 1997. 508 pp. Paper $24.95.

The Name "Negro": Its Origin and Evil Use
Richard B. Moore

Moore's study focuses on the exploitive nature of the word "Negro." Connecting its origins to the African Slave Trade, he shows how the label "Negro" was used to separate African descendants and to confirm their supposed inferiority. ISBN 0-933121-35-0. 1960*, 1992. 108 pp. Paper $10.95.

Wonderful Ethiopians of the Ancient Cushite Empire
Drusilla Dunjee Houston

Mrs. Houston describes the origin of civilization and establishes links among the ancient Black populations of Arabia, Persia, Babylonia, and India. In each case, she concludes that the ancient Blacks who inhabited these areas were all culturally related. ISBN 0-933121-01-6. 1926*, 1985. 280 pp. Paper $14.95.

The Exiles of Florida
Joshua R. Giddings

During the early part of the nineteenth century, the United States conducted a brutal campaign to re-enslave Blacks who escaped slavery and found freedom in Native American settlements in Florida. Giddings' observations document the struggle waged by these brave Africans and their Native American hosts.
ISBN 0-933121-47-4. 1858*, 1997. 338 pp. Paper $16.95.

Ancient Egypt the Light of the World
Gerald Massey

An epic analysis of ancient origins and beliefs, this first volume of Ancient Egypt elaborates how the first humans, who emerged in Africa, created thought. In the second volume Massey examines the Precession of the Equinoxes and the old Kamite sources of Christianity.
ISBN 0-933121-31-8. 1907*, 1992. 944 pp. Paper $59.95.

A Book of the Beginnings
Gerald Massey

In volume one, Massey focuses on Egyptian origins in the British Isles. In the second volume, he explores the African/Egyptian roots of the Hebrews, the Akkado-Assyrians, and the Maori. By linking these diverse cultures and origins to their African roots, Massey demonstrates not only the extent of African influence but its durability as well.
ISBN 0-933121-93-8. 1881*, 1995. 1200 pp. Two volume set. Cloth $84.95.

The Natural Genesis
Gerald Massey

By centralizing Egypt as the root of Western civilization's myths, symbols, religions, and languages, this famed Egyptologist and 'mythographer' challenges conventions of theology as well as fundamental notions of race supremacy. Introduction by Dr. Charles S. Finch.
ISBN 1-57478-009-3. 1883*, 1998. 1087 pp. Two volume set. Paper $59.95.

Christianity, Islam and the Negro Race
Edward W. Blyden

Blyden offers an early African-centered perspective on race, religion, and the development of Africa.
ISBN 0-933121-41-5. 1887*, 1993. 441 pp. Paper $14.95.

To order, send a check or money order to:
Black Classic Press
P.O. Box 13414-b
Baltimore, MD 21203-3414

Include $5 for shipping and handling, and $.50 for each additional book ordered.
Credit card orders call: 1-800-476-8870

For a complete list of titles, please visit our website at www.blackclassic.com

*Indicates first year published

210922-100-3-60W